HEALTH AND OTHER UNASSAILABLE VALUES

Health and Other Unassailable Values sets out to examine health as a core cultural value. Taking 'health', 'evidence' and 'ethics' as her primary themes, Bell explores the edifice that underpins contemporary conceptions of health and the transformations in how we understand it, assess it and enact it. Although health, evidence and ethics have always been important values, she demonstrates that the grounds upon which they are grasped today are radically different from how they were formulated in the past.

Divided into three parts, Part I focuses on the rise of epidemiology, Part II examines the emergence of evidence-based medicine and Part III explores the broader ethical turn in health and medicine. Through an examination of core concepts including health behaviour, the randomised controlled trial, informed consent and human rights, Bell illustrates the ways in which certain entrenched ideas and assumptions about how human beings think and act recur across a variety of settings. An array of topical case studies, including cigarette packaging legislation, the incorporation of male circumcision as an HIV prevention tool, cancer screening technologies and e-cigarettes, ground the arguments presented.

Written in a clear and engaging style, this volume will be of interest to a wide range of scholars and students, especially those in medical anthropology, medical sociology, and public health. Clear chapter delineations make the work easy to engage with at the individual chapter level as well as a whole.

Kirsten Bell is an Honorary Associate in the Department of Anthropology, University of British Columbia, Canada.

HEALTH AND OTHER UNASSAILABLE VALUES

Reconfigurations of health, evidence and ethics

Kirsten Bell

Routledge
Taylor & Francis Group

LONDON AND NEW YORK

First published 2017
by Routledge
2 Park Square, Milton Park, Abingdon, Oxon OX14 4RN

and by Routledge
711 Third Avenue, New York, NY 10017

Routledge is an imprint of the Taylor & Francis Group, an informa business

British Library Cataloguing-in-Publication Data
A catalogue record for this book is available from the British Library

Library of Congress Cataloging-in-Publication Data
Names: Bell, Kirsten, author.
Title: Health and other unassailable values : reconfigurations of health, evidence and ethics / Kirsten Bell.
Description: Abingdon, Oxon ; New York, NY : Routledge is an imprint of the Taylor & Francis Group, an Informa Business, [2017] | Includes index.
Identifiers: LCCN 2016025180 (print) | LCCN 2016043021 (ebook) | ISBN 9781138898554 (hardback : alk. paper) | ISBN 9781138899032 (pbk. : alk. paper) | ISBN 9781315708164 (e-book) | ISBN 9781315708164 (E-book)
Subjects: LCSH: Public health—Social aspects. | Health education. | Medical economics—Political aspects. | Public health—Moral and ethical aspects.
Classification: LCC RA418 .B45 2017 (print) | LCC RA418 (ebook) | DDC 362.1—dc23
LC record available at https://lccn.loc.gov/2016025180

ISBN: 978-1-138-89855-4 (hbk)
ISBN: 978-1-138-89903-2 (pbk)
ISBN: 978-1-315-70816-4 (ebk)

Typeset in Bembo Std
by Swales & Willis Ltd, Exeter, Devon, UK
Printed and bound by CPI Group (UK) Ltd, Croydon, CR0 4YY

CONTENTS

PART III
Ethics   **129**

FIGURES AND TABLES

Figures

Tables

ACKNOWLEDGEMENTS

I knew that I should probably write a book. 'You're not a real anthropologist without a sole-authored book', colleagues admonished. Fifteen years out of my PhD and still disgracefully bookless, I could put this off no longer. But given that my research interests could be politely described as 'eclectic', what book to write? My inimitable colleague, Vinay Kamat, advised me to 'Write a book on smoking. Or cancer. But not health. Who will buy a book on health?' I listened to this advice carefully before dismissing it out of hand. If this book was my academic calling card, I was determined that it would be an ambitious exercise (based on the admittedly optimistic assumption that someone will actually bother to read it). In the writing of this book, it occurred to me *more than once* that I probably should have listened to Vinay.

This book was not like a child I lovingly expelled in a flood of hormones and afterbirth – unless that child is *Rosemary's Baby*: demon spawn that gave me count-less sleepless nights and induced periodic fits of guilt and despondency. The going got slightly easier after a timely conversation with Shaylih Muehlmann made me realise that I was approaching things in completely the wrong way, but this book never became easy to write. Half way through it became clear that I had taken a bite that was too large to swallow; bar spitting the whole thing out, my only option was to try to digest the edges and anticipate that the middle part would soften enough to eventually chew through (and, yes, I recognise that I might have chosen a classier metaphor). The point is that I hope this book is less torturous for the reader to wade through than it was for me to write.

Given this book's lengthy gestation, there are numerous people who've contrib-uted significantly to its content through conversations, discussions and debate over the years. First and foremost, a considerable debt is owed to Ciara Kierans, Darlene McNaughton and Svetlana Ristovski-Slijepcevic – friends and collaborators who have kept me sane in the course of writing this book, and have listened to endless whingeing about 'TFB' (I will leave the reader to fill in the blanks). Ciara, in particular, kept me on track – both through her critical intellectual interventions into the content and by helping me stick to my writing schedule, which at one stage looked completely unsalvageable. The influence of other friends and collaborators such as Simone Dennis, Denielle Elliott, Rebecca Haines-Saah, Helen Keane and Amy Salmon will also be evident, and exchanges with Judy Green, Adam Burgess, Gerry Stimson and Melanie Rock have influenced my thinking about certain topics presented herein. I have mercilessly abused several of these relationships to solicit feedback on chapters and am immensely grateful to Ciara, Darlene, Denielle, Svetlana, Rebecca and Simone for their willingness to wade through drafts that veered heavily towards the 'uncut rock' as opposed to the 'polished gem' side of the scale.

I am also indebted to my husband, Andrew Ham, without whose unstinting support this book would not have been written and who convinced me to finish it when I was at the spit or swallow stage (okay, this metaphor definitely needs some work). My parents, Sue and Tim Bell, and my siblings, Nikki Adshead-Bell and Chris Bell, have always been my biggest supporters. A special thanks goes to my father, a retired academic geologist who spent most of his career being attacked for his controversial theories on porphyroblasts (the inspiration for the porphyroblast paradox is discussed in Chapter 6). He has often encouraged me to persist with work I would otherwise have given up on getting published. 'What?' he'd say. 'You've only had that paper rejected four times? I rewrote one paper *seven times* before it was finally accepted.'

The empirical research drawn on in this book was funded by operating grants from the Canadian Institutes of Health Research, the Canadian Cancer Society Research Institute and the Social Sciences and Humanities Research Council and I gratefully acknowledge their support here, along with that of the folk at Routledge. I'm also indebted to the many people who've willingly shared their experiences with me over the course of a variety of research projects connected with the concerns of this book. I've only included a few of their voices here, but their stories have unquestionably shaped the ways I understand the topics I discuss in the chapters that follow.

Not being a fan of books consisting primarily of previously published papers strung together, I promise the reader that none of the chapters herein duplicates any previously published material, although excerpts from the following publications are used: 'Remaking the self: Trauma, teachable moments and the biopolitics of cancer survivorship', *Culture, Medicine and Psychiatry* 36, 4 (2012): 584–600; 'Cochrane reviews and the behavioural turn in evidence-based medicine', *Health Sociology Review* 21, 3 (2012): 313–321; 'Tobacco control, harm reduction and the problem of pleasure', *Drugs and Alcohol Today* 13, 2 (2013): 111–118; 'HIV prevention: Making male circumcision the "right" tool for the job', *Global Public Health* 10, 5–6 (2015): 552–572; and 'On the perils of invoking neoliberalism in public health critique', *Critical Public Health* 26, 3 (2016): 239–243 (co-authored with Judith Green).

I briefly toyed with the idea of dedicating this book to my beloved (now deceased) cat, Spike, but even I recognise that this tips me too far towards the 'crazy cat lady' side of the scales, so I have officially refrained.

INTRODUCTION

There is a scene in the 1987 Rob Reiner film *The Princess Bride*[1] where the villainous Prince Humperdinck is talking to his right-hand man, Count Rugen, outside of the entrance to Rugen's secret underground laboratory, ominously known as 'the Pit of Despair'. Rugen, who fancies himself something of a scholar of pain, has Westley, the film's hero, trussed up in the Pit and plans to start torturing him shortly – at Humperdinck's behest but also for his own edification. Count Rugen asks, 'Are you coming down into the Pit? Westley's got his strength back. I'm starting him on the Machine tonight.' Prince Humperdinck responds, in tones of utmost sincerity, 'Tyrone, you know how much I love watching you work, but I've got my country's 500th anniversary to plan, my wedding to arrange, my wife to murder and Guilder to frame for it; I'm swamped.' 'Get some rest,' Count Rugen counsels. 'If you haven't got your health, then you haven't got anything.'

Rugen's sentiments are echoed, virtually unchanged, in the influential green paper *Our Healthier Nation*, produced by England's Department of Health. According to the paper:

> No matter what goes wrong in life – money, work or relationship problems – good health helps sustain us. How often have we all heard somebody say that although things may not be going well – at least they have their health. Good health is treasured.
>
> *Department of Health 1998: 7–8*

Clearly, from sociopathic fictional characters to government reports, the importance of health is something we can all agree on. Whatever else might divide us (culture, class, race, religion), as a value health is so self-evident, so universal, it's utterly *unassailable*. As Richard Klein (2010: 15) observes:

To say we are 'against health' is to utter a paradox, a sort of oxymoron in the Greek sense, from *oxus*, meaning 'sharp', and *moros*, meaning 'stupid'. To be against health is to utter a sharp stupidity because, almost by definition, we cannot be against health. The very concept of health implies a positive value that one cannot but choose.

Endorsed as a kind of meta-value, speaking in the name of health is a powerful rhetorical device (Greco 2004). To say that something is 'healthy' or 'unhealthy' is often seen to be all that needs to be said about a topic. In essence, health becomes a trump card wielded to disguise what are fundamentally political, moral and economic arguments – arguments about how people should think, comport themselves and live. According to Jonathan Metzl:

> '[H]ealth' is a term replete with value judgments, hierarchies, and blind assumptions that speak as much about power and privilege as they do about well-being. Health is a desired state, but it is also a prescribed state and an ideological position. We realize this dichotomy every time we see someone smoking a cigarette and reflexively say, 'smoking is bad for your health', when what we really mean is, 'you are a bad person because you smoke'. Or when we encounter someone whose body size we deem excessive and reflexively say, 'obesity is bad for your health', when what we mean is not that this person might have some medical problem, but that they are lazy or weak of will . . . In these and other instances, appealing to health allows for a set of moral assumptions that are allowed to fly stealthily under the radar.
>
> *Metzl 2010: 1–2*

Commentators with a wide variety of disciplinary orientations and theoretical inclinations have illustrated the ways in which the concept of health is not only valorised but *normativised*. A core thread in the work of Michel Foucault, it is succinctly captured in his observation that 'The imperative of health [is] at once the duty of each and the imperative of all' (1980: 170) – a theme taken up in books with titles like *The Imperative of Health: Public Health and the Regulated Body* (Lupton 1995) and *Against Health: How Health Became the New Morality* (Metzl and Kirkland 2010), along with countless studies on governmentality and biopolitics.[2] In discussing the growing array of social phenomena that have been expropriated by medicine and recast as medical issues, medicalisation theorists such as Irving Zola (1975, 1977) and Ivan Illich (1977) have also highlighted the ways in which the ostensibly neutral and objective language of 'health' disguises its moral attributes and socio-political (or rather depoliticising) effects. Likewise, Robert Crawford (1980) developed the concept of 'healthism'[3] to describe the growing preoccupation with health as the primary focus for the definition and achievement of personal well-being and the attendant assumption that it lies in the realm of individual choice.[4] The voices of physicians themselves have also occasionally featured among the critics – the title of Michael Fitzpatrick's book *The Tyranny of Health*

(2001) provides some inkling of the vehement indictment it contains of the various uses and abuses of the concept of health.

In light of how well trodden this ground is, a book with a title like *Health and Other Unassailable Values* will likely generate some eye-rolling. Do we *really* need another book on the rise of health as a master value? [5] However, my goal in this book isn't merely (or even primarily) to unpack the concept of health but to explore the edifice that currently underpins it. To speak of health has always been to speak about morality, but I don't believe that we've just replaced the language of sin with the language of science. I aim to show that the rise of epidemiology has fundamentally transformed the ways we conceive of health. To understand this new conception of health we also need to understand how it intersects with several other equally unassailable values: namely, evidence and ethics. Like health, these, too, have always been important – both in and beyond the field of medicine. However, the grounds upon which 'evidence' and 'ethics' are grasped today are radically different from how these values were formulated in the past.

Although evidence has always been central to the scientific method, it came to take on a new reified form with the rise of evidence-based medicine (itself an epidemiological product) and its intellectual offspring: evidence-based public health, evidence-based health care, evidence-based policy and, well, evidence-based *everything*.[6] Premised on the notion of 'purity', evidence-based medicine entails a number of assumptions about what constitutes evidence of efficacy and what doesn't, and the possibility of separating 'evidence' from 'ideology'. Likewise, the emergence of bioethics and parallel fields such as human rights saw new conceptions of 'ethics' instantiated in ways that impacted both the organisation of health care and research itself. Evidence-based medicine and ethics have generated their own sizeable bodies of literature in much the same way that the concept of health has, but to date they haven't been systematically explored *together*. However, while each constitutes a powerful discourse in its own right, together they form a seemingly impregnable fortress – after all, how can one be *against* health, evidence and ethics? While these values don't always cohere, my interest in this book is particularly in the ways they have intersected (co-constituted each other, even). If the book has a distinctive contribution to make, I believe that this is primarily where it lies – in bringing together topics that are typically studied apart.

Orienting the reader

Although I am a social anthropologist, this book is not an ethnography grounded in my own empirical research (I will have more to say on this shortly). Instead, I'm interested in epidemiology, evidence-based medicine and ethics as transnational movements and their *global* rather than *local* effects on knowledge practices.[7] However, while we can speak of the three movements as transcending national boundaries, different countries had different trajectories in terms of the key figures that drove them and how they were taken up. These differences are far from minor and connect not only to broad cultural and political contrasts between national settings, but the ways these play out in their policies and health care systems.

A related issue is the pitfalls in attempting to characterise fields that are intrinsically broad and diverse. Epidemiologists, ethicists and proponents of evidence-based medicine don't speak in a singular voice and critiques of their theories and practices have just as frequently been levelled by those *among* their ranks as *outside* of them: social epidemiology and feminist bioethics are two cases in point. Any ambition to grapple with topics this large and unwieldy must, of necessity, cut through swathes of history and paint with a relatively broad brush. However, while I recognise the danger of presenting an overly simplistic view that mirrors the same sorts of reductionisms I seek to challenge, I think it's possible to identify certain dominant assumptions and ideas without setting up a triad of straw men to demolish. That said, I want to emphasise at the outset that I am focusing on the 'mainstream' versions of these movements rather than attempting to characterise the fields as a whole.

The book's general disposition is storytelling rather than theorising[8] and it, like my work in general, is underpinned by a promiscuous array of theoretical and methodological influences. However, if pressed, I would probably identify two dominant and interrelated strands: Foucault's genealogical approach to power/knowledge and science and technology studies. Although I would not identify myself as a Foucauldian or an STS scholar per se, the influence of the former is evident in my interest in the fields of epidemiology, evidence-based medicine and ethics in a broadly genealogical sense (see Foucault 1980, 1994 [1973], 2010 [1972]). How did these assemblages, as they exist today, come to be? What were their conditions of possibility? I push strongly against a progressivist view of history – which pervades all three movements in equal measure. The influence of science and technology studies is most evident in my interest in how scientific facts are established (e.g., Latour and Woolgar 1986; Latour 1987; Epstein 1996; Shapin 2010). This is a particular focus of Part II, although it informs the overall project of the book – which, after all, is about the ways health, evidence and ethics intersect and *converge*. These might be conceptually distinct arenas, but they also constitute a larger assemblage.[9]

Although I aim to denaturalise these fields, I should make it clear that my goal isn't merely to debunk them or engage in the sort of empty critique that has become associated with some versions of constructivism. As Bruno Latour (2004) observes, constructivism has a tendency to become *de*construction, where reality is not explained as much as explained *away*, with the author of the critique installed as 'the courageous critic, who alone remains aware and attentive, who never sleeps [and who] turns those false objects into fetishes' (p. 238). The irony, of course, is that such accounts rely themselves on an underlying positivism – because there *is* an objective reality to be found, but it just so happens that only the author can see it! In effect, we become constructivists about everything we don't believe in and positivists about everything we do, an approach that places us in the felicitous position of always being right. I suspect I've been guilty of this in the past, and I may occasionally be guilty of it here, but my *intent* (if intentions actually count) is to treat the topics I explore as 'matters of concern' rather than 'matters of fact' – i.e., shifting attention from the stage itself to the whole machinery of the theatre (Latour 2008: 39; see also Latour 2004). Thus, I don't intend to condemn epidemiology, evidence-based medicine and ethics wholesale or to simplistically assert that they've got it 'wrong', although I do aim to make their underlying logics visible. Perhaps more importantly, I explore the irresistible magnetic pull they exert, such that phenomena initially outside their orbit are eventually drawn into it.

The impetus for the book

As noted above, this book doesn't draw on my own empirical research in a particularly direct or substantive fashion, except in the context of illustrative case studies employed in six chapters. In part, I've chosen this approach because I work across a variety of different topics, and writing a book focusing on something like, say, smoking or cancer (the two topics I've written about most intensively) didn't hold much appeal.[10] However, whether the topic is smoking, cancer, addiction, obesity, circumcision, etc., and whether I've been writing about public health or biomedicine, the same kinds of themes have repeatedly cropped up. It's these *recurrences* that form my central preoccupation in this book. The fact that I work on a number of different topics is something that I see as a particular strength in this context, because it gives me a distinct vantage point on the ways in which the concepts of health, evidence and ethics have been enacted across a variety of settings.

Health and Other Unassailable Values is also strongly informed by experiences that relate not just to research I have conducted but contexts in which I have worked. My interest in the uses of the concept of health began well before I started formally conducting research in the area of medical anthropology[11] and dates from a gender course I used to teach at a regional university in the USA. The course included a section on female circumcision and my approach to the topic was to draw in male circumcision and to ask students to consider them in a comparative fashion. Teaching this material is the first time I recall being explicitly aware of the ways in which the invocation of health could serve to shut down conversation, despite its obvious cultural and moral loading. For my students, male circumcision was actively health promoting and female circumcision was a harmful mutilation so how *dare* I compare them together.[12] I saw health invoked in much the same way when I first arrived in Canada and took a position managing the tobacco research programme at an applied health research centre. A topic I initially had no particular professional interest in (and, if I'm being honest, some personal aversion to), I was nevertheless shocked by the sorts of opinions frequently expressed on tobacco control listservs, where 'smoking is bad for your health' quickly transformed into 'you are a bad person because you smoke' (to repeat Metzl's observation) with little comment or criticism.[13]

My interest in evidence-based medicine and its distinctive forms of knowledge synthesis and production dates from this same period. Between 2006–2007, I led four rapid reviews[14] that aimed to synthesise evidence on various aspects of tobacco control for a national organisation devoted to producing evidence-based guidance in the areas of clinical medicine and public health. Having just left an academic appointment in Australia, I had never heard of a systematic review before (let alone conducted one) and the experience was eye opening. Beyond the intensive exposure it provided to the evidence hierarchies prioritised in evidence-based medicine (EBM) and its methods of knowledge synthesis, it formed the basis for much of my subsequent thinking about the assumptions upon which EBM is founded. The confidentiality agreements I signed make it difficult to write directly about these experiences, but they have unquestionably informed my approach to the book.

Likewise, my interest in ethics stems in large part from service and administrative appointments I have held in the area of research ethics – both as a representative on the Human Research Ethics Committee at Macquarie University in Australia and as a consultant research ethics analyst with the Office of Research Ethics at the University of British Columbia. In these roles, I have had intimate access to the generally 'behind closed doors' processes that constitute institutional ethics review (Stark 2012). Once again, confidentiality agreements preclude me from talking in any direct way about these experiences,[15] but they have been instrumental to my interest in the topics I explore in the book, and provide a background of lived experience through which I have formed opinions on them. Thus, my arguments aren't based primarily on abstract critiques but were formulated in the thick of *enacting* the values I am exploring here.

Overview of the book

Health and Other Unassailable Values is organised into three parts, each of which concentrates on one of the three themes of the book, namely: health, evidence and ethics. By placing the topics in this particular order I don't intend to give the impression of a clear temporal or hierarchical relationship between them. These fields are *complexities* in the sense that Mol and Law (2002: 1) describe: they relate but don't add up; events occur but not within processes of linear time; they share a space but can't be mapped in terms of a single set of three-dimensional coordinates.

Each part of the book follows the same general structure. The first chapter is primarily synthetic and aims to provide a broad overview of the topic at hand, focusing on the circumstances of its emergence, its key assumptions, and how they have been challenged as well as taken up. I see these introductory chapters as providing necessary context for the two chapters that follow, each of which takes up more specific concepts and ideas and uses an illustrative case study, drawn from my own research, to more concretely explore their implications and effects. However, it's challenging (to say the least) to provide enough context for each case study without overriding the larger conceptual focus of each chapter. I'm not convinced I've achieved an appropriate balance in all chapters, but it was a core concern in terms of how I approached the writing process. In focusing on these case studies I also want to make it clear that I intend to illustrate what I see as *broader* processes at work. Although things may not always play out in exactly the ways I describe, I think they point to assumptions and ideas that are operating across a number of areas.

Part I of the book, 'Health', is primarily concerned with the rise of epidemiology and the ways it has transformed our conceptions of health. Chapter 1 focuses on the emergence of the 'new' epidemiology in the period following the Second World War and its emphasis on lifestyle as the answer to the question of how to address chronic disease. Here we see clear evidence of a shift in views of disease causality, with causality now conceptualised in *probabilistic* rather than *mechanistic* terms. Challenging the notion that chronic disease is merely a descriptive category that describes a straightforward epidemiological transition in the nature of disease, I discuss its relationship with these new conceptions of health and disease causality. Although I draw the reader's attention throughout the chapter to the ways in which health is framed as an individual choice, I challenge the view that this is primarily an effect of the rise of neoliberal forms of governance.

In Chapter 2, I focus on the concept of 'health behaviour', which is the primary mode through which the preoccupation with lifestyle has been operationalised in public health. My goal is to denaturalise the concept, both by explicating its roots in behavioural psychology and showing how it has changed over time. Pointing to two underlying models of health behaviour: a 'cognivist' model and a 'behaviourist' model, the latter of which has recently been revitalised in the concept of 'nudging', I discuss their limitations for understanding the complex social practices currently writ as lifestyle 'behaviours'. While the rise of the social determinants of health framework has challenged the individual, behavioural focus of risk factor epidemiology, I argue that it hasn't dislodged it to any substantive degree. To illustrate these points I focus on cigarette packaging legislation as a case study, which exemplifies both the behaviourist and cognitivist paradigms and assumes a great deal about how smokers will respond to warnings about the dangers of smoking.

Chapter 3 shifts focus from the realm of primary (and secondary) prevention to tertiary prevention – which focuses on arresting the progression of diseases that have already emerged clinically. In essence, my interest is in demonstrating the ways in which the lifestyle focus has expanded from the well to the sick. Although there are clear parallels between primary and tertiary prevention in terms of their emphasis on 'health behaviour', there are some important differences as well. These differences are evident in the rise of self-management as a core component of tertiary prevention. They are also evident in the growing emphasis on the 'teachable moment' as a means of promoting behavioural change and its intention of replacing a 'bad' kind of optimism (that a negative outcome won't be realised) with a 'good' kind (that an outcome won't be realised *if* certain 'behaviours' are instituted or eradicated). Using cancer 'survivorship' as a case study, I discuss the growing preoccupation with lifestyle in the field and the assumptions embedded in self-management programmes about the possibility of taking control of the disease.

Part II of the book shifts focus to the topic of 'evidence'. My key interest is in the rise of evidence-based medicine, a term I use to encapsulate the movement in both its initial form and successive iterations as its principles and processes were taken up beyond medicine itself. In Chapter 4, the central question I explore is why its particular notions of what constitutes evidence of effectiveness became so widely disseminated in the 1990s. Given that its central tenets have been articulated from at least the 1970s, I consider why the movement was embraced at this particular historical moment, suggesting that it can't be divorced from a number of concurrent and highly contextual developments. Outlining the intensive criticisms the movement engendered, I reflect on the reasons for their failure to dislodge its grip on medicine and health care, arguing that one of the reasons why EBM has been so successful is its capacity to assimilate objections without changing in essentials. This has seen its notions of 'evidence' taken up in fields far removed from the contexts it was originally designed to address, with important implications for knowledge claims about what 'counts' as health problems and solutions.

Chapter 5 focuses on the installation of the randomised controlled trial as the 'gold standard' evidence of efficacy. I explore what conditions needed to be in place for it to become such, especially given that its key assumptions were anathema to many nineteenth-century scientists and philosophers. I'm also interested in what happened as the randomised control trial (RCT) paradigm was transposed beyond the 'classic' clinical trial and how its logic was sustained in these new, radically different, settings. Via a case study on the emergence of male circumcision as an HIV prevention tool, I demonstrate the ways in which the rise of evidence-based medicine served to transform knowledge claims about the efficacy of the procedure and elided the entanglements between science and politics.

I continue to explore these themes in Chapter 6, although my focus is more explicitly on the transposition of EBM principles to 'behavioural' interventions, which themselves owe a considerable debt to the concepts and theories discussed in Chapter 2. Although the applicability of RCTs to 'complex' settings has been debated for decades, the notion of a 'pristine' intervention divorceable from its context is widely assumed in the ways the method has been taken up in fields such as public and global health. This assumption is compounded in systematic reviews of behavioural interventions, where data are further stripped of context in order to determine an overall 'mean effect' of any given intervention. Focusing on a Cochrane review on the impact of physician advice on smoking cessation, I illustrate the problems with this framework, arguing that the assumption of a stable intervention is an illusion created by the paradigm itself.

Part III of the book shifts gears again, turning to the topic of 'ethics' – a term I use to refer not only to the field of bioethics, but the broader ethical turn in health and medicine (which I take to include the human rights movement). As with the other introductory chapters, Chapter 7 provides necessary background and context for the final two chapters of the book. Focusing on the period following the Second World War, I highlight the assertion of humanist universalism that underpinned the growing preoccupation with ethics as a distinct set of concerns requiring arbitration by figures *outside* the field of medicine. In an effort to knit together the strands of the prior sections, I emphasise the ways that changing conceptions of health served to facilitate the new emphasis on patient agency and autonomy that bioethics introduced. I also argue that many of the same developments that precipitated the rise of evidence-based medicine were integral to the formation of bioethics and that the relationship between these two fields has been primarily one of mutual elaboration.

Chapter 8, the penultimate chapter of the book, focuses on the concept of informed consent, which is the primary mechanism through which 'autonomy' is operationalised in health care. Once again, my gaze is both historical and contemporary: I discuss the roots of the doctrine and its current instantiation as a means of facilitating patient choice. However, the rise of evidence-based medicine has seen the concept of informed consent inflected in particular ways that affect the perceived roles and responsibilities of both physicians and patients. If patients are informed, the logic goes, they can be empowered to make 'rational' decisions about their health. As in previous chapters, I draw on a case study to trouble this view of the informed patient: cancer-screening technologies. Focusing specifically on biomarker tests for prostate and ovarian cancer (the PSA test and the CA125 test), I explore the ways in which the controversies surrounding these tests – controversies that have been produced by the instruments of evidence-based medicine – are problematically mediated via the concept of informed consent.

The final chapter of the book continues to focus on questions of choice, but primarily through the lens of the concept of human rights. Today, the language of 'human rights' is ubiquitous, perhaps because it represents one of the most powerful secular discourses through which to call for reform. However, until the rise of HIV/AIDS it wasn't concretely invoked in the context of health, primarily because of the abstract nature of the concept of health itself. Challenging the assumption that human rights claims to represent freedom from power, I turn to the field of harm reduction, where the concept of human rights has been invoked with increasing frequency since the turn of the twenty-first century. I demonstrate that while human rights are premised on the notion of freedom of choice, this tends to be enacted in a way that reinstates health as an overarching value: one is free to choose, as long as one chooses *health*. Focusing on the debates surrounding electronic cigarettes, I use this as a case study to explore the effects of invoking human rights – which have become a primary means through which advocates have challenged efforts to restrict access to these products. Illustrating the ways in which the language of human rights has become entwined with the languages of evidence-based medicine and health itself, I suggest that they serve to legitimise e-cigarettes in very specific terms.

As the overview of the chapters hopefully makes clear, I have tried to write the book so that readers can dip into individual chapters without reading the whole thing. I imagine that some will want to engage with the book in this manner, especially if they are primarily interested in a particular concept or case study (e.g., 'health behaviours' or e-cigarettes). But I want to make it clear that this isn't just a collection of essays that relate to each other in only a broad sense – if this was the sort of book I was aiming to write, I would have made far more intensive use of previously published work. While I have included excerpts from several prior publications, this material has been substantially reworked and recontextualised, with each chapter aiming to build on what has come before. Thus, the book is intended to be read from cover to cover and I think the connections I draw between the three topics that form its focus will be clearer if it is engaged with in this fashion.

I have one final caveat. While I thought I had a solid grasp of the content at the outset, writing a book is a humbling exercise. In the writing it became starkly apparent how inadequate my knowledge was. To reuse a well-worn aphorism: the more I read, the less I realised I knew. Throughout the writing process, I continued to discover books and papers I had somehow – quite shockingly! – never previously stumbled across, a realisation that became increasingly disturbing as the writing progressed. While this is inevitable to some degree, I'm well aware that there are gaps in my understanding and that a book this ambitious in scope will be – and should be – held to high standards. After all, *I* was the one who decided to take on three large fields (somewhat blithely as it turns out). Despite its deficiencies on this front, I hope that the story I tell about health, evidence and ethics is one that will resonate with at least some readers. If one thing has become clear to me in the writing of this book, it's that these three areas are intimately entangled and that we need to be more frequently examining them together.

Notes

1 The film is based on the book of the same name by William Goldman. I'm quoting from the film rather than the book because the scene plays out a bit differently in the latter and the punch line from Rugen is missing.
2 Any list would be lengthy and rife with omissions, so I will avoid the attempt except to say that the most influential scholar in this area is probably Nikolas Rose (especially Rose 2007 but also Rose 1998, 1999).
3 I say 'developed' because the term was first used in the title of a book chapter by Zola (1977) titled 'Healthism and disabling medicalization' (something Crawford himself acknowledges), although Zola didn't discuss the concept in the chapter.
4 As he has more recently noted:

> Personal responsibility for health is widely considered the *sine qua non* of individual autonomy and good citizenship ... In a health-valuing culture, people come to define themselves in part by how well they succeed or fail in adopting healthy practices and by the qualities of character or personality believed to support healthy behaviors. They assess others by the same criteria.
>
> *Crawford 2006: 401*

5 One colleague responded, 'Oh, so you're basically writing another *Against Health*' upon hearing the title. *Against Health* is an important collection full of stimulating essays, many of which I cite in the course of this book, but hopefully it will be clear by the end of the introduction that my agenda is somewhat different.
6 This is an allusion to the title of a paper by Ann Oakley (2002) titled 'Social science and evidence-based everything'.
7 I am reluctant to make recourse to concepts such as 'the West'; as Annemarie Mol (2008: 2–6) notes, there are a series of clichés that underwrite differentiations between 'the West' and everywhere else. Nevertheless, the movements I discuss in this book are broadly 'Western' products insofar as they emerged primarily from the USA and the UK, although they have been widely taken up in other so-called 'Western' contexts and their core assumptions have been exported beyond them to varying degrees.

8 I have taken this framing from Sean Phelan (2007: 331), who uses it to characterise a book on the history of neoliberalism.
9 The concept of an 'assemblage' itself is largely an STS creation, reaching its epitome in actor-network theory (e.g., Law and Hassard 1999; Latour 2005).
10 Especially as excellent books have recently been published on both of these topics, including Lochlann Jain's (2013) *Malignant: How Cancer Becomes Us* and Simone Dennis's (2016) *Smokefree: A Social, Moral and Political Atmosphere*.
11 Before moving into medical anthropology, my research focused on a new religious movement in South Korea.
12 I later wrote an article inspired by this experience and what it tells us about dominant discourses on male and female genital cutting (Bell 2005).
13 Arguably, tobacco denormalisation strategies rely on the same conflation – a topic I have gone on to explore at some length.
14 A 'rapid review' is one that draws on the principles of systematic review methodologies but is conducted in a much shorter timeframe.
15 While there may be valid reasons for such agreements, conversations are clearly needed about their censoring effects.

References

Bell, K. (2005) Genital cutting and western discourses on sexuality. *Medical Anthropology Quarterly*, 19(2): 125–148.
Crawford, R. (1980) Healthism and the medicalization of everyday life. *International Journal of Health Services*, 10(3): 365–388.
Crawford, R. (2006) Health as a meaningful social practice. *Health: An Interdisciplinary Journal*, 19(4): 401–420.
Dennis, S. (2016) *Smokefree: A Social, Moral and Political Atmosphere*. London: Bloomsbury.
Department of Health (1998) *Our Healthier Nation: A Contract for Health*. London: Stationery Office.
Epstein, S. (1996) *Impure Science: AIDS, Activism, and the Politics of Knowledge*. Berkeley: University of California Press.
Fitzpatrick, M. (2001) *The Tyranny of Health: Doctors and the Regulation of Lifestyle*. London: Routledge.
Foucault, M. (1980) *Power/Knowledge: Selected Interviews and Other Writings 1972–1977*. Edited by Colin Gordon. New York: Pantheon Books.
Foucault, M. (1994 [1973]) *The Birth of the Clinic*. New York: Vintage Books.
Foucault, M. (2010 [1972]) *The Archaeology of Knowledge*. New York: Vintage Books.
Greco, M. (2004) The politics of indeterminacy and the right to health. *Theory, Culture and Society*, 21(6): 1–22.
Illich, I. (1977) *Medical Nemesis: The Expropriation of Health*. New York: Bantam Books.
Jain, S.L. (2013) *Malignant: How Cancer Becomes Us*. Berkeley: University of California Press.
Klein, R. (2010) What is health and how do you get it? In J. Metzl and A. Kirkland (eds), *Against Health: How Health Became the New Morality*. New York: New York University Press, pp. 15–25.
Latour, B. (1987) *Science in Action*. Boston, MA: Harvard University Press.
Latour, B. (2004) Why has critique run out of steam? From matters of fact to matters of concern. *Critical Inquiry*, 30(2): 225–248.
Latour, B. (2005) *Reassembling the Social: An Introduction to Actor Network Theory*. Oxford: Oxford University Press.
Latour, B. (2008) *What is the Style of Matters of Concern?* Assen, The Netherlands: Van Gorcum.
Latour, B. and Woolgar, S. (1986) *Laboratory Life: The Construction of Scientific Facts*. Princeton, NJ: Princeton University Press.

Law, J. and Hassard, J. (1999) *Actor Network Theory and After*. Oxford: Blackwell.

Lupton, D. (1995) *The Imperative of Health: Public Health and the Regulated Body*. London: Sage.

Metzl, J.M. (2010) Introduction: Why 'against health'? In J. Metzl and A. Kirkland (eds), *Against Health: How Health Became the New Morality*. New York: New York University Press, pp. 1–11.

Metzl, J.M. and Kirkland, A. (eds) (2010) *Against Health: How Health Became the New Morality*. New York: New York University Press.

Mol, A. (2008) *The Logic of Care: Health and the Problem of Patient Choice*. London: Routledge.

Mol, A. and Law, J. (2002) Complexities: An introduction. In J. Law and A. Mol (eds), *Complexities: Social Studies of Knowledge Practices*. Durham, NC: Duke University Press, pp. 1–22.

Oakley, A. (2002) Social science and evidence-based everything: The case of education. *Educational Review*, 54(3): 277–286.

Phelan, S. (2007) Messy grand narrative or analytical blind spot? When speaking of neoliberalism. *Comparative European Politics*, 5: 328–338.

Rose, N. (1998) *Inventing Ourselves: Psychology, Power, and Personhood*. Cambridge: Cambridge University Press.

Rose, N. (1999) *Governing the Soul: The Shaping of the Private Self*. London: Free Association Books.

Rose, N. (2007) *The Politics of Life Itself: Biomedicine, Power, and Subjectivity in the Twenty-First Century*. Princeton, NJ: Princeton University Press.

Shapin, S. (2010) *Never Pure: Historical Studies of Science as if It Was Produced by People with Bodies, Situated in Time, Space, Culture, and Society and Struggling for Credibility and Authority*. Baltimore, MD: Johns Hopkins University Press.

Stark, L. (2012) *Behind Closed Doors: IRBs and the Making of Ethical Research*. Chicago, IL: University of Chicago Press.

Zola, I.K. (1975) In the name of health and illness: On some socio-political consequences of medical influence. *Social Science and Medicine*, 9: 83–87.

Zola, I.K. (1977) Healthism and disabling medicalization. In I. Illich, I.K. Zola, J. McKnight, J. Caplan and H. Shaiken, *Disabling Professions*. London: Marion Boyars, pp. 41–67.

PART I
Health

1
LIFESTYLE AND THE RISE OF EPIDEMIOLOGY

Introduction

According to the influential American health economist Victor Fuchs, 'differences in diet, smoking, exercise, automobile driving and other manifestations of "lifestyle" have emerged as the major determinants of health' (Fuchs 2011: 6). In his highly cited book *Who Shall Live? Health, Economics and Social Choice*, Fuchs (2011) makes it clear that health is, at some level, a choice. He writes: 'Positive health can be achieved only through intelligent effort on the part of each individual. Absent that effort, health professionals can only insulate the individual from the more catastrophic results of his ignorance, self-indulgence, or lack of motivation' (Colman cited in Fuchs 2011: 28).

This emphasis on 'lifestyle' is one of the hallmarks of contemporary public health and has been an intensive preoccupation in the field since the 1970s. As Petersen and Lupton (1996: ix) note, '"Lose weight!" "Avoid fat!" "Stop smoking!" "Reduce alcohol intake!" "Get fit!"' is its central rallying cry. Indeed, it wouldn't be too much of a stretch to say that alcohol, tobacco and obesity form public health's 'Axis of Evil': an unholy trinity of 'lifestyle choices' deemed responsible for all manner of preventable chronic diseases, including three of the most common and costly: heart disease, cancer and diabetes (Bell, McNaughton and Salmon 2011).

Contemporary understandings of the health consequences of lifestyle owe a considerable debt to the field of epidemiology, which constitutes our primary means of understanding the distribution and determinants of disease in human populations. Yet, although the science of epidemiology occupies a very prominent place today in the health sciences, and in regulatory affairs and news reports, it's easy to forget that this is a relatively recent development (Kabat 2008). Indeed, it was only during the 1960s and 1970s that it gained legitimacy as a scientific discipline in its own right, although its growth since then has been exponential (Kabat 2008).

In this chapter I am interested in examining the emergence of 'lifestyle' as a core focus in public health. As I aim to show, to understand how lifestyle came to preoccupy the field, we must turn to the rise of the 'new' epidemiology in the second half the twentieth century, and the ways in which it served to transform both public health and medicine, setting the course for its contemporary path of consolidation and development. Although epidemiology is not a monolithic enterprise (Inhorn 1995), my interest in this chapter is its emergence as an institutionalised discipline. Generalised portrayals of the type I attempt here always run the risk of stereotype and caricature; for this reason, I want to make it clear at the outset that my characterisations are true primarily of what has come to be known as 'risk factor epidemiology' and 'mainstream epidemiology' as opposed to the field as a whole.[1] In what follows, I discuss transformations in the object of public health since the nineteenth century, before turning to the concept of lifestyle and exploring what antecedents had to be in place for it to become a meaningful way of understanding the distribution and determinants of disease.

The 'old' public health

Michel Foucault (1980) argues that 'the population' emerged as a problem and object of surveillance, intervention and modification in the eighteenth century, as a result of its explosion in growth in Western Europe.[2] According to Foucault, at this point the project of a technology of population began to be developed, with demographic estimates, differential life expectancies and levels of mortality and so on, calculated. During this period, medicine as a general technique of health (rather than merely a service to the sick) assumed an increasingly instrumental place in the administrative system and its accompanying machinery of power. Ian Hacking (1990: viii) has famously pointed to this era as one in which tabulation began in earnest, highlighting the subsequent 'avalanche of printed numbers' that dominated nineteenth-century Europe. These statistics, in turn, produced the idea that the world was governed by laws of probability – laws that were now visible to the naked eye through the innumerable regularities that appeared in such data (Hacking 1990: 73). Consequently, it was in the nineteenth century that significant changes started to occur in conceptions of and approaches to public health.

According to David Armstrong (1993, 2006, 2011), before the mid-nineteenth century the primary public health strategy was that of quarantine: maintaining a strict *cordon sanitaire* between geographic spaces. However, by the mid-nineteenth century a new model of public health emerged in the form of sanitary science. Equally concerned with maintaining boundaries, the focus instead shifted from geographic boundaries to bodily ones, although a line of total exclusion was impossible, as it had to allow the passage of environmental inputs into the body (food, water, air) and bodily outputs (faeces, urine, etc.) into the environment. Thus, the emphasis was on ensuring the regulation and sanitisation of the conduits between the two.

This model of public health is usually described with reference to the work of the nineteenth-century English physician John Snow – his seminal work on cholera forms one of public health's core 'hero' narratives (Raftery 2004). Contra the prevailing miasmatic theories of disease, Snow posited that the agent of cholera infection must be present in discharges from the alimentary tract. Thus, 'unless these persons are scrupulously clean in their habits, and wash their hands before taking food, they must accidentally swallow some of the excretion, and leave some on the food they handle and prepare' (Snow in Winslow 1943: 273). However, observing that the disease wasn't confined only to crowded dwellings, he suggested that it must extend itself more widely through a second mode of communicability: 'the mixture of cholera evacuations with the water used for drinking and culinary purposes' (Snow in Winslow 1943: 273). His study of a cholera outbreak in London in 1854 was to become a classic illustration of sanitary science at work.[3] Based on an analysis of death records for the affected and a detailed door-to-door survey, he isolated a pump in Broad Street as the source of the infection and eventually persuaded the local Board of Guardians to remove its handle, which effectively disabled it; the epidemic ceased shortly afterwards. Importantly, it wasn't necessary for Snow to understand the precise mechanism of causation (*vibrio cholerae* – discovered in 1883) in order to isolate the roots of the epidemic. Instead, the effectiveness of his approach rested on his ability to isolate factors associated with the disease and potential sources of infection via the intensive use of statistics that tracked its course across the population. Although the epidemic was already on the decline when the pump handle was removed and it took several decades for his ideas about cholera to be taken up (Raftery 2004), Snow is considered to be one of the founding fathers of epidemiology – a discipline that came into its own in the mid-twentieth century.

However, between the era of sanitary science and the rise of modern epidemiology, an intermediate regime emerged that saw a growing emphasis on personal hygiene (Armstrong 1993, 2006, 2011). Unquestionably, Louis Pasteur's experiments on the relationship between germs and disease and the subsequent rise of germ theory and bacteriology were critical to this new regime. Unlike the sanitary science that preceded it, which relied to a significant extent on a centralised administrative structure and formalised legislative framework, it 'opened up the possibility of recruiting people themselves to the surveillance of body boundaries and anatomical spaces' (Armstrong 1993: 401). Armstrong (1983, 1993, 2011) argues that these changing conceptions of disease were reflected in a reconfiguration of tuberculosis. Previously understood to be a disease of poverty and unsanitary conditions, tuberculosis was reformulated as one of interpersonal contact. Here, the experimental work of the German physician and microbiologist Robert Koch was critical; using guinea pigs he was able to demonstrate that the disease was caused by an infectious bacterium that could be readily transmitted from body to body (see Winslow 1943: 307–310). Arguably, the rise of bacteriology and the pathological model of disease it engendered led to a turn away from the kinds of statistical and population-driven methods pioneered by Snow,[4] but these were to reclaim a central place in the mid-twentieth century with the rise of what has been termed the 'new' epidemiology.

Twentieth-century public health and the 'new' epidemiology

A key difference between public health as it was conceived and practiced in the mid-twentieth century and the 'old' public health that preceded it was the latter's primary focus on infectious disease and controlling filth, odour and contagion (Petersen and Lupton 1996). This new public health, on the other hand, was characterised by an intense concern with the health status of populations more broadly and its predominant focus shifted to non-infectious conditions such as cancer and cardiovascular disease. This shift was engendered by a new form of clinical practice stressing the centrality of risk factors and medical surveillance to understanding health and illness (Armstrong 1995, 2006, 2011). These risk factors were understood to exist outside and around the human body: the environment, stress, behaviour, etc., now became legitimate targets for health-related actions (Armstrong 2006, 2011). The effects of this shift were twofold: first, they began to dissolve the distinction between the sick and the well and attendant conceptions of normality and abnormality; second, as these were unseen dangers that could come from anywhere and everywhere, constant vigilance became the new imperative. In this new world, as Armstrong (2011: 411) observes, 'everyone is potentially ill and no one is truly healthy as everyone has a particular risk factor profile that can be managed by a vigilant medicine'.

This new version of public health was intrinsically connected with the rise of the 'new' epidemiology in the era following the Second World War, which subsequently colonised public health to such a degree that it is now commonly considered its basic science (Petersen and Lupton 1996; Inhorn and Whittle 2001; Kabat 2008). The foundations of contemporary epidemiology lie in the landmark studies conducted in the early 1950s linking cigarette smoking with lung cancer (Brandt 1997, 2007; Fitzpatrick 2001; Kabat 2008). Although a variety of researchers worked on this topic,[5] the most important studies were unquestionably those conducted by Richard Doll and Austin Bradford Hill in the United Kingdom. Based on a large-scale survey conducted with cancer patients and comparable controls and a subsequent cohort study that surveyed smoking patterns in physicians and tracked their causes of death, Doll and Hill (1950, 1952, 1954, 1956) were able to show a very strong and direct relationship between smoking and lung cancer. This relationship, they convincingly demonstrated, couldn't be accounted for by other causes – such as atmospheric pollution (a prevailing view at the time). According to the medical historian Allan Brandt (2007), noteworthy about Doll and Hill's work was their awareness of the tobacco industry's interest in discrediting their findings and the ways they pre-emptively countered this by meticulously describing the criteria they had used to designate the association between smoking and lung cancer as genuinely causal.

These studies were tremendously influential on a variety of levels.[6] First, they fundamentally transformed notions of causality in both public health and medicine

(Brandt 1997, 2007; Susser and Stein 2009). The term 'cause' implies a single process in which A leads to B; this is a central premise of germ theory medicine and the biomedical paradigm it established, which aimed to isolate a single cause and demonstrate its core mechanisms (Brandt 2007). However, the rise of the new epidemiology was accompanied by an emphasis on multiple causation in explaining the roots of disease (Krieger 1994, 2011; Brandt 1997, 2007; Susser and Stein 2009). Under this framework, literally hundreds of web-like factors are responsible for disease, so it becomes possible to speak of causality in *probabilistic* rather than *mechanistic* terms. After all, only a minority of smokers end up with lung cancer and numerous non-smokers get the disease, so an assertion that smoking 'causes' cancer – as opposed to merely being associated with it – means that causality must now be conceptualised in a relative rather than absolute sense.

On the basis of his work on smoking and lung cancer, Hill (1965) would later go on to posit nine considerations for distinguishing causation from association: 1) the strength of the association; 2) its consistency across different studies; 3) its specificity, i.e., its limitation to certain members of the population and certain sites and types of disease; 4) a clear temporal relationship between the cause and the effect; 5) evidence of a biological gradient or dose–response relationship between exposure and effect; 6) its biological plausibility; 7) coherence between lab and epidemiological findings; 8) appeals to experimental evidence where possible[7]; and 9) analogy – judging what we know about one drug or disease on the basis of another similar one. These have come to be known as the 'Bradford Hill criteria'[8] and form the basis for establishing causality in contemporary epidemiology.

Secondly, and relatedly, these studies introduced a statistical logic that challenged the authority upon which clinical medicine had traditionally rested (Brandt 2007) – a challenge, as we will see in Part II, which reached its peak in the 1990s with the rise of evidence-based medicine. The new epidemiology deals with probabilities that apply to individuals as members of a group, rather than to the individual him or herself. Indeed, its ability to predict events on an individual level is actually quite limited (Kabat 2008). As Richard Klein (2010: 21) observes, 'it tells the truth of an aggregate. By definition, epidemiology says nothing about a particular person's mortal destiny or the health that accompanies it.' Nevertheless, the field focused attention on questions of comparative risk and excess mortality, with researchers recognising that there were hundreds of variables affecting the incidence of disease (Brandt 2007).

Finally, they made commonplace the idea that specific 'lifestyle behaviours'[9] affect health – offering the prospect that many chronic diseases might be radically reduced by curtailing such behaviours (Brandt 2007; Kabat 2008). According to Brandt (2007), the publication of the 1964 Surgeon General's report *Smoking and Health* was a watershed moment for epidemiology and public health more broadly in the twentieth century because of the way it marked this transition 'from institutions and approaches that centered on infections to a critical reorientation to approaching chronic disease' (p. 437). The report also played a crucial role in legitimising these new epidemiologic notions of causality and the population-based studies 'that would offer the core methods of public health and medical assessment of causality and efficacy from that time' (Brandt, 2007: 438). The fact that never again have such strong and direct associations between a 'behaviour' and a disease been witnessed[10] has done little to dislodge the assumption that lifestyle presents the key answer to stemming the tide of chronic disease (Fitzpatrick 2001).

Challenging the epidemiological transition model

As should now be evident, the practice of public health from the middle of the twentieth century reflected a shift in focus from infectious to chronic disease – a shift that has been most explicitly theorised in the influential 'epidemiological transition' model, which posits that we have experienced a transition 'in which degenerative and man-made disease [e.g., cardiovascular disease, cancer] displace pandemics of infection as the primary causes of morbidity and mortality' (Omran 2005 [1971]: 732). However, although the notion of an epidemiological transition has proved an influential way of explaining the emergence of chronic disease during the second half of the twentieth century,[11] Armstrong (2014a) observes that subscribing to this view means accepting that the diagnostic labels of any given period straightforwardly reflect an underlying biological reality – a view at odds with his genealogical approach and the perspective I take in this book. Based on an analysis of articles referencing 'chronic illness' and 'chronic disease' published in the *Journal of the American Medical Association* since its inception in 1883, he instead illustrates the ways in which the concept has changed over time and its implications for the projects of medicine and public health.

According to Armstrong (2014a), in the late nineteenth and early twentieth century the distinction between acute and chronic disease was exclusively temporal, relating to the duration of the disease. This attribute was merely one, among many, characteristics of disease that could be used to group them – in much the same manner that diseases causing pain or fever might be classified together. It wasn't until the 1930s that the appearance of chronic illness as a distinctive construct began to crystallise. What differentiated it from prior usage was the incorporation of a new attribute: one that identified it with disabling illness. However, its disabling impact couldn't be easily identified using standard medical tools such a stethoscope or X-ray. Instead, 'new technologies emerged to capture this novel medical construct and, given the population framework of this new medical object, it propelled epidemiology and public health from their former sanitary realm to engage with these new illness/diseases with disabling attributes' (2014a: 18–19).

Armstrong (2014a) argues that this new way of practising medicine no longer involved close physical examination of the individual body; instead, the body of the population was studied via the survey.[12] Thus, chronic disease was, in essence, the emergence of a new form of morbidity based less on pathology and more on the patient's capacity to function. This, in turn, led to a new conceptualisation of health, which could no longer be equated merely with the absence of pathological disease. This was reflected in the definition promulgated by the newly formed World Health

Organization in 1948, which defined health as 'a state of complete physical, mental and social well-being and not merely the absence of disease or infirmity' (WHO 2006 [1946]) – a conceptual shift that arguably precipitated the 'ethical' turn in medicine and public health (see Chapter 7).

According to Armstrong, a similar transformation occurred in conceptions of ageing during this same period. In particular, over the first half of the twentieth century, the line demarcating the domains of pathological processes and natural ageing became increasingly blurred. What had previously been known as degenerative diseases (especially cancer and heart disease) began to discursively metamorphose into preventable and/or treatable – even curable – pathological ones. This was partly an effect of the population-level approaches that by now characterised epidemiology. The variations they revealed in the prevalence of these diseases within populations, and the implication that these might be due to lifestyle, 'marked the appearance of a crack in the edifice of natural ageing' (Armstrong 2014a: 22). Thus, in the second half of the twentieth century there was no longer any need for a degenerative disease label – the ageing process had been successfully colonised by pathology.[13] As Armstrong observes, these changing conceptions were reflected in obituary columns in *JAMA* itself.[14] After 1972, no one died of 'myocardial degeneration' anymore; 'thereafter it was no longer possible to die from natural causes' (Armstrong 2014a: 23). In sum, while chronic illness may have replaced acute disease as the leading preoccupation of medicine and public health, this pattern was arguably[15] connected with a transformation in the classification of its problems as much as a fundamental change in the nature of the problems themselves. This, in turn, created the conceptual space in which the notion of 'lifestyle' could flourish (Armstrong 2009).

Lifestyle and its socio-political effects

As previously noted, an emphasis on 'lifestyle' has become ubiquitous in public health since the 1970s. This is perhaps most evident in the rise of health promotion – a field primarily concerned with identifying and changing 'risky' lifestyles (Bunton 1992; Lupton 1995; Petersen and Lupton 1996; Bunton, Nettleton and Burrows 2003). At once a descriptor of a way of living and a sum of everyday activities, 'lifestyle' is simultaneously understood to constitute a catalogue of hazardous 'behaviours' adopted by the individual that predispose them to illness (Coreil and Levin 1984–1985; Coreil, Levin and Jaco 1985; Lupton 1995; Coveney 2006). As Lewis Thomas (1991) observes, 'lifestyle' has become a perceived answer to the question of how to stall death. Indeed, it has become a truism in public health that if people didn't smoke, drank less, consumed healthier diets, were more active and so on, the burden of chronic disease would be dramatically reduced (Petersen and Lupton 1996; Fitzpatrick 2001; Bell, McNaughton and Salmon 2011).

Some have asserted that the rise of what has been labelled the 'new public health' since the 1970s[16] has served to erode the emphasis on lifestyle (e.g., Baum 2008) by broadening the emphasis of public health to environmental, technological and social hazards as well as behavioural and biological ones. However, various scholars have argued that this broadened scope hasn't displaced the underlying individualism of mainstream epidemiological theory (e.g., Gifford 1986; Petersen and Lupton 1996; Krieger 1994, 2008, 2011). For example, Sandra Gifford (1986) argues that models of multiple causation are based on an underlying assumption of specific aetiology. Thus, 'we find an emerging rhetoric speaking of holistic, multi-causal relationships yet a practice which continues to adopt a reductionistic, mechanistic approach towards understanding and managing disease' (Gifford, 1986: 217). Part of the problem, as Nancy Krieger observed in 1994, is that notions of multiple causation and attendant multivariate analyses have become so embedded in contemporary epidemiological reasoning that they hardly merit discussion as a model or as an approach to understanding disease: 'the "web" as such is "given"' (1994: 891). Thus, although the web of causation *seems* to challenge the traditional pathological model of disease, it typically focuses attention on risk factors 'closest' to the outcome under investigation, which translates into an emphasis on the direct biological causes of disease in individuals and/or lifestyle 'behaviours'. More recently she has argued that the web and its focus on an individualistic, biomedical, lifestyle approach has continued to endure (see Krieger 2008, 2011), pointing to the ways in which contrasts between 'proximal' (or 'downstream') and 'distal' (or 'upstream') causes implicitly reproduce it.

Krieger (1994, 2011) points to the importance of the Cold War and McCarthyism in explaining the individualism underwriting epidemiological discourse on disease causation from the 1950s[17] and the tendency to eschew speculation about the social determinants of health. Arguing along somewhat different lines, Robert Crawford (2006) observes that while the politicisation of health in the 1970s in the USA led to growing government efforts to regulate industry, such perspectives typically reinforced the emphasis on individual behaviour change. Thus, controversies surrounding government regulation of industrial and environmental hazards 'reinforced a rapidly deteriorating sense of safety,[18] which in turn contributed to the growing awareness of lifestyle hazards' (Crawford 2006: 407). For example, the politics of air pollution legitimised the growing anti-smoking sentiment and political controversies over additives and pesticides affected individual dietary changes as much as medical attention to the prevention of heart disease. Indeed, Crawford asserts that the allocation of health protection to the sphere of lifestyle ultimately 'enfeebled' government health and safety regulations (2006: 408), paving the way for the neoliberal reforms introduced under the Reagan administration. In his words, the entrenchment of 'privatized, market solutions to public problems cannot be grasped without a clear understanding of how personal responsibility triumphed over a political morality premised on collective responsibility for economic and social well-being' (2006: 409; see also Crawford 1977, 1980).

Although Crawford focuses primarily on the US context, countless scholars have highlighted the relationship between neoliberalism and public health across the globe, from the United Kingdom and continental Europe to the Antipodes and the Global south (Bell and Green 2016). However, although the conceptual intelligibility of the term is often taken for granted (Garland and Harper 2012), in these accounts 'neoliberalism' is used as shorthand for a number of distinct phenomena. Broadly speaking, the term refers to the capitalist restructuring that has occurred in a variety of countries since the 1970s in the name of a 'post-Cold War, post-welfare state model of social order that celebrates unhindered markets as the most effective means of achieving economic growth and public welfare' (Maskovsky and Kingfisher 2001: 105). Thatcherism in the UK and Reaganism in the USA are often highlighted as prototypical manifestations of neoliberalism, although policies informed by a similar market-centric logic were introduced in a more moderate form in a variety of social democracies (Maskovsky and Kingfisher 2001; Brenner and Theodore 2002). However, in recent years the term has broadened to include a wide variety of meanings. As James Ferguson notes:

> One is as a sloppy synonym for capitalism itself, or as a kind of shorthand for the world economy and its inequalities . . . a kind of abstract causal force that comes in from outside to decimate local livelihoods. Another . . . usage sees 'neoliberalism' as the name of a broad, global cultural formation characteristic of a new era of 'millennial capitalism' – a kind of global meta-culture, characteristic of our newly de-regulated, insecure, and speculative times. And finally, 'neoliberalism' can be indexed to a sort of 'rationality' in the Foucauldian sense, linked less to economic dogmas or class projects than to specific mechanisms of government, and recognizable modes of creating subjects.
>
> *Ferguson 2010: 171*

This latter usage treats neoliberalism as synonymous with governmentality and focuses on the ways in which the relations among and between people and things have been successively re-imagined, reinterpreted and reassembled to effect governing at a distance (Ward and England 2007). In accounts focusing on public health and health promotion,[19] attention is paid to the ways in which 'lifestyle theory posits the individual subject as a rational, calculating actor who adopts a prudent attitude in respect to risk and danger' (Petersen and Lupton 1996: 15). This imagined subject-citizen is autonomous and self-regulating and, above all, *responsible*, with choices and desires that align with the state and other social institutions and authorities (Petersen and Lupton 1996; Brown and Baker 2013).

However, although there is much to these analyses, and I will be considering their implications in the chapters that follow, in some accounts there is a tendency for the 'neoliberalism' frame to become so totalising and monolithic that it starts to assume causal properties in its is own right; 'that is, it becomes the "it" that does the explaining, rather than the political phenomenon that needs to be explained' (Phelan 2007: 328). It therefore runs the risk of eliding *other* processes that deserve analytic attention.[20] For example, Andrew Kipnis (2008) points out that the key defining features of neoliberalism-as-governmentality (governing from a distance; the emphasis on calculability; and the promotion of self-activating, disciplined, individuated subjects) can be found in a variety of contexts that are historically and culturally distant from Western neoliberal or liberal governing philosophies. In his words, 'These three categories correspond to broad human potentialities that have been imagined in a wide variety of ways in a broad range of settings and that have become more prevalent in *all* state-governed and industrial societies' (Kipnis, 2008: 284, emphasis added). Indeed, as Petersen and Lupton (1996) recognise,[21] the 'discovery' of lifestyle as a key source of ill health since the 1970s is more accurately a 'rediscovery' 'since the discourse of lifestylism can be traced back at least as far as the late nineteenth century' (p. 15).

Scandals of the appetite: the precursors to 'lifestyle risk behaviours'

According to Ruth Clifford Engs (2000), contemporary attitudes towards lifestyle 'risk factors' in public health share marked similarities with sentiments expressed well over a hundred years ago. Focusing on the US context, she argues that it has witnessed cyclical clean living movements: 'broad periods in history when concerns about alcohol, tobacco, other mood-altering substances, sexuality, diet, physical fitness, diseases and other health-related issues have manifested themselves on multiple fronts' (Engs, 2000: 2). Engs suggests that each of these movements, including the latest millennial reform era (dating from the 1970s), share common features. In each instance, we see health elevated to an almost religious status and constituted as a moral obligation, along with the demonisation of particular substances or activities: the 'demon drink', 'the little white slaver' and 'gluttony' in one era; 'alcohol consumption', 'smoking' and 'overnutrition' in the next. Generally, the acquisition of one bad habit is seen as a 'stepping stone' to another (a view most recently reincarnated in the form of the 'gateway theory'). During these periods, alternative perspectives are downplayed or censored and medical orthodoxies are rejected to varying degrees. The movements are invariably middle class in composition and there is an emphasis on 'purity', along with 'rights' and 'values' (e.g., women's rights, family values), accompanied by fear and targeting of so-called 'dangerous classes' (migrants, minority groups, youth).

Although Engs restricts her arguments to the USA, they are also clearly applicable to varying degrees to other cultural contexts. For example, temperance movements gained mass support in a number of predominantly Protestant countries in the nineteenth century, particularly among the middle classes (Aaron and Musto 1981; Levine 1993; Valverde 1998). As is now well documented, temperance reformers perceived alcohol as the root of social, moral and physical decay, linking it to familial violence, crime, poverty, insanity and a litany of other social evils. At its height, the temperance movement was influential in a number of countries, leading to a variety of alcohol restrictions and culminating in the USA's failed experiment with alcohol prohibition between 1920 and 1933.

Likewise, although far smaller in scale and influence, anti-tobacco reformers emerged in the late nineteenth and early twentieth centuries in the UK (Hilton 2000), Canada (Rudy 2005) and Australia (Tyrell 1999), although reformers in the USA were by far the most successful in limiting circulation (see Tate 1999). Tobacco use was linked to various medico-moral issues that were the mainstay of Victorian medicine, such as insanity, idleness, hysteria and impotence (Hilton and Nightingale 1998; Hilton 2000). However, a key concern for social reformers was its association with the 'corruption' of innocents, and smoking and drinking were often were often teamed together as 'an evil partnership threatening to undermine physical and moral health' (Aaron and Musto 1981: 176). Indeed, a number of temperance advocates endorsed their titular principle in its broader sense, advocating changes in diet and exercise as well as abstention from stimulants. American reformers such as Sylvester Graham and John Harvey Kellogg are some of the best-known examples (see Schwartz 1986; Engs 2000; Warner 2008), but the connections between the temperance and dietetics movements were equally strong in the UK (see Shapin 2010). Indeed, the roots of the vegetarian movement in England were intimately entwined with the temperance movement, with the former understood in some quarters to be a logical outgrowth of the latter (Gregory 2007).

In each instance, these movements were connected with larger Protestant-infused values that ascribed moral worth to self-restraint and self-regulation and condemned 'pathological' excess – values clearly evident in the contemporary emphasis on the links between lifestyle and health (Lupton 1995; Brandt and Rozin 1997; Engs 2000; Fitzpatrick 2001; Metzl and Kirkland 2010; Bell, McNaughton and Salmon 2011). They are also connected with the embrace of the Enlightenment ideals of rational control and humanistic progress (Crawford 2006) and its presumption of the rational, autonomous subject – a figure that will rear its head repeatedly in the chapters that follow.

While such 'scandals of the appetite' (Berlant 2011: 105) and the attendant emphasis on self-control and responsibility have a long history, it nevertheless wouldn't do to overplay these continuities.[22] The contemporary regulation of lifestyle in the name of health may be a 'mechanism for deterring vice and for disciplining society as a whole' (Fitzpatrick 2001: 8), but clearly the context in which, say, the 'demon drink' was problematised in the nineteenth century was radically different from contemporary assessments of 'alcohol consumption' as a 'lifestyle risk behaviour'. Although the temperance movement occurred under the broader mantle of social as opposed to 'health' reform and reformers had an overtly moral agenda, the differences aren't just lexical, with the language of science superficially cloaking the language of morality. In other words, I'm not convinced that we can speak about the substance in question in these two eras as the 'same thing'.[23] As I've illustrated throughout this chapter, the epidemiological edifice supporting the view of alcohol as a lifestyle risk behaviour required fundamental changes in conceptions of the object of public health and new conceptions of disease causality before 'lifestyle' in its contemporary sense was able to emerge as a *health* problem.

Conclusion

Clearly, the turn to lifestyle in the twentieth century is the result of a number of interrelated phenomena. Although twentieth-century assertions about the deleterious impacts of lifestyle on health echo sentiments that have been expressed for centuries, there were important differences as well as continuities with earlier eras. In essence, new methods and approaches for studying health, a shift from an emphasis on mechanical causes to probabilistic risk factors, and the rise of the notion of 'chronic disease', evolved synergistically to converge in an emphasis on lifestyle as a core – really, *the* core – problem confronting public health. As I will go on to discuss in Chapter 2, although challenges to the lifestyle frame have been mounted, primarily in the form of a focus on the *social* rather than *physiological* and *behavioural* determinants of health, the idea that 'health behaviours' represent the key to reducing chronic disease, once installed, has proved almost impossible to dislodge.

Notes

1 Indeed, some of those most critical of epidemiological approaches have been epidemiologists themselves (Inhorn and Whittle 2001).
2 Thomas Malthus's work (1798) exemplified this growing emphasis on the population as a 'problem' that, left unchecked, would lead to the impoverishment of society.
3 Actually, he did two separate studies, and his follow-up to the Broad Street study is probably the more significant (Koch and Denike 2006); nevertheless, the removal of the pump handle has taken on great historical and symbolic significance in the field of epidemiology (Trostle 1986; Raftery 2004; Hempel 2007). Such narratives typically posit 'a series of causal events in which the advance of science plays an independent and key role in improvements in life expectancy and population well-being' – starting from the 'Golden Age' of public health in the nineteenth century and continuing apace into the present (Petersen and Lupton 1996: 2).
4 For example, Susser and Stein (2009: 165) argue that, 'some of the maturational lag of epidemiology can be attributed to the enormous successes of germ theory . . . [which] displaced the population-based inferences typical of the work of the earliest modern epidemiologists.'
5 Indeed, the Nazis were the first to link tobacco use with lung cancer (see Proctor 1996).
6 That said, I don't want to give the impression that the medical community just straightforwardly accepted these studies. As Matthew Hilton (2000) documents, considerable scepticism was expressed in medical journals when Doll and Hill presented their initial results, but the fact that they were able to demonstrate the connection through two distinct types of studies eventually convinced most critics.
7 As I will outline in Chapter 5, in 1948 Hill spearheaded what is typically characterised as the first truly randomised controlled trial.
8 Although they are now treated as a checklist, Hill made it clear that he didn't believe that

> we can usefully lay down some hard-and-fast rules of evidence that *must* be obeyed before we accept cause and effect. None of my nine viewpoints can bring indisputable evidence for or against the cause-and-effect hypothesis and none can be required as a *sine qua non*.
>
> *1965: 11, emphasis in original*

9 As Nancy Krieger (2011:147) notes, it wasn't until the 1950s that the concept of 'lifestyle' acquired its contemporary meaning as 'a characteristic of individuals, who could then be aggregated into distinctive groups based on their patterns of consumption'.
10 Even diseases like type II diabetes, which obesity is increasingly touted as the core 'risk factor' for, are extremely complex in their aetiology (see McNaughton 2013).

11 This isn't to suggest that the model has been without criticism; however, critics typically take it as given that Omran is broadly right in his identification of core 'transitions', even if the specifics of his argument require adjustment and refinement (e.g., Mackenbach 1994). As Julie Livingston (2012) illustrates, the effects of this framework are evident in the relative invisibility of cancer in Africa, where assumptions about cancer as a 'disease of civilisation' have been partially responsible for its marginalisation and relative invisibility.

12 As Doll and Hill's work on the relationship between smoking and lung cancer illustrates.

13 See also Susser and Stein (2009: 166) for similar points.

14 Interestingly, they are also reflected in discussions of epidemiological transition theory itself. While in 1971 Omran referred to cardiovascular disease and cancer as 'degenerative diseases', the term was subsequently criticised for being confusing and vaguely moralistic, with commentators advocating the use of the terms 'non-communicable diseases' and 'chronic diseases' instead. To quote one critic, writing in 1994: 'current views of the pathogenesis of ischaemic heart disease and cancer do not see these as age-related biological processes of "degeneration" any more' (Mackenbach 1994: 330).

15 See Gilleard and Higgs' (2014) rebuttal of his arguments and Armstrong's (2014b) response.

16 It's worth noting that there isn't universal agreement on what constitutes the 'new public health' or when it emerged. These differences go beyond questions of timing and relate to how the core underpinnings of the new public health are characterised. For example, Fran Baum (2008) dates its origins to the mid-1980s, arguing that the 'lifestyle' era was succeeded by the 'new public health' era. This is primarily because Baum uses the term as largely synonymous with the rise of conceptual frameworks emphasising the social determinants of health – a concept I will be discussing in more detail in Chapter 2. This, she argues, has placed the pursuit of equity at the very heart of public health, while broadening its scope beyond epidemiological approaches and recognising the value of other methodologies (e.g., qualitative research). However, although more optimistic about the new public health than Petersen and Lupton, Baum acknowledges that its ideals haven't been fully realised in practice and that the transition from the 'lifestyle' to the 'new public health' era cannot just be understood in terms of a one-becomes-the-other typology.

17 Krieger (2011) argues that the effects of these ideological battles were felt not only in the USA but internationally, as the US exported its ideologies and products around the world. Similarly, Macintyre, Ellaway and Cummins (2002) argue that methodological, conceptual and political individualism was dominant in many industrialised countries. As previously noted, I will discuss models of the social determinants of health in more detail in Chapter 2.

18 Crawford doesn't explicitly reference work on the rise of 'risk society', but Anthony Giddens (1990) and Ulrich Beck (1992), among others, have discussed at length the pervasiveness of the concept of risk in late industrial capitalism and its social and political effects.

19 The literature here is far too voluminous to enumerate in any comprehensive way, but for some book-length treatments see Lupton (1995), Petersen and Lupton (1996), Petersen and Bunton (1997), Bunton, Nettleton and Burrows (2003) and Brown and Baker (2013).

20 For such reasons, there have been growing calls to explore neoliberalism in terms of 'concrete projects that account for specific people, institutions and places' (Kingfisher and Maskovsky 2008: 118) – an approach that Brenner and Theodore (2002) refer to as 'actually existing neoliberalism'. Some prefer the term 'neoliberalisation' as a means of stressing its partial and incomplete nature (see Ward and England 2007); others treat neoliberalism as a discourse rather than a 'thing' (Springer 2012).

21 Crawford (2006) also points to continuities between contemporary notions of health and those evident in the late nineteenth century and attributes to this period the roots of the privatisation of the struggle for well-being.

22 There is something of this tendency in Engs' (2000) work.
23 Stevin Shapin (2010) makes a related point about changes in dietetics over time and the ways in which the modern biochemistry of food has served to transform the old adage that 'you are what you eat'. As he notes, 'the cultures of moral discourse and of medical expertise have gone their separate ways' (Shapin 2010: 284) insofar as medical discourse today is divorced from explicit moral considerations. In his words, 'the medical profession has almost wholly given up the role of counseling individuals on their way of life, *save with respect to disease-specific conjunctures*' (Shapin 2010: 284, emphasis added).

References

Aaron, P. and Musto, D. (1981) Temperance and prohibition in America: An overview. In M.H. Moore and D.R. Gerstein (eds), *Alcohol and Public Policy: Beyond the Shadow of Prohibition*. Washington, DC: National Academy Press, pp. 125–181.

Armstrong, D. (1983) *Political Anatomy of the Body: Medical Knowledge in Britain in the Twentieth Century*. Cambridge: Cambridge University Press.

Armstrong, D. (1993) Public health spaces and the fabrication of identity. *Sociology*, 27(3): 393–410.

Armstrong, D. (1995) The rise of surveillance medicine. *Sociology of Health and Illness*, 17(3): 393–404.

Armstrong, D. (2006) Embodiment and ethics: Constructing medicine's two bodies. *Sociology of Health and Illness*, 28(6): 866–881.

Armstrong, D. (2009) Origins of the problem of health-related behaviours: A genealogical study. *Social Studies of Science*, 39(6): 909–926.

Armstrong, D. (2011) The invention of patient-centred medicine. *Social Theory and Health*, 9: 410–418.

Armstrong, D. (2014a) Chronic illness: A revisionist account. *Sociology of Health and Illness*, 36(1): 15–27.

Armstrong, D. (2014b) Revisionist or simply wrong? A rejoinder. *Sociology of Health and Illness*, 36(7): 1116–1117.

Baum, F. (2008) *The New Public Health*. Third Edition. Melbourne: Oxford University Press.

Beck, U. (1992) *Risk Society: Towards a New Modernity*. London: Sage.

Bell, K. and Green, J. (2016) Editorial. On the perils of invoking neoliberalism in public health critique. *Critical Public Health*, 26(3): 239–243.

Bell, K., McNaughton, D. and Salmon, A. (eds) (2011) *Alcohol, Tobacco and Obesity: Morality, Mortality and the New Public Health*. London: Routledge.

Berlant, L. (2011) *Cruel Optimism*. Durham, NC: Duke University Press.

Brandt, A.M. (1997) Behavior, disease, and health in the twentieth-century United States: The moral valence of individual risk. In A.M Brandt and P. Rozin (eds), *Morality and Health*. New York: Routledge, pp. 53–78.

Brandt, A.M. (2007) The first Surgeon General's Report on Tobacco: Science and the state in the new age of chronic disease. In J.W. Ward and C. Warren (eds), *Silent Victories: The History and Practice of Public Health in Twentieth-Century America*. Oxford: Oxford University Press, pp. 437–456.

Brandt, A.M. and Rozin, P. (eds) (1997) *Morality and Health*. New York: Routledge.

Brenner, N. and Theodore, N. (2002) Cities and the geographies of 'actually existing neoliberalism'. *Antipode*, 34(3): 349–379.

Brown, B.J. and Baker, S. (2013) *Responsible Citizens: Individuals, Health and Policy Under Neoliberalism*. London: Anthem Press.

Bunton, R. (1992) More than a woolly jumper: Health promotion as social regulation. *Critical Public Health*, 3(2): 4–11.

Bunton, R., Nettleton, S. and Burrows, R. (eds) (2003) *The Sociology of Health Promotion: Critical Analyses of Consumption, Lifestyle and Risk*. London: Routledge.

Coreil, J. and Levin, J.S. (1984–1985) A critique of the life style concept in public health education. *International Quarterly of Community Health Education*, 5(2): 103–114.

Coreil, J., Levin, J.S. and Jaco, E.G. (1985) Life style: An emergent concept in the socio-medical sciences. *Culture, Medicine and Psychiatry*, 9: 423–437.

Coveney, J. (2006) *Food, Morals and Meaning: The Pleasure and Anxiety of Eating*. Second Edition. London: Routledge.

Crawford, R. (1977) You are dangerous to your health: The ideology and politics of victim blaming. *International Journal of Health Services*, 7(4): 663–680.

Crawford, R. (1980) Healthism and the medicalization of everyday life. *International Journal of Health Services*, 10(3): 365–388.

Crawford, R. (2006) Health as a meaningful social practice. *Health: An Interdisciplinary Journal*, 19(4): 401–420.

Doll, R. and Hill, A.B. (1950) Smoking and carcinoma of the lung. *British Medical Journal*, 2(4682): 739–748.

Doll, R. and Hill, A.B. (1952) A study of the aetiology of carcinoma of the lung. *British Medical Journal*, 2(4797): 1271–1286.

Doll, R. and Hill, A.B. (1954) The mortality of doctors in relation to their smoking habits: A preliminary report. *British Medical Journal*, 1(4877): 1451–1455.

Doll, R. and Hill, A.B. (1956) Lung cancer and other causes of death in relation to smoking. *British Medical Journal*, 2(5001): 1071–1081.

Engs, R.C. (2000) *Clean Living Movements: American Cycles of Health Reform*. Westport, CT: Praeger.

Ferguson, J. (2010) The uses of neoliberalism. *Antipode*, 41(S1): 166–184.

Fitzpatrick, M. (2001) *The Tyranny of Health: Doctors and the Regulation of Lifestyle*. London: Routledge.

Foucault, M. (1980) *Power/Knowledge: Selected Interviews and Other Writings 1972–1977*. Edited by Colin Gordon. New York: Pantheon Books.

Fuchs, V.R. (2011) *Who Shall Live? Health, Economics and Social Choice*. Second Expanded Edition. Singapore: World Scientific Publishing.

Garland, C. and Harper, S. (2012) Did somebody say neoliberalism?: On the uses and limitations of a critical concept in media and communication studies. *tripleC*, 10(2): 413–424.

Giddens, A. (1990) *The Consequences of Modernity*. Cambridge: Polity Press.

Gifford, S.M. (1986) The meaning of lumps: A case study of the ambiguities of risk. In C.R. Janes, R. Stall and S.M. Gifford (eds), *Anthropology and Epidemiology*. Dordrecht: D. Reidel Publishing, pp. 213–246.

Gilleard, C. and Higgs, P. (2014) Revisionist or simply wrong? A response to Armstrong's article on chronic illness. *Sociology of Health and Illness*, 36(7): 1111–1115.

Gregory, J. (2007) *Of Victorians and Vegetarians: The Vegetarian Movement in Victorian Britain*. London: Tauris Academic Studies.

Hacking, I. (1990) *The Taming of Chance*. New York: Cambridge University Press.

Hempel, S. (2007) *The Strange Case of the Broad Street Pump: John Snow and the Mystery of Cholera*. Berkeley: University of California Press.

Hill, A.B. (1965) The environment and disease: Association or causation? *Proceedings of the Royal Society of Medicine*, 58: 295–300.

Hilton, M. (2000) *Smoking in British Popular Culture 1800–2000*. Manchester: Manchester University Press.

Hilton, M. and Nightingale, S. (1998) 'A microbe of the devil's own make': Religion and science in the British anti-tobacco movement, 1853–1908. In S. Lock, L.A. Reynolds and E.M. Tansey (eds), *Ashes to Ashes: the History of Smoking and Health*, Amsterdam: Rodopi, pp. 41–63.

Inhorn, M.C. (1995) Medical anthropology and epidemiology: Divergences or convergences? *Social Science and Medicine*, 40(3): 285–290.

Inhorn, M.C. and Whittle, K.L. (2001) Feminism meets the 'new' epidemiologies: Toward an appraisal of antifeminist biases in epidemiological research on women's health. *Social Science and Medicine*, 53: 553–567.

Kabat, G.C. (2008) *Hyping Health Risks: Environmental Hazards in Daily Life and the Science of Epidemiology*. New York: Columbia University Press.

Kingfisher, C. and Maskovsky, J. (2008) Introduction: The limits of neoliberalism. *Critique of Anthropology*, 28(2): 115–126.

Kipnis, A.B. (2008) Audit cultures: Neoliberal governmentality, socialist legacy, or technologies of governing? *American Ethnologist*, 35(2): 275–289.

Klein, R. (2010) What is health and how do you get it? In J. Metzl and A. Kirkland (eds), *Against Health: How Health Became the New Morality*. New York: New York University Press, pp. 15–25.

Koch, T. and Denike, K. (2006) Rethinking John Snow's South London study: A Bayesian evaluation and recalculation. *Social Science and Medicine*, 63: 271–283.

Krieger, N. (1994) Epidemiology and the web of causation: Has anyone seen the spider? *Social Science and Medicine*, 39(7): 887–903.

Krieger, N. (2008) Proximal, distal, and the politics of causation: What's level got to do with it? *American Journal of Public Health*, 98: 221–230.

Krieger, N. (2011) *Epidemiology and the People's Health: Theory and Context*. Oxford: Oxford University Press.

Levine, H.G. (1993) Temperance cultures: Alcohol as a problem in Nordic and English-speaking cultures. In M. Lader, G. Edwards and D.C. Drummon (eds), *The Nature of Alcohol and Drug-Related Problems*. New York: Oxford University Press, pp. 16–36.

Livingston, J. (2012) *Improvising Medicine: An African Oncology Ward in an Emerging Cancer Epidemic*. Durham, NC: Duke University Press.

Lupton, D. (1995) *The Imperative of Health: Public Health and the Regulated Body*. London: Sage.

Macintyre, S., Ellaway, A. and Cummins, S. (2002) Place effects on health: How can we conceptualise, operationalise and measure them? *Social Science and Medicine*, 55: 125–139.

Mackenbach, J.P. (1994) The epidemiologic transition theory. *Journal of Epidemiology and Community Health*, 48: 329–332.

McNaughton, D. (2013) 'Diabesity' down under: Overweight and obesity as cultural signifiers for type 2 diabetes mellitus. *Critical Public Health*, 23(3): 274–288.

Malthus, T.R. (1798) *An Essay on the Principle of Population*. London: J. Johnson.

Maskovsky, J. and Kingfisher, C. (2001) Introduction: Global capitalism, neoliberal policy and poverty. *Urban Anthropology and Studies of Cultural Systems and World Economic Development*, 30(2–3): 105–121.

Metzl, J. and Kirkland, A. (eds) (2010) *Against Health: How Health Became the New Morality*. New York: New York University Press.

Omran, A.R. (2005 [1971]) The epidemiologic transition: A theory of the epidemiology of population change. *Milbank Quarterly*, 83(4): 731–757.

Petersen, A. and Bunton, R. (eds) (1997) *Foucault, Health and Medicine*. London: Routledge.

Petersen, A. and Lupton, D. (1996) *The New Public Health: Health and Self in the Age of Risk*. London: Sage.

Phelan, S. (2007) Messy grand narrative or analytical blind spot? When speaking of neoliberalism. *Comparative European Politics*, 5: 328–338.

Procter, R.N. (1996) The anti-tobacco campaign of the Nazis: A little known aspect of public health in Germany, 1933–1945. *British Medical Journal*, 313(7070): 1450–1453.

Raftery, J. (2004) Critical perspectives on public health history. In H. Keleher and B. Murphy (eds), *Understanding Health: A Determinants Approach*. Melbourne: Oxford University Press, pp. 127–133.

Rudy, J. (2005) *The Freedom to Smoke: Tobacco Consumption and Identity*. Montreal: McGill-Queen's University Press.

Schwartz, H. (1986) *Never Satisfied: A Cultural History of Diets, Fantasies and Fat*. New York: Doubleday.

Shapin, S. (2010) *Never Pure: Historical Studies of Science as if It Was Produced by People with Bodies, Situated in Time, Space, Culture, and Society and Struggling for Credibility and Authority*. Baltimore, MD: Johns Hopkins University Press.

Springer, S. (2012) Neoliberalism as discourse: Between Foucauldian political economy and Marxian poststructuralism. *Critical Discourse Studies*, 9(2): 133–147.

Susser, M. and Stein, Z. (2009) *Eras in Epidemiology: The Evolution of Ideas*. Oxford: Oxford University Press.

Tate, C. (1999) *Cigarette Wars: The Triumph of the Little White Slaver*, New York: Oxford University Press.

Thomas, L. (1991) Science and health: Possibilities, probabilities, and limitations. In A. Mack (ed.), *In Time of Plague: the History and Social Consequences of Lethal Epidemic Disease*. New York: New York University Press, pp. 57–73.

Trostle, J. (1986) Early work in anthropology and epidemiology: From social medicine to the germ theory, 1840 to 1920. In C.R. Janes, R. Stall and S.M. Gifford (eds), *Anthropology and Epidemiology*. Dordrecht: D. Reidel Publishing, pp. 35–57.

Tyrell, I. (1999) *Deadly Enemies: Tobacco and its Opponents in Australia*. Sydney: University of New South Wales Press.

Valverde, M. (1998) *Diseases of the Will: Alcohol and the Dilemmas of Freedom*. Cambridge: Cambridge University Press.

Ward, K. and England, K. (2007) Introduction: Reading neoliberalization. In K. England and K. Ward (eds), *Neoliberalization: States, Networks, Peoples*. Hoboken, NJ: Blackwell, pp. 1–22.

Warner, J. (2008) *All or Nothing: A Short History of Abstinence in America*. Toronto: McClelland and Stewart.

WHO (2006 [1946]) Constitution. *World Health Organization*. Available at: www.who.int/governance/eb/who_constitution_en.pdf (accessed 15 December 2015).

Winslow, C.-E. A. (1943) *The Conquest of Epidemic Disease: A Chapter in the History of Ideas*. Princeton, NJ: Princeton University Press.

2

NUDGING AND OTHER THEORIES OF 'HEALTH BEHAVIOUR'

Introduction

In 2001, Canada became the first country in the world to introduce graphic warning labels on cigarette packets. The legislation was ostensibly designed to inform smokers about the health effects of smoking, but its purpose was clearly *persuasive* as well as *informational*. In other words, the Canadian government explicitly recognised that graphic warning labels might have a role to play in reducing tobacco consumption as well as warning smokers about its risks (Health Canada 2000). Although not explicitly framed in such terms, the assumption was clearly that repeated exposure to the warning labels on the packet would potentially 'nudge' the smoker away from the habit. According to one tobacco control researcher: 'An individual who smokes one pack per day, for example, is potentially exposed to the health warning 7,300 times in a single year' (Fong 2001: 2).

Another paradigmatic shift occurred in December 2012, when Australia became the first country in the world to implement plain packaging legislation to remove all industry branding from cigarette packets. The assumption underpinning the legislation was that such packets would reduce the appeal of smoking, increase the salience of health warnings and correct misperceptions about the harms of tobacco use, thereby decreasing the number of young people who start smoking and increasing the number of people who quit (WHO 2011). In May 2016, the English government followed Australia's lead in implementing such legislation and plain packaging has also been identified as a priority for Canada's new Liberal government.

Cigarette packaging legislation, along with innumerable other public health initiatives, is implicitly based on theories of 'health behaviour' – theories that form the focus of this chapter. If, as argued in Chapter 1, a preoccupation with 'lifestyle' has shaped much of contemporary epidemiology and public health, equally important is its corollary: 'health behaviour'. As Coreil, Levin and Jaco (1985: 428) note, when the term 'lifestyle' is used in the health sciences it is typically intended to refer to 'specific behaviors identified as risk factors for disease and accidental death . . . These applications are oriented toward behavioral intervention at the level of the individual'. Although a variety of health behaviours have been targeted, the most intensively studied are what are commonly referred to as public health's 'Big Four', namely: smoking, alcohol consumption, diet and exercise.

Although behaviour change has become the 'Holy Grail' of public health and primary care, only recently has the concept of health behaviour been articulated and formalised as a major health care problem (Armstrong 2009). As David Armstrong (2009) has shown, when the concept of 'behaviour' was used in medical journals in the nineteenth and early twentieth centuries, it typically referred to the actions of *inanimate* objects – such as the tubercle bacillus – as opposed to denoting *human* activity. The concept of 'health behaviour' as it is conceptualised today was a product of the mid-twentieth century and it's largely developments that occurred from this period onwards that I'm concerned with in this chapter. Following an overview of the rise of the concept of health behaviour and the various theories positing how behaviour change occurs, including recent interest in the concept 'nudging', I return to smoking and tobacco control policy. As the most intensively studied of the 'Big Four', it's frequently touted as a model for the others. However, as I aim to show, the concept of health behaviour has serious limitations as a means of grasping (and responding to) the complex domains that are currently framed within the rubric of 'lifestyle'.

The concept of 'health behaviour'

The concept of 'health behaviour' derives from health psychology and has today become ubiquitous in health-related research and interventions (Armstrong 2009; Cohn 2014). According to Simon Cohn (2014: 157), 'The assumption that there are easily identifiable and observable forms of health behaviour has almost universally been adopted by those involved in (and funded to do) healthcare research'. However, the concept is indebted to the emergence of behaviourism in the early part of the twentieth century, which saw 'behaviour' rise to the status of a major explanatory variable (Armstrong 2014; Cohn 2014). As formulated in the work of John Watson and, later, B.F. Skinner, behaviourism postulated that it was possible to understand human actions without recourse to introspection. To quote Watson:

> The behaviorist asks: Why don't we make what we can observe the real field of psychology? Let us limit ourselves to things that can be observed, and formulate laws concerning only those things. Now what can we observe? Well, we can observe *behavior – what the organism does or says.*
>
> *Watson 2009 [1924]: 6, emphasis in original*

Clearly a reaction to psychoanalysis and the 'fiction'[1] of consciousness it had promulgated, behaviourism was also connected with psychology's concern to be 'a purely objective, experimental branch of natural science which needs introspection as little as do the sciences of chemistry and physics' (Watson cited in Willis and Giles 1978: 17). The attraction this more 'scientific' approach held for practitioners is illustrated by the rise of the notion of 'behaviour modification', which achieved widespread representation in the psychological literature more rapidly than any prior conceptual innovation (Willis and Giles 1978). Indeed, the term 'behavioural science' (still in wide use today) is a direct product of this reorientation of psychology and the subsequent naturalisation of the concept of behaviour it engendered. Thus, while behaviourism began to lose favour in the 1950s, its legacy is evident in the continued importance of 'behaviour' in psychology, epidemiology and a variety of other fields.

Jane Ogden (1995) argues that while psychological theories up until the 1950s tended to describe the individual as a passive responder to external events, with behaviour seen to be the product of external stimuli, a more animated version of the individual began to emerge from the 1960s, formed around the notion of an *interactive* alignment of the individual and environment (see also Armstrong 2011 for similar points). Such theories emphasised the cognitive and processing capacities of the individual. In this framework 'behaviour was conceptualized as being mediated by selective processing and as a product of interactions between individuals, and between the individual and the outside world. The individual was characterized by an increasing sense of agency' (Ogden 1995: 410).

During this period, social psychologists began to develop models to explain health 'behaviours' (e.g., smoking, alcohol consumption, screening practices) that reproduced this figure of the interactive individual (Ogden 1995). The health belief model was one of the first specific theories of health behaviour and remains highly influential today (Glanz and Bishop 2010). Developed in the 1950s by psychologists[2] employed by the newly formed Behavioral Science Section of the US Public Health Service, the model was an attempt to theorise why people did and didn't make use of tuberculosis screening programmes (Steckler, McLeroy and Holtzman 2010). The health belief model posits that people's beliefs about whether they are at risk for a health problem, and their perceptions of the benefits of taking action to avoid it, influence their readiness to take action (Glanz and Bishop 2010). In this framework, education becomes a core intervention to transform unhealthy behaviours, based on the assumption that if people just know how ill health occurs – and stop being in denial about it – positive change will naturally follow (cf. Basu 2004). As Armstrong (2014) notes, the model had radical implications in positing the value of a staged reconstruction of the self and its sense of agency as a means of promoting healthier 'behaviours'. In his words: 'The health belief model was less a theoretical framework and more a technology that promoted the idea of actions based on psychological readiness' (Armstrong 2014: 167).

Although echoes of the health belief model have remained in the many theories that have been advanced since, and health education continues to be a primary 'intervention', Ogden argues that in the late 1970s another subtle shift occurred in conceptions of health behaviour. Instead of a dyadic model in which the individual interacts with the environment via external cues to action that are perceived and appraised at a cognitive level, a third moderating variable was introduced. Thus, 'The individual is no longer conceptualized as passively responding to external cues, nor as interacting with their environment, but as interacting with their own inner self' (Ogden 1995: 411) – a model Ogden labels *intra-active* as opposed to *interactive*. Here, Albert Bandura's (1986) social learning theory (later reformulated as social cognitive theory) and the construct of 'self-efficacy' were pivotal. Broadly speaking, this approach explains human behaviour in terms of a tripartite reciprocal model in which personal factors, environmental influences and behaviour continually interact; in this framing, self-efficacy – the individual's confidence in her ability to take action and persist with it despite obstacles – is critical to influencing health behaviour change (Glanz and Bishop 2010). Its traces are evident in other highly influential models, such as the transtheoretical or 'stages of change' model (Prochaska and DiClemente 1985; Prochaska and Velicer 1997), and the theory of planned behaviour change (Ajzen 1991).

Ogden argues that these shifts in psychological theories paralleled changing conceptions of risks to health over the course of the twentieth century, with such risks now deemed to stem from the presence or absence of *self-control* in managing and mastering the drives that expose the body to external threats. As she notes, in this framing it's not, for example, HIV that presents the risk to health, but individuals' *inability* to control their sexual behaviour; likewise, it's not cervical cancer that constitutes the risk to health but women's *unwillingness* to undergo regular screening and take preventive action. Thus, the greatest risk to individual health in the late twentieth century was now the individual him or herself (Ogden 1995; see also Crawford 1977; Greco 1993; Petersen and Lupton 1996; Armstrong 1995, 2009, 2011).

However, although the focus on the individual's actions (or inactions, as it were) as posing the greatest risk to her health is still dominant today, a fourth model of health behaviour has increasingly supplemented, albeit not supplanted, the models Ogden identified two decades ago: the concept of 'nudging.'[3] The growing popularity of nudge initiatives is a result of the failures of the interactive and intra-active models of health behaviour to make noticeable strides in transforming so-called 'problem' behaviours. That said, in many respects it is more of a return to the old behaviourist model as opposed to an entirely new regime.

Nudging and the (re)turn to behaviourism

Nudging has its roots in the disciplines of psychology and economics, among others; as Adam Burgess (2012: 4) observes, 'The boundaries between behavioural economics, various forms of "nudging", social marketing and psychology are not clear, but they all inform the policy mix that is now generally known as "nudging".' Although precise definitions of the concept are difficult to come by, like the behaviourist models of old, nudging emphasises the importance of environmental stimuli in determining behaviour (Marteau *et al.* 2011).

The term was first used in the book *Nudge: Improving Decisions About Health, Wealth, and Happiness* by Thaler and Sunstein (2008). The premise of the book is straightforward: environment dictates our behaviour to a large extent, so if you want people to make better decisions, rearrange their environments to facilitate this. It begins with a hypothetical case study about 'Carolyn', the director of food services for a large city school system, who sets up a series of experiments with the layout of school cafeterias to determine whether the way food is displayed and arranged might influence students' decisions about what to eat. 'Simply by rearranging the cafeteria, Carolyn was able to increase or decrease consumption of many food items by as much as 25 per cent,' Thaler and Sunstein assert (2008: 1). In their formulation, by rearranging the environment in this fashion, Carolyn has become a 'choice architect': someone who 'has the responsibility for organizing the context in which people make decisions' (Thaler and Sunstein 2008: 3). The authors identify this approach as 'libertarian paternalism' based on the view that 'in general, people should be free to do what they like' but that 'it is legitimate for choice architects to try to influence people's behavior in order to make their lives longer, healthier, and better' (Thaler and Sunstein 2008: 5).

In essentially re-importing classic behaviourist principles, the concept of nudging might seem incompatible with the health behaviour models posited above but it is typically reconciled in the following way:

> Most people value their health yet persist in behaving in ways that undermine it . . . This gap between values and behaviour can be understood by using a dual process model in which human behaviour is shaped by two systems. The first is a reflective, goal oriented system driven by our values and intentions. It requires cognitive capacity or thinking space, which is limited . . . The second is an automatic, affective system that requires little or no cognitive engagement, being driven by immediate feelings and triggered by our environments.
>
> *Marteau* et al. *2011: 263*

Nudging shifts the focus away from a purely rational actor and posits instead an individual who makes imperfect choices based on a tension between short-term pleasure and long-term goals (Burgess 2012). Intended to represent 'a "third way" between the regulation associated with the left and the "leave it to the markets" approach of the right' (Burgess 2012: 6), its core assumptions have been tremendously influential. Witness the British government's Behavioural Insights Team, for which Thaler is an adviser (Oliver 2013). Billing itself as 'the world's first government institution dedicated to the application of behavioural sciences', it has three core objectives: 1) making public services more cost-effective and easier to use; 2) improving outcomes by applying a more realistic model of human behaviour to public policy; and 3) 'enabling people to make "better choices for themselves"' (Behavioural Insights Team 2016). A US counterpart, the Social and Behavioral Sciences Team (frequently referred to on social media as 'Obama's Nudge Brigade'), has also been established in the White House, and similarly aims to 'use behavioral science insights to better serve the American people' (Social and Behavioral Sciences Team 2016). Clearly, the promise of offering more effective and cost-effective public policies has been extremely attractive to governments, despite the fact that nudging, like the theories of health behaviour that preceded it, 'is not driven by compelling evidence that it works' (Burgess 2012: 6).

Critiques of health behaviour theories

Although these theories of health behaviour differ in a variety of ways, they share the assumption that their object is a verifiable 'thing' that can be isolated, intervened into and transformed. In this framework the everyday activities of eating, smoking, exercise, drinking and so on become transformed into the problems of eating behaviour, smoking behaviour, exercise behaviour and drinking behaviour respectively (Armstrong 2009). They are treated as equivalent and interchangeable: smoking, drinking, eating and exercise become activities of the same type of order;[4] they are taken to be unitary in character, easily identified and with meanings that don't change across the diverse array of contexts in which they might be carried out (Cohn 2014; Horrocks and Johnson 2014).

Such models are also equally mechanistic and deterministic. In the cognitivist view, human beings are predominantly shaped by cognitive blueprints that guide individual actions along predetermined lines: 'These mental constructions are generally seen as ready-made schemes that scientists can learn to "read" in order to predict actual behaviors of individuals' (Bibeau 1997: 251). Likewise, behaviourist models such as the nudge paradigm are based on a framework in which humans are equally shaped by blueprints that can be used to predict – and transform – future behaviour, except the blueprints in question are environmental (actually, architectural in a quite literal sense) as opposed to cognitive. In both instances, the underlying framework is positivistic and evokes a 'science of behaviour' modelled on the natural sciences (Coreil and Levin 1984–1985: 107). In such renderings, as Cohn (2014) observes, the notion of 'behaviour' becomes so reified that it provides little critical insight into what people actually do and why:

> In this, then, lies the inherent conservatism of adopting categories of behaviour a priori. The issue is not simply that they continuously get reproduced from one research project to another but that they increasingly become naturalised the more they are 'understood'.
>
> *Cohn 2014: 160*

In many respects, the reification of the concept of behaviour has been facilitated by the assumption that it *can't* be reified because it's something concrete and observable. Recall that this was precisely why proponents of behaviourism advocated the study of behaviour in the first place – because it would enable the field to evolve into a purely objective branch of natural science. However, by forcing behaviours into a natural science paradigm, the behaviour itself becomes abstract and removed from any comprehensive or detailed description of what people are actually doing when they eat, drink, smoke, etc. (Cohn 2014). Thus, research questions tend to become focused on 'discrete variables that are technocratic at best or completely arbitrary at worst' (Bourgois, Lettiere and Quesada 1997: 166).

Consider, for example, drinking as a health behaviour. First, as Michael Fitzpatrick (2001) observes, it's not immediately obvious why alcohol should have assumed its current prominence in the fields of public health and health promotion, because, unlike smoking, it isn't linked to a particular disease that has increased dramatically in prevalence. Fitzpatrick argues that the relexicalisation of 'drinking' as 'alcohol consumption' enabled it to become discursively transformed into a health behaviour, despite the somewhat arbitrary character of the limits set for safe and risky consumption and the fact that it can't be condemned as something uniformly 'bad'. However, as Blue and colleagues (2016) point out, drinking (along with eating, exercising and smoking) is not a single behaviour in the way that public health conventionally defines it. Instead, it is a broad domain of human activity – a practice that is reproduced and transformed through re-enactment and performance across time and space. As they note, focusing on *practices* rather than *behaviours* completely changes the questions to be asked and answered. Accordingly,

> whilst the practice of consuming alcohol involves the action of ingesting ethanol, what is drunk, how much is drunk, how it is drunk, what is said, varies considerably from a dinner at high table in an Oxford College, a group of teenagers planning a Friday evening out, a gang of workmen from a building site relaxing after a hard day's work, drinking 'on the street', or someone drinking alone at home; they constitute significantly different variants of 'the' practice. Efforts to change 'drinking behaviour' as if this was a single entity are doomed to failure because drinking is manifestly not like that.
>
> *Blue* et al. *2016: 38–39*

As we saw in Chapter 1, another feature of such models of health behaviour is the assumption that individuals are capable of making 'better' choices for themselves and that their well-being is in part an outcome of the decisions they make (Blue *et al.* 2016; see also Petersen and Lupton 1996; Fitzpatrick 2001; Cohn 2014). This assumption is equally embedded in both cognitivist and behaviourist models – according to the former, 'it is finally up to the individual to choose whether to change their behaviour to a healthier one'; likewise, the latter asks: 'How can individuals best be encouraged to take more responsibility for their well-being?'[5] Cohn (2014: 160) points out that models of health behaviour are therefore unavoidably morally loaded, 'as issues of responsibility and agency are distributed in specific ways along causal pathways that inevitably converge on the individual'.

The social determinants of health: a rejoinder?

In light of these criticisms, growing prominence has been accorded in the field of public health to models that take the *social* rather than *individual* determinants of health as their starting point and primary object of analysis. Since the late 1990s, literature on the social determinants of health has grown exponentially (Braveman, Egerter and Williams 2011) and its status as a mainstream concept was cemented in 2005, when the World Health Organization established its Commission on the Social Determinants of Health.[6] However, it is debatable whether such frameworks have dislodged the focus on individual health behaviours to any substantive degree. For example, in the Canadian context – arguably a country early to embrace the framework at a policy level – lifestyle approaches have continually trumped those focusing on the social determinants of health (Raphael 2008, 2011). Indeed, some scholars have argued that the social determinants of health perspective actively lends itself to depoliticised approaches because it accords relatively little attention to the underlying political-economic systems that give rise to the material and social circumstances that are labelled as 'social determinants' (see Krieger 2011).

Part of the issue is that the social determinants of health tend to operate as a conceptual black box.[7] For example, as Macintyre, Ellaway and Cummins (2002: 125) have noted of the oft-observed relationship between area deprivation and health, '"place effects" often appear to have the status of a residual category, an unspecified black box of somewhat mystical influences on health'. Arguably, this fuzziness stems from the fact that the social determinants of health framework is often embraced as a response to the biomedical bias of existing definitions of health rather than as a fully articulated concept in its own right.[8] Thus, it often seems to be defined more by what it *isn't* than what it *is*. Indeed, this is precisely how Braveman, Egerter and Williams (2011) define the concept: 'the term social determinant of health is often used to refer broadly to any *nonmedical factors* influencing health' (p. 383, emphasis added).

The extraordinary breadth of the concept means that there is little consistency in overviews of what exactly constitutes it. Consider the following three definitions of the social determinants of health:

1) Freedom, including equal access to participation in the political process, equal opportunity, safe jobs, health care, and the social bases of self respect.
2) Income, education, employment, housing and the environment, as well as their effect on lifestyle.
3) The social gradient, stress, early life, social exclusion, work, unemployment, social support, addiction, food, and transport.

Regidor 2006: 899

The first focuses primarily on rights, the second retains a focus on lifestyle (albeit with an emphasis on 'distal' factors that affect it), and the third includes issues like addiction and transport. Thus, the differences relate not only to the specific factors that constitute 'social determinants', but how they are more broadly conceptualised; even within any given definition, the listed elements are not of the same order.

According to Dennis Raphael (2006, 2011), the framework seems to encompass a number of distinct discourses; while some advocate more radical political and economic action, others are merely dressed-up versions of the prevailing lifestyle model and see the social determinants of health as primarily a means of identifying individuals with modifiable medical and behavioural risk profiles.[9] In health policy, there's also a tendency to conceptualise determinants as single reducible categories, rather than seeing them as complex social locations that shape the experience of health (Hankivksy and Christoffersen 2008). Indeed, various models don't challenge the validity or utility of the concept of health behaviour itself. Instead, social determinants are understood as additional variables that impact health *beyond* personal health behaviours – such as the conceptual framework used by the Robert Wood Johnson Foundation Commission to Build a Healthier America[10] (see Figure 2.1). Thus, by preserving the delineated characteristics of health behaviour, the inclusion of 'the social' frequently serves simply to *maintain* rather than *revise* it (cf. Cohn 2014) – as prevailing public health approaches to smoking attest.

Tobacco control policy and models of smoking 'behaviour'

As outlined in Chapter 1, in many respects smoking is the prototypical unhealthy 'behaviour' – the one that legitimised epidemiology as a discipline, not only in terms of the compelling evidence it provided of the adverse health effects of the habit, but the inroads it enabled in reducing its prevalence. Indeed, observers have frequently touted tobacco control policy as exemplary in its focus on the social and systemic, as opposed to individualistic, sources of the 'tobacco epidemic'.

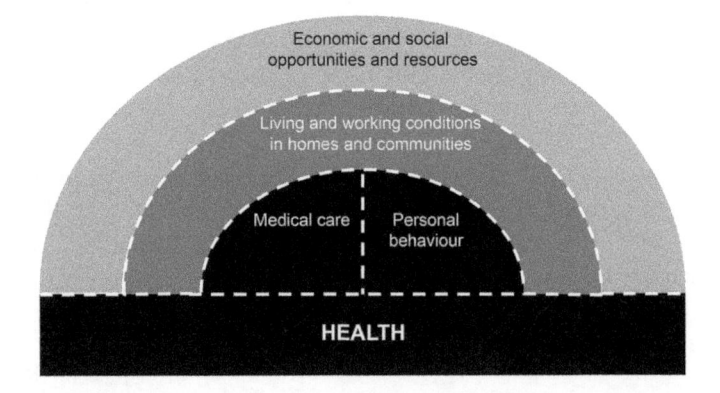

FIGURE 2.1 Conceptual framework for social determinants of health produced by the Robert Wood Johnson Foundation Commission to Build a Healthier America

Source: adapted from Braveman, Egerter and Williams 2011.

Typically such observations are made in comparing tobacco control policy to prevailing approaches to obesity (e.g., Yach *et al.* 2003, 2005; West 2007; Kinmonth 2016). However, tobacco control policy is increasingly being positioned as a case study from which various other areas of public policy, especially pertaining to food, alcohol and transport, might learn (Smith 2013: 64).

The six-stranded tobacco control policy package endorsed by the World Health Organization for 'defeating the global tobacco epidemic' is known by the acronym 'MPOWER': Monitor tobacco use and prevention polices; Protect people from tobacco smoke; Offer help to quit tobacco use; Warn about the dangers of tobacco; Enforce bans on advertising, promotion and sponsorship; and Raise taxes on tobacco (WHO 2013). The package therefore consists of strategies that target the *environment* (e.g., smoking bans, advertising bans) and the *individual* (support for quitting, information campaigns, etc.). However, has this ostensibly more structural approach dislodged the focus on smoking as an individual 'risk behaviour'? Consider the use of the term 'epidemic' to describe smoking.[11] As Mair and Kierans observe:

> The implication of such phraseology is that smoking is a disease or disorder, and that smokers should be thought of in much the same way as any other category of individual with a disease or disorder. When researching questions relating to tobacco use among populations, the objective is to uncover the processes through which individuals contract that disease or disorder.
>
> *Mair and Kierans 2007: 106*

In this framing, what 'causes' an individual to smoke is modelled on analyses of the relationship that connects exposure to tobacco smoke to lung cancer, with the processes treated as structurally analogous (Mair 2011). According to Mair and Kierans (2007), a causal, linear narrative about problem/solution and pathology/treatment is established: that people use tobacco because they are addicted and can't stop; that they lack an awareness of the health consequences of tobacco use; and they lack the self-control or self-efficacy to resist peer pressure and/or manipulation by the tobacco industry.

In a similar vein, Macnaughton, Carro-Ripalda and Russell (2012) have more recently noted that the principles that guide mainstream tobacco control research articulate a particular vision of 'the smoker' based on two seemingly contradictory models of personhood. The rational agent view assumes that smokers 'need only be presented with the facts to respond appropriately' (Macnaughton *et al.* 2012: 458). The non-agent view, on the other hand, understands smokers as 'Pavlovian automatons' (Macnaughton *et al.* 2012: 459) fuelled by their addiction and need for instant gratification. Here, we see yet further incarnations of the cognitivist and behaviourist paradigms outlined above. Despite their differences, both models equally assume a unitary being consisting of a stable core and a movable periphery: smoking thus becomes an appendage of the core person. 'What follows is a logic of addition and subtraction: something added can also be taken away' (Macnaughton *et al.* 2012: 460).

The first generation of tobacco control policies were based primarily on the rational agent model: 'The individual targeted by those policies was a free, responsible, autonomous subject, capable of making the right choice insofar as she received the correct information' (Alemanno 2012: 38). However, the newer generation of measures attempt to keep consumers away from the habit by reducing the visibility and appeal of smoking. Now those wanting to purchase a packet of cigarettes face a series of physical and moral obstacles in order to do so (Alemanno 2012). In British Columbia, these obstacles are twofold: first, venues selling cigarettes are required to hide them from view and the server must retrieve them from a locked cupboard after the smoker requests a specific brand; second, the packet itself is dominated by hard-hitting graphic warnings, which cover 75 per cent of its exterior (see Figure 2.2).

Alberto Alemanno (2012) argues that cigarette packaging legislation implicitly relies on nudging strategies. In his words, 'none of these policies . . . is set to correct ignorance. Instead, they aim at fighting inertia – by discouraging automatic behaviour – and akrasia, i.e. the weakness of the will' (p. 38). There's little question that such strategies aim to target a presumed automatic, affective system that requires no cognitive engagement. For example, in a commentary on plain packaging, Hastings, Gallopel-Morvan and Rey (2008: 361) state: 'It is abundantly clear that young people are drawn into smoking by branding and that liveried packs play an active role in this process'. In such framings, the industry-branded packet becomes a 'silent salesman', which enacts a 'poisonous seduction' against susceptible minds, with a rebranded packet logically seen to reverse these effects (see Chantler 2014; Chapman and Freeman 2014). Accordingly, the branded aesthetics of the cigarette packet – of either danger or desire, depending on who is in charge – are seen to unconsciously shape smokers' responses to its content.

FIGURE 2.2 Front and back of Canadian cigarette packet

Source: photo by Kirsten Bell.

Although such legislation implicitly posits the smoker as a Pavlovian automaton, it simultaneously relies on an assumption of the rational human who will respond predictably to information about the health effects of tobacco use. According to the World Health Organization report *Warning About the Dangers of Tobacco* (WHO 2011), 'Despite clear evidence about the dangers of tobacco use, many tobacco users worldwide underestimate the full extent of the risk to themselves and others' (p. 18). The report argues that it is therefore critical that tobacco packaging contains 'evidence-based health warnings' (p. 20). The underlying message is that education about the dangers of tobacco will cause many individuals to consciously *choose* not to smoke.[12] Interestingly, despite the different logics informing each model, their conclusions are strikingly similar: the bigger and bolder the warning label, the better. Although in one case the impact of an unattractive packet is deemed to be unconscious and in the other it's understood to evoke a conscious choice, both models presume an equal effect on smoking 'behaviour'.

Cigarette packaging out of and in context

But what exactly is being studied in tobacco control research on cigarette packaging? As Simone Dennis (2013) observes, research tends to fall into two interrelated categories: 1) surveys or qualitative studies that assess the impact of cigarette packaging via respondents' awareness of and reactions to warning labels; or 2) experimental studies that make links between graphic warnings, text-based information and perceptions of harm and appeal. In both instances, participant responses are taken as a proxy for future 'smoking behaviour'.

To provide an illustration of the first type of study, Mead and colleagues (2015) explored the ways that 25 low-income smokers in Baltimore engaged with graphic warning labels. In describing their methods they note that: 'participants were asked about their cognitive and affective reactions to each label (such as what was the main message of the label and how it made them feel) and which labels were most likely to motivate them to quit' (Mead *et al.* 2015: 3). Based on responses in focus groups, the authors conclude: 'We found that participants were most motivated by labels portraying the negative consequences of smoking' (Mead *et al.* 2015: 8). As should be evident, this study falls primarily into the 'rational human' paradigm and is influenced by cognitive theories of behaviour change – indeed, social cognitive theory forms the explicit conceptual core of the study. Here, participants' assertions of a sense of fear and vulnerability in response to the labels are seen as indicators of their motivation to quit, which, in turn, is understood to predict future behaviour change.

An illustration of the latter type of study is found in the work of Munafò and colleagues (2011), who utilised eye-tracking technology to measure the responses of 43 English smokers and non-smokers to cigarette packets. Participants were shown images of branded and unbranded packets on a computer screen and their eye movements (or 'saccades') were tracked. The researchers found that non-smokers and weekly smokers (although not daily smokers) had more eye movements towards health warnings on plain versus branded packs. In focusing on such, the researchers' goal was clearly to try and get at respondents' automatic, *preconscious* response to the packet, with its visual architecture seen to determine the form of engagement. They conclude:

> [I]t is plausible that increased visual attention towards health warning information may increase the impact of this information and lead to a reduction in the likelihood of smoking initiation (among non-smokers) and an increase in the likelihood of smoking cessation (among light smokers).
>
> *Munafò* et al. *2011: 1509*

Despite the caveats posed ('plausible', 'may'), the assumption is clearly that such 'looking behaviour' is a proxy for future 'smoking behaviour', because the smoker is implicitly nudged towards an awareness of the harms of the habit. However, such assumptions are severely tested when confronted with smoking (and smokers) in everyday context.

I met Imran in the fall of 2013 at an outdoor seating area in downtown Vancouver where he was enjoying a quiet cigarette while studying for an upcoming exam. Young and well dressed, it quickly became apparent that Imran was from the UK. He told me that his family had migrated from east India to England before he was born and he had arrived in Vancouver the previous year to study for a technical degree. As we chatted, Imran informed me that had been smoking on and off since the age of 17. In his words, 'when it was on, it was *a lot* of smoking. And when it was off it was completely off'. Imran was currently smoking about 10 cigarettes daily, although he had recently cut back from a pack a day. However, despite intermittently going 'cold turkey', he insisted that he wasn't concerned about the long-term health effects of smoking – 'there's some people say, "Oh, it's cancer," and all that. You say, "Oh, I'll smoke. I'll die at 40 instead of 80." People on average are dying at 75, so who cares?' At 21, Imran was years away from such consequences, if indeed they happened at all.[13] For him, smoking was an ingrained habit, one inextricably bound up with sociality and drinking coffee – which he sipped from a disposable cup as we talked. In his words,

> I started smoking in England and I don't regret it. People are more social. I find that coffee – coffee is just the same as cigarettes. People sit down and have a cup of coffee, talk, have some conversation and smoke.

When I quizzed Imran about the warning label on the pack he was currently smoking (now ensconced in the pocket of his black trench coat), he confidently informed me that it was 'the guy with the hole' (see Figure 2.2). However, when we checked out his packet together, it was clear that he had misremembered it. Sheepish at having misrecalled the label, Imran explained: 'it's too creepy to look at! So I don't look at it at all'. I responded by drawing his attention to the actual label on the packet itself: 'So, it's the heart disease one' (a picture of gloved hands holding a meaty-looking heart) and Imran reflected: 'I thought it was the lungs, though. They *always* show the lungs.'

This exchange is revealing on a variety of levels. First, Imran clearly didn't know what label was on his packet, a pattern that has been consistently found among smokers in various countries with graphic warning labels in place (Bell *et al.* 2015). Second, he admitted that he intentionally didn't look at the warning labels – also a frequently reported response (Bell *et al.* 2015; Hardcastle *et al.* 2016). Third, he expressed his surprise that the label didn't contain 'the pair of lungs'. The problem is that there are no lungs depicted on any of the Canadian warning labels, so he was recalling a label that doesn't actually exist,[14] although it's precisely the sort of thing that one would *expect* to see on a cigarette packet. As this exchange revealed, encountering one's cigarette packet, like the larger practice of smoking itself, is intimately bound up with habitual, bodily engagements (Bell *et al.* 2015) – engagements that bear little resemblance to 'looking behaviour'. In essence, it simply isn't possible to parse the 'elements' that constitute smoking into a series of discrete 'variables' (e.g., looking at the pack, motivation to quit); to do so is to reproduce on a micro-level the mistaken assumptions that comprise prevailing approaches to the larger 'behaviour' itself.

But let's imagine for a moment that Imran did respond to his cigarette packet in the ways assumed by the studies above. Can we draw any implications from this about his 'smoking behaviour'? When I asked him, point blank, whether he thought the warning labels had an effect on his smoking, he immediately responded, 'No! I mean, why? It just doesn't make any sense. We know that, it's common sense. Every smoker knows that. No one smoking thinks it's a benefit.' He continued: 'The picture's not gonna make any difference.' At this point Imran became somewhat irate, drawing comparisons to other unhealthy substances.[15] 'I mean, it's not fair – for alcohol I don't think you see any pictures. Do you have any pictures of alcohol for the liver?' As a self-declared teetotaller, singling out smoking smacked of hypocrisy to Imran. He also drew comparisons with chocolate bars, stating:

> Chocolate! You eat it in excess – write on it 'you might get obese. You might get fat' – write on it! Why don't you write on chocolates or liquor like you do with smoking? I'm not promoting smoking but I'm just saying it's kind of unfair. It's *very* unfair.

He concluded: 'People are just gonna light on regardless. The more you write.'

I'm not necessarily suggesting that we just take Imran at face value here and conclude that cigarette packaging doesn't 'work',[16] but his arguments (of which I have heard countless variants) and his individual smoking history do illustrate the flaws in the prevailing model(s) of 'health behaviour'. If we think of smoking as a bundle of practices that are themselves inextricably entwined with other practices, we are forced to consider the social, affective, material and interrelational features of this activity (cf. Cohn 2014; see also Klein 1996; Poland *et al.* 2006; Dennis 2011). Certainly, we can't understand Imran's smoking without reference to drinking coffee and talking with friends. Nor can we understand it without reference to his habitual bodily engagements – not just with cigarettes themselves, but with their packs. As Dennis (2011: 31) notes, 'In and through frequent interactions between body and (cigarette) object, smoking practice both creates and maintains patterns of body use; our own bodies become ingrained through our interactions with objects', including both cigarettes themselves and the other accoutrements of the habit. And while his comparisons with alcohol and obesity might sound like defensive posturing, they also speak to smokers' growing sense of themselves as a marginalised and put upon minority and the way this, too, becomes tied up in the practice and identity of being 'a smoker', who will 'light on' regardless – or even because of – increasingly aggressive injunctions to quit. In sum, despite their differences, we have good grounds to be suspicious of the core assumptions upon which the cognitivist and behaviourist models of 'health behaviour' rest, both of which are equally reductionist in their understanding of how human beings think and act.

Conclusion

Although the concept of 'health behaviour' has become thoroughly naturalised today, in many respects it is a legacy of behaviourism and its attempts to create a science of behaviour modelled upon the natural sciences. While the rise of 'lifestyle' as the primary answer to the question of how to prevent chronic disease was a necessary precursor to the concept, much of its seductiveness rests on its apparent irrefutability. After all, we can *see* such behaviours whenever we glance around: people smoking, drinking too much, eating too much fast food, sitting at their desks all day and so on. But the notion of a 'health behaviour' is, in fact, an illusion. What *looks* like a stable behaviour that can be isolated and intervened into, is in actuality a complex bundle of practices that can't be divorced from its context without seriously misapprehending it – a theme I will return to in Chapter 6. Thus, we seem to bounce back and forth between two equally limiting frames: the rational human who will respond in a predictable fashion to educational interventions and the Pavlovian automaton at the whim of environmental stimuli. As I will discuss in Chapter 3, their assumptions about how to facilitate 'behaviour' change have dictated the terms of engagement with the concept of prevention – not just in the context of preventing disease, but arresting its effects once it has actually emerged.

Notes

1 For Watson (2009 [1924]: 5), 'consciousness' was a fundamentally unscientific concept – 'a plain assumption just as unprovable, just as unapproachable, as the old concept of the soul'.
2 Several figures are associated with the model, including Godfrey Hochbaum and Irwin Rosenstock; the model itself was outlined and refined in various publications between 1958–1966.
3 Which in any case can't be understood in terms of a one-replaces-the-other typology.
4 This is how 'obesity', something intrinsically different from 'smoking', came to be treated as conceptually equivalent and policies in the latter context were treated as potential models in the former. In this framing, 'obesity' becomes the 'new smoking'.

5 The former quote is from the 1998 report *Our Healthier Nation: A Contract for Health* produced by the England's Department of Health (Department of Health 1998: 48); the latter quote is from the blurb for the book *Behavioural Public Policy* (Oliver 2013).

6 I don't have space to address the rise of the 'social determinants of health' concept in any depth, but its growing influence is connected with the emergence of social epidemiology as a distinct subfield of epidemiology in the late 1990s (see Berkman, Kawachi and Glymour 2014). Complicating matters further is the fact that 'social epidemiology' itself is an umbrella term for a number of distinct theoretical perspectives, some of which are quite critical of the social determinants of health framework (see Krieger 2011 for a discussion). It's also worth noting that the assumptions underpinning the social determinants of health (and, indeed, social epidemiology) aren't especially new; they are essentially a repetition of themes that were well developed more than a century ago (Trostle 1986; Inhorn and Whittle 2001).

7 While this criticism has been made of conceptions of 'the environment' (Krieger 2011) and 'context' (Poland *et al.* 2006; Shoveller *et al.* 2016) in public health, it also applies equally to the social determinants of health. In many respects, this is a reflection of the ways that concepts such as 'society' and 'the social' are invoked – as pre-packaged and ready-made explanations for a variety of disparate phenomena (see Latour 2005: 22–23).

8 To clarify, I'm not suggesting that all those who have theorised the social determinants of health are guilty of this. My point is simply that this is often how the term has come to be used – both at a policy level and in terms of how public health practitioners conceptualise it.

9 Discussing the National Health Service in England, Katherine Smith (2013) highlights that interventions designed to change lifestyle behaviours are frequently being promoted as key policy responses to health inequalities. Thus, the *framing* may have changed, but the interventions themselves haven't.

10 I've used this as an illustration because it demonstrates the ways that social determinants of health frameworks have been taken up at a policy level, but it's worth noting that this model closely echoes the one introduced by Dahlgren and Whitehead (1991).

11 Of course, the metaphor is frequently employed in discussions of the 'Big Four' – the notion of a 'global obesity epidemic' is a case in point.

12 There are echoes of this in the MPOWER strategy itself, which is presumably a play on the word 'empower' – as in 'empowering' smokers to quit.

13 Many smokers 'reject a reductive causal link between risky present practice and a catastrophic future' (Diprose 2008: 143). Indeed, most smokers I've interviewed readily cite examples of relatives who 'smoked like a chimney' and lived to a ripe old age. And, of course, they are not wrong insofar as epidemiology cannot definitively speak to an individual's mortal destiny (see Chapter 1). I will discuss this in further detail in Chapter 3 in relation to the concept of 'risk denial'.

14 In Canada, at least, although it's common elsewhere – including the UK, where Imran was from. It's possible that he was thinking of the British labels.

15 These comparisons are reasonably common among smokers I've interviewed in Vancouver, many of whom feel that in a world of 'risks' (drinking, unhealthy food, pollution, etc.) smoking has been hypocritically singled out for attack.

16 Indeed, proponents of nudging would suggest that he is largely unaware of the impact of packaging on his smoking and his introspections therefore tell us little of value.

References

Ajzen, I. (1991) The theory of planned behavior. *Organizational Behavior and Human Decision Processes*, 50(2): 179–211.

Alemanno, A. (2012) Nudging smokers: The behavioural turn of tobacco risk regulation. *European Journal of Risk Regulation*, 3(3): 32–42.

Armstrong, D. (1995) The rise of surveillance medicine. *Sociology of Health and Illness*, 17(3): 393–404.

Armstrong, D. (2009) Origins of the problem of health-related behaviours: A geneaological study. *Social Studies of Science*, 39(6): 909–926.

Armstrong, D. (2011) The invention of patient-centred medicine. *Social Theory and Health*, 9: 410–418.

Armstrong, D. (2014) Actors, patients and agency: A recent history. *Sociology of Health and Illness*, 36(2): 163–174.

Bandura A. (1986) *Social Foundations of Thought and Action: A Social Cognitive Theory*. Englewood Cliffs, NJ: Prentice-Hall.

Basu, S. (2004) AIDS, empire and public health behaviorism. *International Journal of Health Services*, 34(1): 155–167.

Behavioural Insights Team (2016) Who we are. Available at: www.behaviouralinsights. co.uk/about-us/ (accessed 3 January 2016).

Bell, K., Dennis, S., Robinson, J. and Moore, R. (2015) Does the hand that controls the cigarette packet rule the smoker? Findings from ethnographic interviews with smokers in Canada, Australia, the United Kingdom and the USA. *Social Science and Medicine*, 142: 136–144.

Berkman, L.F., Kawachi, I. and Glymour, M.M. (eds) (2014) *Social Epidemiology*. Second edition. Oxford: Oxford University Press.

Bibeau, G. (1997) At work in the fields of public health: The abuse of rationality. *Medical Anthropology Quarterly*, 11(2): 246–255.

Blue, S., Shove, E., Carmona, C. and Kelly, M.P. (2016) Theories of practice and public health: Understanding (un)healthy practices. *Critical Public Health*, 26(1): 36–50.

Bourgois, P., Lettiere, M. and Quesada, J. (1997) Social misery and the sanctions of substance abuse: Confronting HIV risk among homeless heroin addicts in San Francisco. *Social Problems*, 44(2): 155–173.

Braveman, P., Egerter, S. and Williams, D.R. (2011) The social determinants of health: Coming of age. *Annual Review of Public Health*, 32: 391–398.

Burgess, A. (2012) 'Nudging' healthy lifestyles: The UK experiments with the behavioural alternative to regulation and the market. *European Journal of Risk Regulation*, 3(3): 3–16.

Chantler, C. (2014) *Standardised Packaging of Tobacco: Report of the Independent Review Undertaken by Sir Cyril Chantler*. London: Department of Health. Available at: www.kcl.ac.uk/health/10035-TSO-2901853-Chantler-Review-ACCESSIBLE.PDF (accessed 9 July 2015).

Chapman, S. and Freeman, B. (2014) *Removing the Emperor's Clothes: Australia and Tobacco Plain Packaging*. Sydney: Sydney University Press.

Cohn, S. (2014) From health behaviours to health practices: An introduction. *Sociology of Health and Illness*, 36(2): 157–162.

Coreil, J. and Levin, J.S. (1984–1985) A critique of the life style concept in public health education. *International Quarterly of Community Health Education*, 5(2): 103–114.

Coreil, J., Levin, J.S. and Jaco, E.G. (1985) Life style: An emergent concept in the sociomedical sciences. *Culture, Medicine and Psychiatry*, 9: 423–437.

Crawford, R. (1977) You are dangerous to your health: The ideology and politics of victim blaming. *International Journal of Health Services*, 7(4): 663–680.

Dahlgren, G. and Whitehead, M. (1991) *Policies and Strategies to Promote Social Equity in Health*. Copenhagen: Institute for Futures Studies. Available at: https://core.ac.uk/download/files/153/6472456.pdf (accessed 17 February 2016).

Dennis, S. (2011) Smoking causes creative responses: On state anti-smoking policy and resilient habits. *Critical Public Health*, 21(1): 25–35.

Dennis, S. (2013) Golden chocolate olive tobacco packaging meets the smoker you thought you knew: The rational agent and new cigarette packaging legislation in Australia. *Contemporary Drug Problems*, 40(1): 71–97.

Department of Health (1998) *Our Healthier Nation: A Contract for Health.* London: Stationery Office.

Diprose, R. (2008) Biopolitical technologies of prevention. *Health Sociology Review,* 17: 141–150.

Fitzpatrick, M. (2001) *The Tyranny of Health: Doctors and the Regulation of Lifestyle.* London: Routledge.

Fong, G.T. (2001) A review of the research on tobacco warning labels, with particular emphasis on the new Canadian warning labels. *Tobacco Labelling Resource Centre.* Available at: www.tobaccolabels.ca/wp/wp-content/uploads/2013/12/Canada-2002-A-Review-of-the-Research-on-Tobacco-Warning-Labels-With-Particular-Emphasis-on-the-New-Canadian-Warning-Labels-Report-Fong1.doc (accessed 17 March 2015).

Glanz, K. and Bishop, D.B. (2010) The role of behavioural science theory in development and implementation of public health interventions. *Annual Review of Public Health,* 31: 399–418.

Greco, M. (1993) Psychosomatic subjects and the 'duty to be well': Personal agency within medical rationality. *Economy and Society,* 22(3): 357–372.

Hankivsky, O. and Christophersen, A. (2008) Intersectionality and the determinants of health: a Canadian perspective. *Critical Public Health,* 18(3): 271–283.

Hardcastle, S.J., Chan, D.C.K., Caudwell, K.M., Sultan, S., Cranwell, J., Chatzisarantis, N.L.D. and Hagger, M.S. (2016) Larger and more prominent graphic health warnings on plain-packaged tobacco products and avoidant responses in current smokers: A qualitative study. *International Journal of Behavioral Medicine,* 23(1): 94–101.

Hastings, G., Gallopel-Morvan, K. and Rey, J.M. (2008) The plain truth about tobacco packaging. *Tobacco Control,* 17(6): 361–362.

Health Canada (2000) *The Tobacco Act: History of Labelling.* Ottawa: Health Canada.

Horrocks, C. and Johnson, S. (2014) A socially situated approach to inform ways to improve health and wellbeing. *Sociology of Health and Illness,* 36(2): 175–186.

Inhorn, M.C. and Whittle, K.L. (2001) Feminism meets the 'new' epidemiologies: Toward an appraisal of antifeminist biases in epidemiological research on women's health. *Social Science and Medicine,* 53: 553–567.

Kinmonth, H.A. (2016) *The Social Construction of Obesity in an Australian Preventative Health Policy.* Doctoral Dissertation. Australian National University.

Klein, R. (1996) *Cigarettes are Sublime.* Durham, NC: Duke University Press.

Krieger, N. (2011) *Epidemiology and the People's Health: Theory and Context.* Oxford: Oxford University Press.

Latour, B. (2005) *Reassembling the Social: An Introduction to Actor-Network-Theory.* Oxford: Oxford University Press.

Macintyre, S., Ellaway, A. and Cummins, S. (2002) Place effects on health: How can we conceptualise, operationalise and measure them? *Social Science and Medicine,* 55: 125–139.

Macnaughton, J., Carro-Ripalda, S. and Russell, A. (2012) 'Risking enchantment': How are we to view the smoking person? *Critical Public Health,* 22(4): 455–469.

Mair, M. (2011) Deconstructing behavioural classifications: tobacco control, 'professional vision' and the tobacco user as a site of governmental intervention. *Critical Public Health,* 21(2): 129–140.

Mair, M. and Kierans, C. (2007) Critical reflections on the field of tobacco research: the role of tobacco control in defining the tobacco research agenda. *Critical Public Health,* 17(2): 103–112.

Marteau, T., Oglivie, D., Roland, M., Suhrcke, M. and Kelly, M.P. (2011) Judging nudging: Can nudging improve population health? *British Medical Journal,* 342: 263–265.

Mead, E.L., Cohen, J.E., Kennedy, C.E., Gallo, J. and Latkin, C.A. (2015) The role of theory-driven graphic warning labels in motivation to quit: A qualitative study on perceptions from low-income, urban smokers. *BMC Public Health*, 15: 92.

Munafò, M.R., Roberts, N., Bauld, L. and Leonards, U. (2011) Plain packaging increases visual attention to health warnings on cigarette packs in non-smokers and weekly smokers but not daily smokers. *Addiction*, 106: 1505–1510.

Ogden, J. (1995) Psychosocial theory and the creation of the risky self. *Social Science and Medicine*, 40(3): 409–415.

Oliver, A. (2013) Introduction. In A. Oliver (ed.) *Behavioural Public Policy*. Cambridge: Cambridge University Press, pp. 1–15.

Petersen, A. and Lupton, D. (1996) *The New Public Health: Health and Self in the Age of Risk*. London: Sage.

Poland, B., Frohlich, K., Haines, R.J., Mykhalovskiy, E., Rock, M. and Sparks, R. (2006) The social context of smoking: the next frontier in tobacco control? *Tobacco Control*, 15: 59–63.

Prochaska, J.O. and DiClemente, C.C. (1985) Stages and processes of self-change and smoking: Toward an integrative model of change. *Journal of Consulting and Clinical Psychology*, 51(3): 390–395.

Prochaska, J.O. and Velicer, W.F. (1997) The transtheoretical model of health behavior change. *American Journal of Health Promotion*, 12(1): 38–48.

Raphael, D. (2006) Social determinants of health: Present status, unanswered questions, and future directions. *International Journal of Health Services*, 36(4): 651–677.

Raphael, D. (2008) Grasping at straws: A recent history of health promotion in Canada. *Critical Public Health*, 18(4): 483–495.

Raphael, D. (2011) A discourse analysis of the social determinants of health. *Critical Public Health*, 21(2): 221–236.

Regidor, E. (2006) Social determinants of health: A veil that hides socioeconomic position and its relation with health. *Journal of Epidemiology and Community Health*, 60: 896–901.

Shoveller, J., Viehbeck, S., Di Ruggiero, E., Greyson, D., Thomson, K. and Knight. R. (2016) A critical examination of representations of context within research on population health interventions. *Critical Public Health*, DOI: 10.1080/09581596.2015.1117577.

Smith, K. (2013) *Beyond Evidence-Based Policy in Public Health: The Interplay of Ideas*. Basingstoke: Palgrave Macmillan.

Social and Behavioral Sciences Team (2016) About. *General Services Administration*. Available at: https://sbst.gov/about/ (accessed 3 January 2016).

Steckler, A., McLeroy, K.R. and Holtzman, D. (2010) Godfrey H. Hochbaum (1916–1999): From social psychology to health behavior and health education. *American Journal of Public Health*, 100(10): 1864.

Thaler, R. and Sunstein, C. (2008) *Nudge: Improving Decisions About Health, Wealth, and Happiness*. New Haven, CT: Yale University Press.

Trostle, J. (1986) Early work in anthropology and epidemiology: From social medicine to the germ theory, 1840 to 1920. In C.R. Janes, R. Stall and S.M. Gifford (eds), *Anthropology and Epidemiology*. Dordrecht: D. Reidel Publishing, pp. 35–57.

Watson, J.B. (2009 [1924]) *Behaviorism*. New Brunswick, NJ: Transaction Publishers.

West, R. (2007) What lessons can be learned from tobacco control for combating the growing prevalence of obesity? *Obesity Reviews*, 8(Suppl. 1): 145–150.

Willis, J. and Giles, D. (1978) Behaviorism in the twentieth century: What we have here is a failure to communicate. *Behavior Therapy*, 9: 15–27.

WHO (2011) *WHO Report on the Global Tobacco Epidemic, 2011: Warning About the Dangers of Tobacco*. Geneva: World Health Organization.

WHO (2013) *MPOWER in Action: Defeating the Global Tobacco Epidemic.* Geneva: World Health Organization.

Yach, D., Hawkes, C., Epping-Jordan, J.E. and Galbraith, S. (2003) The World Health Organization's Framework Convention on Tobacco Control: Implications for global epidemics of food-related deaths and disease. *Journal of Public Health Policy*, 24(3): 274–290.

Yach, D., McKee, M., Lopez, A.D. and Novotny, T. (2005) Improving diet and physical activity: 12 lessons from controlling tobacco smoking. *British Medical Journal*, 330: 898–900.

3

TERTIARY PREVENTION AND THE TEACHABLE MOMENT

Introduction

In June of 2010, the biennial *Cancer Survivorship Research: Recovery and Beyond* conference was held in Washington, DC. Sponsored by the National Cancer Institute, the American Cancer Society, the Livestrong Foundation and the Centers for Disease Control and Prevention, the meeting is devoted to the topic of cancer survivorship and its stated aim is to 'bring together investigators, clinicians, and survivors to share and learn about the most up-to-date cancer survivorship research' (NCI, ACS, Livestrong, CDC 2010). The first day of the 2010 conference was devoted to the topic of lifestyle and presenters included a number of leading lights in the field. 'It's never too late to start an exercise programme', counselled a speaker on energy balance and cancer prognosis. Noting that most patients diagnosed with cancer decreased their exercise levels by 50 per cent, she stressed the 'need to encourage survivors to increase their physical activity after diagnosis'. Despite acknowledging in passing that treatment side effects were one of the main reasons why patients tended to reduce their exercise levels, the presenter made it clear that such reticence needed to be overcome. Another speaker emphasised the need to 'capitalise on the teachable moment caused by the cancer diagnosis' in promoting weight loss among overweight cancer patients. In her closing remarks, the moderator of the final session tasked the audience with spreading this message far and wide. 'Talk about exercise to the survivors you come into contact with,' she urged; 'we're charging you to get the message out.'

In Chapter 2, I focused on the 'health behaviours' understood to prevent – or at the very least reduce – the risk of developing chronic disease. However, the concept of prevention is emphasised not only in the context of *preventing* disease but *arresting* its course once it has emerged, a phenomenon known today as 'tertiary prevention'. This concept forms the focus of the current chapter, where I consider the expansion of the focus on lifestyle from the well to the sick. In some respects, the insistence on the power of behaviour change to arrest chronic disease can be seen as the result of a spillover from its general pre-eminence in the field of public health. But it also relates to the rise of the idea that people diagnosed with disease are distinctively *susceptible* to lifestyle change: a view that crystallises most explicitly in the concept of the 'teachable moment'. Following an examination of the rise of the concept of tertiary prevention more broadly, especially its growing connection with self-management models of chronic disease, I return to cancer as a case study. My goal is to use it as a way of exploring the effects of contemporary models of chronic disease management on patients themselves.

The rise of tertiary prevention and self-management

The first attempt to subdivide the concept of prevention dates from the 1950s. In 1957, the US Commission on Chronic Illness proposed the classification of disease prevention into the categories 'primary' and 'secondary', with primary prevention defined as prevention practised prior to the biological origin of disease and secondary prevention defined as that occurring after the disease can be recognised but before it has caused suffering or disability (Gordon 1983). A third term, 'tertiary prevention', was introduced the following year[1] and was defined as rehabilitation that focused on the period *after* the disease had caused disability in order to prevent sequelae and further deterioration (Gordon 1983).

It hardly needs stating that this conceptualisation of prevention required various precursors – namely, the emergence of the notion of 'chronic illness' and the rise of surveillance medicine – in order to acquire meaning (see Chapter 1). A core assumption underpinning it is that chronic diseases have latent, early and late manifestations, and that intervention towards the beginning of this natural history can change, or even prevent, an otherwise assured outcome (Armstrong 2012). Cancer screening programmes, discussed in more detail in Chapter 8, exemplify this logic, although early detection was often conflated with primary prevention in terms of how they were sold to the public (Fosket 2010). However, implicit in this view of prevention is that intervention *at any point* – even when the disease has emerged clinically – can be beneficial.

By the 1980s this tripartite classification had become 'ubiquitous in textbooks of epidemiology and preventive medicine' (Gordon 1983: 107), but in the 1990s observers noted that tertiary prevention for chronic conditions tended to fall through the cracks because neither the public health nor personal medical care systems adequately addressed it (e.g., Lorig 1996). On one level, this explanation makes sense: through its identification of threats to the health of populations, public health focuses largely on primary and secondary prevention. Medical care, on the other hand, deals largely with acute issues – i.e., the diagnosis, treatment and relief of suffering among individuals (Mann 1997). The predominant temporal mode of the latter is therefore the immediate present: treating cancer with surgery and chemotherapy, the provision of medication to lower the blood sugar levels of someone diagnosed with type II diabetes and so on. However, while the lack of focus on tertiary prevention was seen as an outcome of each system assuming it was the responsibility of the other to handle, as I detail below, it is also a symptom of the intrinsic ambiguity of the term itself.

Although the categories of primary, secondary and tertiary prevention are typically treated as self explanatory, there is considerable variability in the way they have been defined and used – especially the latter two concepts (Froom and Benbassat 2000). If 'prevention' is conceptualised as medical interventions aiming to *obviate* the need for treatment, then tertiary prevention, by definition, becomes an oxymoron. Indeed, the question of how 'tertiary prevention' differs from 'treatment' – if at all – is not particularly straightforward. For example, chemotherapy is simultaneously a treatment for cancer and a means of preventing cancer from recurring.[2] Likewise, medications for type II diabetes both treat the condition and aim to prevent the morbidities associated with it.

Despite – or perhaps more accurately because of – these ambiguities, tertiary prevention has come to be inflected in ways that have seen a growing association with activities undertaken *outside* of the formal medical system by the *individual* patient. In particular, it has increasingly converged with concept of 'chronic disease self-management'. For example, in the mid-1990s Kate Lorig (1996) advocated self-management as a means of addressing the problem of tertiary prevention and has been a key figure in promoting it since. Drawing its primary impetus from Bandura's[3] social cognitive theory and the concept of self-efficacy (see Chapter 2), this approach to self-management emphasises the importance of instilling five core skills: problem solving, decision making, resource utilisation, the formation of a patient/health care provider partnership and taking action (Lorig and Holman 2003). Clearly, the dominant frame employed is that of the 'partnership'; under this model, the patient is an 'active partner' in his or her health care (Lorig and Holman 2003; Holman and Lorig 2004).

Although it's tempting to see self-management as a product of the patient advocacy movement, David Armstrong (2014: 169) argues that it was 'not a strategy driven by patients but rather one incited by medicine and complicit social sciences'. While there were lay efforts from the 1970s to promote self-management agendas, self-management as it became instantiated in health care policy at the turn of the twenty-first century was aimed primarily at reducing health care costs (Morden, Jinks and Ong 2012; Horrocks and Johnson 2014; Ong *et al.* 2014). This orientation is evident in the primary forms of evidence used to determine whether self-management programmes are effective: increases in positive 'health behaviours', improvements in health status and reductions in health care utilisation (Lorig and Holman 2003). Perhaps unsurprisingly, the latter outcome has been intensively studied and promoted (e.g., Lorig *et al.* 1999, 2001; Kennedy *et al.* 2007), although all three are clearly conceptually entangled, with a transformation in lifestyle seen to naturally lead to an improved health status and, in turn, reductions in health care utilisation.

The US Centers for Disease Control and Prevention treats self-management as the fourth strand of tertiary prevention, in conjunction with rehabilitation services, psycho-social strategies and medical treatment. However, self-management programmes typically incorporate many of these elements, among others. For example, one literature review of international self-management programmes found the most common components to include: information about the condition, drug management, symptom management, management of psychological consequences, social support and communication strategies and, of course, lifestyle change (Barlow *et al.* 2002). As Morden *et al.* (2012: 82) observe, 'Self-management policy advocates providing the "right" information and offering support and advice. The logic underpinning "correct" self-management is managing lifestyle risk factors with a view to ensuring "correct" health outcomes.'

The assumption that self-management improves such outcomes is evident in the slogan of Stanford University's influential Chronic Disease Self-Management Program: 'Better Choices, Better Health®'. This programme was adopted by Kaiser Permanente in the USA and was the inspiration for the National Health Service's Expert Patients Programme in the UK (Morden *et al.* 2012; Ong *et al.* 2014; Armstrong 2014). As its slogan makes clear, although 'Better Choices, Better Health' evokes notions of autonomy and choice, there's an underlying assumption that there are better and worse choices to be made and that patients will 'choose' health (Armstrong 2014) – a theme that largely replicates public health discourses on lifestyle and health behaviours more broadly (see Chapters 1 and 2). This figure of the rational decision-maker 'self-managing' his or her condition is thus underwritten by a narrative of responsibility, 'in that, if we are unable to self-manage our health and wellbeing, then we are in deficit at a very personal level' (Horrocks and Johnson 2014: 177).

The teachable moment

Although instilling behavioural change has proved notoriously difficult in the context of primary prevention, the concept of the 'teachable moment' has facilitated the view that it might be more successfully undertaken in the context of tertiary prevention. Widely invoked in an array of contexts,[4] in the health literature the term is used to describe naturally occurring life transitions or health events (e.g., cancer diagnosis, hospitalisation, pregnancy) that have the potential to motivate individuals to adopt health-protective behaviours (McBride, Emmons and Lipkus 2003; Ganz 2005). In other words, there are seen to be predictable temporal moments wherein individuals are particularly susceptible to health promotion messages aimed at facilitating behaviour change. Papers with titles like 'Smoking cessation among patients with head and neck cancer: Cancer as a "teachable moment"' (Sharp *et al.* 2007) speak to the power of the idea that these 'moments' aren't just serendipitous events, but opportunities actively *created* through patient–clinician interactions (Flocke *et al.* 2014).

This version of the teachable moment holds considerable appeal because of the assumption that formal interventions timed to coincide with key health events 'might increase the effectiveness of self-directed and low-intensity interventions that are also low in cost and amenable to widespread dissemination' (McBride *et al.* 2003: 156). However, Lawson and Flocke (2009) observe that the wholesale embrace of the concept in the health field hasn't actually been driven by empirical research demonstrating its validity; instead, it seems to operate more along the lines of a self-evident truism. Nevertheless, partially as a result of the growing emphasis on 'evidence-based' practice (see Chapter 4), attention has increasingly focused on identifying the elements that constitute a teachable moment and empirically testing the efficacy of such (see Lawson and Flocke 2009; Flocke *et al.* 2014).

One of the most influential attempts to empirically describe the teachable moment in the health literature is found in the work of McBride *et al.* (2003), writing specifically about smoking cessation – the context where the teachable moment has been most studied. They suggest that for health (or 'cueing') events to become teachable moments, three interrelated elements are necessary (see Figure 3.1). First, the event must increase perceptions of personal risk and outcome expectancies. Second, it must prompt a strong affective or emotional response. Finally, it must be significant enough to redefine self-concept or social role. In other words, the more anxious patients are, the more fundamentally their prior sense of self is undermined, the higher their motivation is to change their lifestyle – as long as they perceive the change to have some potential benefit. That fear is central to this model becomes explicit in statements such as 'Negative affect, i.e. fear, may be particularly impactful because it increases vigilant attention and prompts the survival instinct'[5] (McBride *et al.* 2003: 163). As should be evident, this model has been strongly influenced by the theories of health behaviour discussed in Chapter 2, especially the health belief model. Indeed, McBride *et al.* explicitly reference this theory in explaining how teachable moments work.

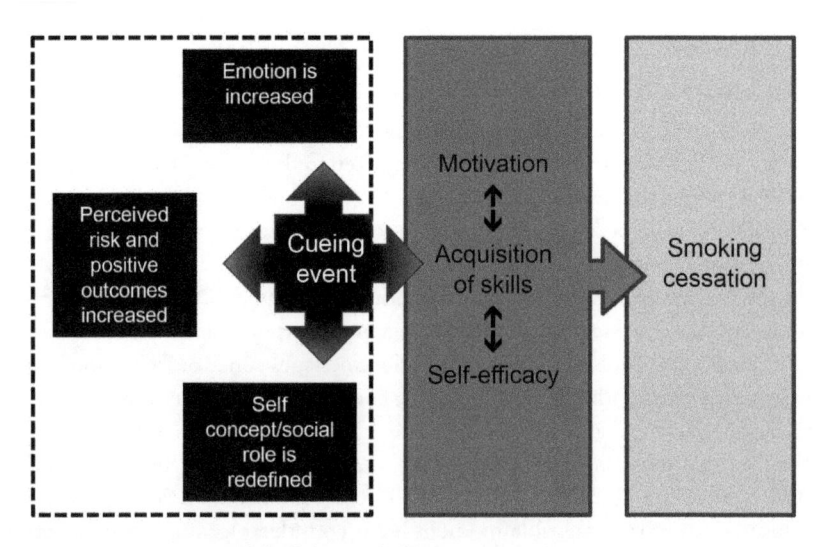

FIGURE 3.1 Heuristic model of the teachable moment

Source: adapted from McBride, Emmons and Lipkus 2003.

Central to the attraction of the teachable moment is its perceived capacity to counteract individuals' tendency to downplay risk. As Ulrich Beck (1992: 34) observes, 'the center of risk consciousness lies not in the present, but in the future'. Thus, the prevailing paradigm of pre-emption insists on a fearful comportment towards the future, pathologising those who assert its indeterminacy (Diprose 2008). This is evident in the language used to describe individuals, such as Imran from Chapter 2, who refuse to take epidemiologically determined risks seriously in the *present*. Although a variety of terms have been used to describe this phenomenon, including 'risk denial', 'wishful thinking', 'self-exempting beliefs', 'unrealistic optimism' and 'optimism bias', each articulates the view that humans have an illusion of relative invulnerability that needs to be eradicated in order for them to adopt health protective behaviours. For example, McBride *et al.* (2003) note, 'our TM [teachable moment] heuristic suggests that events which provide individuals with direct or vivid vicarious experience of risk may *over-ride optimistic biases*, and prompt increased motivation and smoking cessation' (p. 163, emphasis added).

In some respects, the negative meaning attached to optimism in this context would seem to contradict the growing body of scholarship highlighting its ideological value in late consumer capitalist societies (e.g., Ehrenreich 2009; Berlant 2011; Petersen 2015). However, closer inspection of the teachable moment reveals that it relies on replacing one kind of 'bad' or 'faulty' optimism (optimism that a risk won't happen) with another 'good' kind: optimism that a risk can be avoided *if appropriate steps are taken*. After all, the success of the teachable moment relies on two types of outcome expectancies: that negative health outcomes will occur if the behaviour continues, and that positive outcomes will result if the behaviour stops (or conversely that *not* engaging in a behaviour will lead to negative outcomes and introducing it will lead to positive ones). As Alan Petersen observes,

> Some writers have begun to warn of the harms associated with patients' possession of 'false hope', that is, hope based upon an improbable outcome. Such hope is distinguished from 'true hope' that is based on a probable outcome that may only be realised far into the future. While the latter is judged to be legitimate, given available evidence, the former is viewed as illegitimate and dangerous, being based upon a lack of evidence or a misunderstanding of evidence.
>
> *Petersen 2015: 48*

The attempt to differentiate 'false' and 'true' hope is based on an unquestioned faith in the 'proof' offered by epidemiological research (Petersen 2015). However, as I discussed in Chapter 1, this statistical logic says nothing about one's individual destiny – a point I will explore in further detail in Chapter 8. Thus, while the distinction is naturalised in epidemiological accounts of risk and attendant theories of health behaviour, it is simultaneously 'something non-existent, invented, fictive' (Beck 1992: 34). Moreover, such attempts to harness affect are not without attendant risks. As Lauren Berlant and others have pointed out, while affect is a powerful intellectual, aesthetic and political tool, it can't be instrumentalised for predictable ends (Houser 2014: 25). There is always a danger that anxiety 'might lead to a form of psychological paralysis or even denial' (Armstrong 2014: 167). Alternatively, as Imran highlighted in Chapter 2, it may lead to contrarian responses – such as the smokers who respond to progressively stronger warning labels emphasising the risks of the habit by 'lighting on'.

Interestingly, such possibilities are explicitly recognised in the literature on the teachable moment; McBride *et al.* (2003) warn: 'Emotions . . . prompt cognitive and behavioural coping responses that may include denial, avoidance or steps to remediate threat via behavior change' (p. 163). Self-management programmes therefore have a complicated dual aim: they have to instil and maintain a level of anxiety sufficient to motivate risk-reducing behaviours, but simultaneously ensure that these levels of anxiety are not so high that they become counter-productive (van der Pligt 1998). The delicate balancing act required becomes particularly apparent in the context of cancer – so feared it was addressed for much of the twentieth century only through euphemism.

Cancer, fear and prevention

As Lochlann Jain (2013) notes, today there are two widely circulating images of cancer that seem fundamentally counter to each other: while the disease continues to evoke extreme fear – 'a disease horrific enough to warrant virtually any treatment' (p. 181), it has simultaneously been transformed into a banal everyday occurrence. Indeed, if cancer was unspeakable only a few decades ago, today it has become a disease to publicly lay claim to and even celebrate. In North America, a plethora of books, television shows and feature films highlight the experiences of cancer 'survivors', who can also buy cookbooks catering to their distinct needs and bedeck themselves in lines of survivor jewellery. Cancer survivors, it would seem, are finally having their day in the sun (quite literally, as the first Sunday in June has been designated National Cancer Survivors Day).

Comparing such representations of cancer with Joseph Masco's (2010) description of the domestication of the threat of nuclear holocaust during the Cold War,[6] Jain observes the ways in which the disease has been similarly transformed from 'an unthinkable apocalypse into an opportunity for psychological self-management, civic responsibility, and ultimately, governance' (2013: 182). Focusing on the cognitive dissonance caused by the two irreconcilable faces of cancer (horrific enough to warrant atomic-level treatment, yet simultaneously reduced to pink bracelets and BMW test drives), she points to the ways in which fear is elided in medical and popular discourses on the disease. As she observes: 'little literature addresses, head on, the question of precisely how fear should be considered in the mix that we call cancer' (Jain 2013: 183). However, its traces are clearly present in the literature on cancer as a 'teachable moment' and the emphasis on the way in which diagnosis and treatment may spark positive behavioural change. After all, if fear is a necessary element in the creation of successful teachable moments, a cancer diagnosis – or the threat of such – is singularly well placed to facilitate them (Bell 2012).[7]

As the 2010 *Cancer Survivorship Research* conference attests, among oncology care providers there has been growing interest in ways to 'exploit' the teachable moment presented by diagnosis via active interventions that promote adherence to recommended behavioural guidelines. This has continued to be a theme in subsequent *Cancer Survivorship Research* conferences – for example, the 2012 conference contained numerous presentations on encouraging behaviour change in patients and a plenary session devoted to obesity and the importance of interventions to facilitate weight loss.

Commentaries published over the past decade also consistently call for oncologists to intervene more actively in promoting lifestyle change in patients. For example, in 2005 Demark-Wahnefried and colleagues wrote:

> For decades the cancer diagnosis has been acknowledged as a life-changing event. It is time for oncology care providers to not only lead their patients away from disease but also to capitalize on the teachable moment that cancer provides and guide their patients to better health.
>
> *2005: 5827*

Ten years later, their message is largely unchanged:

> The oncologist and the oncology care team now stand at a unique interface – delivering acute care aimed at a life-threatening disease while at the same time readying the patient for a long and healthy life free of comorbidity. Good nutrition and a physically active lifestyle are central to both pursuits, and it is becoming increasingly apparent that these factors need to be routinely integrated into the delivery of optimal cancer care.
>
> *Demark-Wahnefried* et al. *2015: 1*

In this framing, a failure to capitalise on cancer patients' perceived openness to health promotion messages is conceptualised as a 'missed opportunity' (e.g., Flocke *et al.* 2014). This speaks to the ways in which the growing emphasis on patient agency has simultaneously served to responsibilise physicians as well. As Armstrong (2014) observes, while patients had little option except to take the road of 'choice', the medical profession has been caught within the same machinery of power that elicits and instils agency in everyone – lay or professional. Arguing in a similar vein, Thomas Osborne (1997: 186) notes that:

> it is not only, as some critics have noted, that people are made responsible for their own health, with all the 'victim-blaming' consequences this implies. Rather, the principle of responsibilisation works like a moving force throughout the whole system, giving it coherence as its principle of functioning.

Here, the patient's role is to be *active*; the health care professional's role is to *activate* her. Indeed, this was the crux of a session at the 2014 *Cancer Survivorship Research* conference, which was titled 'Activating cancer survivors through self-management: the opportunity, challenges, and future directions'.

Although there has long been debate about whether cancer should be classified as a chronic disease (e.g., Tritter and Calnan 2002), the growing emphasis on cancer 'survivorship' as a distinct phase in the cancer trajectory has arguably facilitated the embrace of such models in the field of cancer care.[8] Today, the most influential self-management intervention is 'Cancer Transitions®: Moving Beyond Treatment', which was created in 2006 by the Cancer Support Community (then the Wellness Community) and the Livestrong Foundation. Both are non-profit organisations that receive primarily corporate funding and speak to the rise of the 'third sector'[9] and the government–corporate–charity partnerships that increasingly support care for cancer 'survivors', and much else besides. Although a US creation, Cancer Transitions is being offered at a number of cancer treatment centres in Canada and the UK; according to one report it has also 'generated interest in Australia and Italy' (Ward *et al.* 2010: 14). For example, in Canada, a federally-funded version 'tailored' to the local context was piloted at cancer treatment centres across the country (Ward *et al.* 2010) and is now available at numerous tertiary treatment centres and community organisations.

Tertiary prevention and the 'active' patient

Cancer Transitions is designed to help cancer survivors 'redefine how we live our lives from this point forward', and to 'support and empower survivors as they transition from active treatment to post-treatment' (CSC 2015a). Running over 6 weeks, it aims to encourage patients to 'take control' of their survivorship through information and training in a variety of areas, including exercise, emotional health and well-being, nutrition and how to manage their follow up medical care. At the heart of the programme is the concept of the 'Patient Active', although it appears to have been downplayed in newer iterations for reasons that will perhaps be obvious when I provide the original definition. According to Dr Harold Benjamin, the founder of the Wellness Community, 'Patients who participate in their fight for recovery along with their healthcare team, *rather than acting as hopeless, helpless, passive victims of the illness*, will improve the quality of their lives and may enhance the possibility of recovery' (Golant and Thiboldeaux 2010: 474, emphasis added).

Today, the more offensive aspects of the definition – especially the judgemental tone – have disappeared. Indeed, many sections of the website now refer to the 'Patient Empowered' instead (slogan: 'Be informed. Take action. Connect with others'). Nevertheless, while the terminology has softened, the concept doesn't appear to have changed in essentials. Like Stanford University's self-management programme, the emphasis is very much on 'Better Choices, Better Health'. For example, in its discussion of nutrition, the Cancer Support Community (CSC 2015b) states, 'There are no guarantees that anything you do will keep cancer away, but being Patient Active means doing everything you reasonably can to maintain your health'.

Read in the context of the prevailing images of cancer Jain has highlighted, these sorts of statements become intensely loaded. On one level they recognise the precariousness of the 'survivor' identity ('there are no guarantees . . .') and the looming threat of recurrence, but on another level they present a means of controlling the threat ('doing everything you reasonably can to maintain your health'). This message becomes even more explicit in the 'Defeat[10] Cancer' programme at the St. Charles Medical Centre in Oregon, USA, which is a similar 'survivorship empowerment program for cancer survivors and their caregivers focusing on nutrition, physical activity, education and inspiration' (Defeat Cancer 2015). While Cancer Transitions is more tempered in its claims about the efficacy of diet and physical activity in preventing cancer recurrence,[11] Defeat Cancer, as its name suggests, rather more forcefully asserts the possibility of 'taking control' of the disease. Here, we see variations of what Barbara Ehrenreich (2009) has bluntly labelled the 'smile or die' approach to cancer, where a positive attitude and a healthy lifestyle are all that is required to help one successfully navigate their 'survivorship'.

The problem is that this confidence flies in the face of the current state of knowledge about cancer aetiology, where what we *don't* know greatly exceeds what we *do*. Although cures for cancer have been promised throughout the twentieth century, scientists still furiously debate how cancer arises and whether it's actually one disease or hundreds (Jain 2013). Nevertheless, echoing the broader focus on lifestyle and behaviour in chronic disease prevention, a growing body of epidemiological literature stresses the relationship between weight, diet, exercise and cancer risk (see WCRF and AICR 2007 for a summary). Likewise, the past decade has also witnessed an intensified emphasis on the need for lifestyle modifications not only to prevent cancer, but to arrest its progression (e.g., Demark-Wahnefried *et al.* 2008; Irwin and Mayne 2008; Gritz and Demark-Wahnefried 2009; Winzer *et al.* 2011).

Some of the emphasis on lifestyle and self-management in tertiary cancer prevention can clearly be attributed to the growing 'neoliberalisation' of health care discussed in Chapter 1 and the concomitant rolling back of the state. Certainly, chronic disease self-management programmes have widely analysed such terms, although primarily from a neoliberalism-as-governmentality frame (e.g., Morden *et al.* 2012; Horrocks and Johnson 2014). There's little question that through such programmes 'survivors' are recruited into their responsibilities as 'good' biological citizens (Rose 2007) – ones who take responsibility to manage their risk of recurrence (here reduced to a matter of choice) in order to alleviate the financial burden otherwise imposed upon the tertiary health care system. However, as I showed in Chapter 1, this emphasis on personal responsibility for health is far from new. Indeed, it has always attached to cancer as a master illness – one that has long been 'used to propose new critical standards of individual health' (Sontag 1990: 73). It also speaks to the distinctive 'political economy of hope' (Novas 2006) that today marks the complex network of alliances between patient advocacy groups, cancer charities, government agencies and corporate entities (Bell and Ristovski-Slijepcevic 2015).

In this environment, where admitting ignorance is not a feasible option, lifestyle research and concomitant interventions become an important means of showing that 'Something Is Being Done' (Jain 2013: 185).

This emphasis comes across strongly on the website of the American Institute for Cancer Research – a corporate-sponsored non-profit organisation that provides funding for cancer research in the USA:

> Only decades ago, most believed that cancer simply strikes the unlucky – and that nothing can be done about it. Today, thanks to millions of dollars of AICR research, the world knows better. Our research sheds unique light on the cancer process – and pinpoints the specific lifestyle choices that will save hundreds of thousands of lives every year in the US alone. Our research also offers hope that cancer patients and survivors can take control of their health during and after treatment.
>
> *AICR 2014*

However, regardless of its origins (which clearly stem from multiple sources), the emphasis on the possibility of control over the course of one's disease has a number of consequences.

Taking control and assuming responsibility

Although commentators argue – occasionally in tones of some annoyance – that the lifestyle behaviours of people treated for cancer are far from ideal (Bell 2012), studies from the USA, Canada, the UK and Australia have reported a strong emphasis on diet and exercise among many people diagnosed with cancer as a way of managing the disease[12] (e.g., Stewart *et al.* 2001; Maskarinec *et al.* 2001; Sinding and Gray 2005; Markovic *et al.* 2006; Broom and Tovey 2008; English, Wilson and Keller-Olaman 2008; Nelson and Macias 2008; Bell 2010; Maley, Warren and Devine 2013; Gibson, Lee and Crabb 2015). Patients who take up such ideas are clearly 'engaging in practices of the self that they consider are vital to their own well-being' (Lupton 1997: 105). Indeed, there are obvious benefits to, say, exercise in terms of improving one's physical functioning during and after cancer treatment. Yet, when lifestyle becomes the perceived answer to the question of how to stall death, the *meaning* of something like exercise changes – a difference Lewis Thomas captures in the following observation:

> We jog, skip, attend aerobic classes, eat certain 'food groups' as though food itself was a new kind of medicine, even try to change our thoughts to make our cells sit up and behave like healthy cells; meditation is taken as medication by some of the most ardent meditators. We do these things not so much to keep fit, which is a healthy exercise and good for the mind, but to fend off dying, which is an effort not so good for the mind.
>
> *Thomas 1991: 58*

As the quote from Thomas alludes, there is clearly a problematic potential to the forms of self-governance these discourses inscribe. Based on research with Australian women treated for breast cancer, Gibson *et al.* (2015) observe that while there are clear benefits to being able to position oneself as empowered and in control of one's health, cancer is reinstated as a risk that requires individual management (see also Sinding and Gray 2005; Broom and Tovey 2008; Bell 2010). The problem with this view is that at the end of the day the *illusion* of control is just that. Moreover, motivations for healing in this context rely on retaining a sense of 'unwellness' or pathology (Broom and Tovey 2008). As Sinding and Gray (2005: 157) illustrate:

> Survivors are required to act as if cancer is over, and at the same time they are required to act to prevent recurrence. The first requirement rejects or pathologizes an ongoing sense of vulnerability to cancer; the latter is premised on it.

Once again, we see the dual quality of cancer as simultaneously horrific and banal, and the ways that optimism of a certain kind mediates the relations between the two.

In essence, dominant discourses on cancer survivorship aim to eradicate one kind of 'bad' optimism (that one's individual actions don't influence the course of the disease) and replace it with another 'good' kind that is premised on the assumption that the vulnerability thereby instilled can be remediated if appropriate steps are taken. Viewed in this way, the form of optimism such discourses engender bears a distinct resemblance to that which Lauren Berlant has characterised as 'cruel'. According to Berlant:

> A relation of cruel optimism exists when something you desire is actually an obstacle to your flourishing. It might involve food, or a kind of love; it might be a fantasy of the good life, or a political project. It might rest on something simpler, too, like a new habit that promises to induce in you an improved way of being. These kinds of optimistic relation are not inherently cruel. They become cruel only when the object that draws your attachment actively impedes the aim that brought you to it initially.
>
> *Berlant 2011: 1*

This potential is perhaps best illustrated by an example – one of many I have documented over years of hearing the stories of men and women diagnosed with cancer. I met Susanna in 2007 at a fortnightly support group for women with metastatic cancer held at a local cancer treatment centre in Vancouver. I conducted fieldwork at the group for an eight-month period and Susanna attended sporadically for its duration. I also visited her at her homely little apartment in North Vancouver, which was about an hour away by bus from the cancer treatment centre – being on a pension, Susanna lived in subsidised housing and couldn't afford anything more central. A divorced white woman of 66, Susanna had been diagnosed with metastatic breast cancer the year before we met. Unlike other women in the support group, many of whom had experienced periods of remission before being diagnosed with incurable cancer, Susanna's initial cancer diagnosis was with metastatic disease.

In her words, 'I think the kids probably got it more than I did. And of course stage IV – I looked it up and it was like "Well, there's no stage V".'

Despite issues with pain and depression, Susanna was strongly opposed to anti-depressants and ambivalent about pain medications – opinions she readily voiced in meetings. Indeed, Susanna was something of a polarising figure in the group, in part because she frequently expressed views that other women found patronising and dismissive. A staunch proponent of the idea that cancer patients needed to be their own advocates, Susanna often counselled newcomers to meetings about the need to be 'proactive'. Indeed, she recounted being advised along precisely these lines by her physician when she was first diagnosed, in a pep talk she had clearly taken to heart. In her words, 'And so that was what the general practitioner said to me right from the beginning: "You cannot go home and throw the covers over your head and just stay there. You have *got* to be proactive".'

Susanna's proactive approach to managing her disease was strongly evident in her everyday life. She was actively trying to lose weight to divest herself of the 'extra four-year-old child I'm carrying', she took yoga classes at the cancer treatment centre, saw a kinesiologist and did regular exercise at home, along with making an effort to walk 'every other day' when the weather allowed it. Susanna also regularly met with a nutritionist at a local holistic cancer treatment centre and had made substantial changes to her diet, now choosing to shop a couple of times a week at two expensive organic supermarkets across town, despite not owning a car and living on a low income. She also attended the cancer support group to help deal with her emotional needs, did visualisation exercises and made an effort to 'be positive' – although she acknowledged that this was something she had struggled with following her diagnosis. In Susanna's words:

> And you just have to kind of take a deep breath I'm learning now, after a year and a half, and kind of go with the flow. It is what it is. And so you know, I visualise that the cancer that's in the wall in my chest is just, you know, a few cells doing nothing. They're just, you know, they're not active at all. And rather than get uptight and upset, you know, what can I do that's positive? Can I ignore it? Should I just go for a walk? Shall I just make a cup of tea? Shall I find a funny movie to laugh at? Whatever works to keep you in that kind of positive mode.

Although Susanna acknowledged the fact that she didn't have as much energy now ('I call it my gas gauge, and when it's on empty I used to be able run it for a while, but I can't do that anymore'), most striking about her account of living with 'mets' was the amount of time and effort she devoted to activities that might extend her life.

The pressure she placed upon herself to 'be positive' was also strongly in evidence. Susanna's self-declared motto (frequently repeated in support group meetings) was 'fake it till you make it' and, true to form, during our individual conversation she downplayed her issues with pain and depression. When I asked her how she was feeling at the moment she responded 'I, right now, I'm feeling terrific!' She went on to confide her plans: to get her teeth fixed, to travel, to climb the *Arc de Triomphe* in Paris. Although a number of other women in the support group were coming to grips with their own mortality, Susanna was up front about the fact that she wasn't 'ready to go there'. It was clear that she planned to beat the odds she had been given when she was initially diagnosed. As she explained:

> And when I had walked into the clinic for the first time I saw a radiologist and he sat down with me and said 'Oh well, you know, I think we can give you a couple of good years right off the bat. And I kind of looked at him and I said 'What do you mean, a couple? Like, you mean like two or three?' And he said 'Well yeah, maybe'. I just burst into tears, because I'm thinking five or 10, maybe 15.

Unfortunately, not long after we talked she received news from her oncologist that her treatment was no longer working to keep her cancer in stasis. In a later support group meeting she expressed her utter shock at this news, because she had expected to be able to go along as she was for 'another five years or so'. After all, she was doing everything right! Despite worsening health, she continued to try to beat the odds for the remainder of my fieldwork. Sadly, she died less than six months later.

Obviously, Susanna's circumstances differed from those of someone declared cancer-free following treatment: the population for whom tertiary prevention ostensibly 'counts' most. However, as Jain (2007, 2013) has shown, the cancer-free 'survivor' and the one harbouring incurable disease are both 'living in prognosis', with the former always in danger of being reclassified as the latter via the prognostic act: one day in remission, the next day 'an asymptomatic person with an almost invariably deadly cancer' (2007: 77). In such circumstances, a bulwark painstakingly built of daily exercise, organic food, weight loss, positive thinking, meditation, etc., comes at a high price (figuratively and literally), but if the wolf arrives at the gate it will be about as effective as a house made of straw.

Conclusion

Clearly, the expansion of the focus on lifestyle from primary to tertiary prevention replicates a futural logic in which not-yet-realised outcomes can be averted by actions taken in the present. However, its consequences are rather different in this context because the 'present' in question is one in which certain outcomes have *already* been realised. Here we see the Janus-faced nature of health as a 'choice': it becomes simultaneously an ideal to be realised and a fact of life – for it's the choices we have *already made* that are seen to dictate our health today (Mol 2008). In this context, the moral loading of the concept becomes starkly highlighted and the optimism upon which it is premised takes a particularly coercive form. It both *relies* on a sense of personal vulnerability and promises to *remediate* it via lifestyle change and other forms of self-management. Central to these promises is the question of evidence itself and the ways it is made to speak – this topic forms the focus of Part II of the book.

Notes

1 The term appears to have been introduced by Leavell and Clark (1958).
2 This is particularly true of adjuvant chemotherapy, which aims to remove microscopic traces of cancer cells that the primary treatment (e.g., surgery or radiation) has not destroyed, but is primarily preventive in intent.
3 Bandura was one of the investigators on the original study that formed the basis of Stanford University's influential Chronic Disease Self-Management Program, which Lorig co-developed (see Stanford School of Medicine 2016).
4 However, one unifying feature is its invocation of distinct spatial and temporal moment in which ignorance can be successfully overcome (Alexander 2005).
5 McBride, Emmons and Lipkus (2003) acknowledge that positive affect may also influence behaviour change; thus, their definition includes any events that elicit 'strong emotional responses, be they negative or positive' (p. 163). However, virtually all empirical research conducted on teachable moments focuses on events that are seen to elicit anxiety – e.g., notification of abnormal test results, hospitalisation and disease diagnosis, clinical visits for an acute illness, pregnancy and so on.
6 As Jain (2013) observes, the metaphor is appropriate on many levels, not just because of the ways that cancer has been metaphorically associated with war (see Sontag 1990), but because of its utilisation of nuclear technology (radiation) as a core means of treatment.
7 Which explains why smoking, abnormal test results and cancer diagnoses have been so well studied as teachable moments.
8 The publication of the *From Cancer Patient to Cancer Survivor: Lost in Transition* report (Institute of Medicine and National Research Council 2006) had an important role to play in drawing attention to the 'survivorship' phrase and the ways in which patients who had successfully completed treatment, but who were still dealing with the physical and emotional aftermath of cancer, tended to fall through the cracks and received inadequate follow up care. This report, in turn, facilitated the creation of the *Cancer Survivorship Research* conference, a new journal devoted to the topic, etc.
9 The 'third sector' is the term frequently used to characterise the part of the service sector consisting of community-based organisations, non-profits, charities, etc. The rise of the third sector is often linked to the restructuring that has occurred under neoliberal forms of governance and the attendant deregulation and decentralisation of goods and services that has accompanied them (e.g., Evans, Richmond and Shields 2005).
10 'Defeat' is actually an acronym that stands for Diet Exercise Family Education Attitude Thriving.
11 Interestingly, while the Cancer Support Community is careful in making no direct claims about the efficacy of diet and exercise in staving off a recurrence (in its online materials, at least; I have not seen the content of the programme itself), it directs the reader to the Defeat Cancer website for overviews of the evidence.
12 The available literature suggests that patients receive this message from a variety of sources – from oncologists but also from practitioners of complementary and alternative medicine and self-help manuals.

References

AICR (2014) Our History. *American Institute for Cancer Research.* Available at: www.aicr.org/about/about_history.html (accessed 25 April 2014).

Alexander, B.K. (2005) Embracing the teachable moment: The black gay body in the classroom as embodied text. In E.P. Johnson and M.G. Henderson (eds), *Black Queer Studies: A Critical Anthology.* Durham, NC: Duke University Press, pp. 249–265.

Armstrong, D. (2012) Screening: Mapping medicine's temporal spaces. *Sociology of Health and Illness,* 24(2): 177–193.

Armstrong, D. (2014) Actors, patients and agency: A recent history. *Sociology of Health and Illness*, 36(2): 163–174.

Barlow, J., Wright, C., Sheasby, J., Turner, A. and Hainsworth, J. (2002) Self-management approaches for people with chronic conditions: A review. *Patient Education and Counseling*, 48: 177–187.

Beck, U. (1992) *Risk Society: Towards a New Modernity*. London: Sage.

Bell, K. (2010) Cancer survivorship, mor(t)ality, and lifestyle discourses on cancer prevention. *Sociology of Health and Illness*, 32(3): 349–364.

Bell, K. (2012) Remaking the self: Trauma, teachable moments and the biopolitics of cancer survivorship. *Culture, Medicine and Psychiatry*, 36(4): 584–600

Bell, K. and Ristovski-Slijepcevic, S. (2015) Communicating 'evidence': Lifestyle, cancer and the promise of a disease-free future. *Medical Anthropology Quarterly*, 29(2): 216–236.

Berlant, L. (2011) *Cruel Optimism*. Durham, NC: Duke University Press.

Broom, A. and Tovey, P. (2008) Exploring the temporal dimension in cancer patients' experiences of nonbiomedical therapeutics. *Qualitative Health Research*, 18(12): 1650–1661.

CSC (2015a) About Cancer Transitions. *Cancer Support Community*. Available at: www.cancersupportcommunity.org/MainMenu/About-Cancer/Cancer-Survivorship/Cancer-Transitions/About-Cancer-Transitions.html (accessed 10 October 2015).

CSC (2015b) Eating right. *Cancer Support Community*. Available at: www.cancersupport community.org/MainMenu/About-Cancer/Cancer-Survivorship/Nutrition-for-Wellness/Eating-Right.html (accessed 10 October 2015).

Defeat Cancer (2015) About. *Defeat Cancer*. Available at: http://defeatcancer.info/defeatcancer-program/about/ (accessed 10 October 2015).

Demark-Wahnefried, W., Aziz, N., Rowland, J. and Pinto, B. (2005) Riding the crest of the teachable moment: Promoting long-term health after the diagnosis of cancer. *Journal of Clinical Oncology*, 23(24): 5814–5830.

Demark-Wahnefried, W., Rock, C.L., Patrick, K. and Byers, T. (2008) Lifestyle interventions to reduce cancer risk and improve outcomes. *American Family Physician*, 77(1): 1573–1578.

Demark-Wahnefried, W., Rogers, L.Q., Alfano, C.M., Thomson, C.A., *et al.* (2015) Practical clinical interventions for diet, physical activity, and weight control in cancer survivors. *CA: A Cancer Journal for Clinicians*, 65(3): 167–89.

Diprose, R. (2008) Biopolitical technologies of prevention. *Health Sociology Review*, 17: 141–150.

Ehrenreich, B. (2009) *Bright Sided: How the Relentless Promotion of Positive Thinking Has Undermined America*. New York: Metropolitan Books.

English, J., Wilson, K. and Keller-Olaman, S. (2008) Health, healing and recovery: Therapeutic landscapes and the everyday lives of breast cancer survivors. *Social Science and Medicine*, 67(1): 68–78.

Evans, B., Richmond, T. and Shields, J. (2005) Structuring neoliberal governance: The nonprofit sector, emerging new modes of control and the marketisation of service delivery. *Policy and Society*, 24(1): 73–97.

Fosket, J.R. (2010) Breast cancer risk as disease. In A.E. Clarke, L. Mamo, J.R. Fosket, J.R. Fishman and J. Shim (eds), *Biomedicalization: Technoscience, Health and Illness in the US*. Durham, NC: Duke University Press, pp. 331–352.

Flocke, S.A., Clark, E., Antognoli, E., Mason, M.J., Lawson, P.J., Smith, S. and Cohen, D.J. (2014) Teachable moments for health behavior change and intermediate patient outcomes. *Patient Education and Counseling*, 96: 43–49.

Froom, P. and Benbassat, J. (2000) Inconsistencies in the classification of preventive interventions. *Preventive Medicine*, 31: 153–158.

Ganz, P. (2005) A teachable moment for oncologists: Cancer survivors, 10 million strong and growing! *Journal of Clinical Oncology*, 23(4): 5458–5460.

Gibson, A.F., Lee, C. and Crabb, S. (2015) 'Take ownership of your condition': Australian women's health and risk talk in relation to their experiences of breast cancer. *Health, Risk and Society*, 17(2): 132–148.

Golant, M. and Thiboldeaux, K. (2010) The Wellness Community's integrative model of evidence-based psychosocial programs, services and interventions. In J.C. Holland, W.S. Breitbart, P.B. Jacobsen, M.S. Lederberg, M.J. Loscalzo and R.S. McCorkle (eds), *Psycho-Oncology*. Second edition. Oxford: Oxford University Press, pp. 437–478.

Gordon, R.S. (1983) An operational classification of disease prevention. *Public Health Reports*, 98(2): 107–109.

Gritz, E.R. and Demark-Wahnefried, W. (2009) Health behaviors influence cancer survival. *Journal of Clinical Oncology*, 27(12): 1930–1932.

Holman, H. and Lorig, K. (2004) Patient self-management: A key to effectiveness and efficiency in care of chronic disease. *Public Health Reports*, 119: 239–243.

Horrocks, C. and Johnson, S. (2014) A socially situated approach to inform ways to improve health and wellbeing. *Sociology of Health and Illness*, 36(2): 175–186.

Houser, H. (2014) *Ecosickness in Contemporary U.S. Fiction: Environment and Affect*. New York: Columba University Press.

Institute of Medicine and the National Research Council (2006) *From Cancer Patient to Cancer Survivor: Lost in Transition*. Washington, DC: National Academies Press.

Irwin, M.L. and Mayne, S.T. (2008) Impact of nutrition and exercise on cancer survival. *Cancer Journal*, 14(6): 435–441.

Jain, S.L. (2007) Living in prognosis: Toward and elegiac politics. *Representations*, 98: 77–92.

Jain, S.L. (2013) *Malignant: How Cancer Becomes Us*. Berkeley: University of California Press.

Kennedy, A., Reeves, D., Bower, P., Lee, V., Middleton, E., Richardson, G., Gardner, C., Gately, C. and Rogers, A. (2007) The effectiveness and cost effectiveness of a national lay-led self care support programme for patients with long-term conditions: A pragmatic randomised controlled trial. *Journal of Epidemiology and Community Health*, 61: 254–261.

Lawson, P. and Flocke, S. (2009) Teachable moments for health behavior change: A concept analysis. *Patient Education and Counseling*, 76: 25–30.

Leavell, H.R. and Clark, E.G. (1958) *Preventive Medicine for the Doctor in His Community: An Epidemiologic Approach*. New York: McGraw Hill Book Company.

Lorig, K.R. (1996) Chronic disease self-management: A model for tertiary prevention. *American Behavioral Scientist*, 39(6): 676–683.

Lorig, K.R. and Holman, H.R. (2003) Self-management education: History, definition, outcomes, and mechanisms. *Annals of Behavioral Medicine*, 26(1): 1–7.

Lorig, K.R., Sobel, D.S., Stewart, A.L., Brown Jr, B.W., Bandura, A., Ritter, P., Gonzalez, V.M., Laurent, D.D. and Holman, H.R. (1999) Evidence suggesting that a Chronic Disease Self-Management Program can improve health status while reducing hospitalization: A randomized trial. *Medical Care*, 37(1): 5–14.

Lorig, K.R., Ritter, P., Stewart, A.L., Sobel, D.S., Brown Jr, B.W., Bandura, A., Gonzalez, V.M., Laurent, D.D. and Holman, H.R. (2001) Chronic Disease Self-Management Program: 2-year health status and health care utilization outcomes. *Medical Care*, 39(11): 1217–1223.

Lupton, D. (1997) Foucault and the medicalisation critique. In A. Petersen and R. Bunton (eds), *Foucault, Health and Medicine*. London: Routledge, pp. 94–110.

McBride, C., Emmons, K. and Lipkus, I. (2003) Understanding the potential of teachable moments: The case of smoking cessation. *Health Education Research*, 18(2): 156–170.

Maley, M., Warren, B.S. and Devine, C.M. (2013) A second chance: Meanings of body weight, diet, and physical activity to women who have experienced cancer. *Journal of Nutrition Education and Behavior*, 45(3): 232–239.

Mann, J.M. (1997) Medicine and public health, ethics and human rights. *Hastings Center Report*, 27(3): 6–13.

Markovic, M., Manderson, L., Wray, N. and Quinn, M. (2006) Complementary medicine use by Australian women with gynecological cancer. *Psycho-Oncology*, 15: 209–220.

Masco, J. (2010) Atomic health, or how the bomb altered American notions of death. In J. Metzl and A. Kirkland (eds), *Against Health: How Health Became the New Morality*. New York: New York University Press, pp. 133–155.

Maskarinec, G., Murphy, S., Shumay, D.M. and Kakai, H. (2001) Dietary changes among cancer survivors. *European Journal of Cancer Care*, 10: 12–20.

Mol, A. (2008) *The Logic of Care: Health and the Problem of Patient Choice*. London: Routledge.

Morden, A., Jinks, C. and Ong, B.N. (2012) Rethinking 'risk' and self-management for chronic illness. *Social Theory and Health*, 10(1): 78–99.

NCI, ACS, Livestrong, CDC (2010) Cancer Survivorship Research: Recovery and Beyond 2010 Conference. Available at: www.cancer.org/subsites/Survivorship2010/index (accessed 1 August 2011).

Nelson, J. and Macias, T. (2008) Living with a white disease: Women of colour and their engagement with breast cancer information. *Women's Health and Urban Life*, 7(1): 20–39.

Novas, C. (2006) The political economy of hope: Patients' organizations, science and bio-value. *BioSocieties*, 1: 289–305.

Ong, B.N., Rogers, A., Kennedy, A., Bower, P., Sanders, T., Morden, A., Cheraghi-Sohi, S., Richardson, J.C. and Stevenson, F. (2014) Behaviour change and social blinkers? The role of sociology in trials of self-management behaviour in chronic conditions. *Sociology of Health and Illness*, 36(2): 226–238.

Osborne, T. (1997) Of health and statecraft. In A. Petersen and R. Bunton (eds), *Foucault, Health and Medicine*. London: Routledge, pp. 173–188.

Petersen, A. (2015) *Hope for Health: The Socio-Politics of Optimism*. New York: Palgrave Macmillan.

Rose, N. (2007) *The Politics of Life Itself: Biomedicine, Power, and Subjectivity in the Twenty-First Century*. Princeton, NJ: Princeton University Press.

Sharp, L., Johannson, H., Fagerstrom, K. and Rutqvist, L.E. (2007) Smoking cessation among patients with head and neck cancer: Cancer as a 'teachable moment'. *European Journal of Cancer Care*, 17(2): 114–119.

Sinding, C. and Gray, R. (2005) Active aging – spunky survivorship? Discourses and experiences of the years beyond breast cancer. *Journal of Aging Studies*, 19: 147–161.

Sontag, S. (1990) *Illness as Metaphor and AIDS and its Metaphors*. New York: Picador.

Stanford School of Medicine (2016) Chronic Disease Self-Management Program (Better Choices, Better Health ® Workshop). *Stanford Medicine*. Available at: http://patient edcation.stanford.edu/programs/cdsmp.html (accessed 2 February 2016).

Stewart, D.E., Cheung, A.M., Duff, S., Wong, F., McQuestion, M., Cheng, T., Purdy, L. and Bunston, T. (2001) Attributions of cause and recurrence in long-term breast cancer survivors. *Psycho-Oncology*, 10: 179–183.

Thomas, L. (1991) Science and health: Possibilities, probabilities, and limitations. In A. Mack (ed.), *In Time of Plague: The History and Social Consequences of Lethal Epidemic Disease*. New York: New York University Press, pp. 57–73.

Tritter, J.Q. and Calnan, M. (2002) Cancer as a chronic illness? Reconsidering categorization and exploring experience. *European Journal of Cancer Care*, 11: 161–165.

van der Pligt, J. (1998) Perceived risk and vulnerability as predictors of precautionary behaviour. *Journal of Health Psychology*, 3: 1–14.

Ward, A., Doll, R., Ristovski-Slijepcevic, S., Kazanjian, A. and Golant, M. (2010) Cancer Transitions: A supportive care program for cancer survivors. *Oncology Exchange*, 9(2): 12–14.

WCRF and AICR (2007) *Food, Nutrition, Physical Activity, and the Prevention of Cancer: a Global Perspective*. Washington, DC: World Cancer Research Fund and American Institute for Cancer Research.

Winzer, B.M., Whiteman, D.C., Reeves, M.M. and Paratz, J.D. (2011) Physical activity and cancer prevention: A systematic review of clinical trials. *Cancer Causes and Control*, 22(6): 811–826.

PART II
Evidence

4

MEDICINE ACQUIRES A BASE

Introduction

In 2007, the editors of the *British Medical Journal* accepted nominations for the most important medical milestones accomplished since 1840, when its first issue hit the shelves of libraries and physician offices. A list of 70 candidates was developed based on reader suggestions and whittled down to 15; these were then referred back to readers for a formal vote (Ferriman 2007; Godlee 2007). The victors are relatively predictable, with the 'sanitary revolution' topping the list, followed closely by the discovery of antibiotics and the development of anaesthesia (Ferriman 2007). Somewhat more surprising is the inclusion of 'evidence-based medicine' in the final 15 candidates, alongside such luminaries as the contraceptive pill and oral rehydration therapy. Aspirin didn't even make the list.

How did evidence-based medicine come to be defined as one of the most 'extraordinary medical advances' (Godlee 2007) of the past 150 years? This is the central preoccupation of this chapter, in which I intend to lay the groundwork for the two that follow. In a strikingly short timeframe, its notions of 'evidence' (what it is and how best to get it) served to largely displace other ways of conceptualising how to organise health care policy and practice. My primary aim is to discuss the circumstances that facilitated the emergence of evidence-based medicine[1] and why its core principles came to be so widely embraced in fields both near and far removed from medicine, despite the intensive criticisms the movement engendered. What I will not be doing is providing a straightforward definition of evidence-based medicine, or 'EBM': the diminutive by which the movement is generally known. While technical definitions can be found in any of the core texts of evidence-based medicine, 'EBM is a slippery and amorphous creature' (Lambert 2009: 17; see also Wahlberg and McGoey 2007), although, as I shall demonstrate, it's this quality that partially accounts for its success.

Evidence-based medicine emerges

'A new paradigm for medical practice is emerging.' This is the portentous opening line of 'Evidence-based medicine: A new approach to teaching the practice of medicine', published in 1992 by a collection of clinical epidemiologists from McMaster University in Canada working under the leadership of David Sackett (EBM Working Group 1992). Although the term 'evidence-based medicine' was coined the previous year (Guyatt 1991), this paper is generally attributed with heralding its arrival (Tonelli 1998; Haynes 2002; Cronje and Fullan 2003; Mykhalovskiy and Weir 2004; Wyer and Silva 2009; Solomon 2015). Part doctrinal tract, part promotional brochure,[2] the authors self-consciously framed evidence-based medicine in terms of a 'paradigm shift', stating: 'when defects in an existing paradigm accumulate to the extent that the paradigm is no longer tenable, the paradigm is challenged and replaced by a new way of looking at the world' (EBM Working Group 1992: 2420).

To illustrate the way their 'new paradigm' differed from the existing one, the authors present the reader with a clinical scenario involving a 43-year-old man who is admitted to hospital after experiencing a grand mal seizure. Various causes are ruled out (recent head injury, excessive alcohol intake) and a physical examination reveals no abnormalities. The patient is given an intravenous dose of an anti-convulsant drug and head and brain scans are conducted, although they provide little clarity regarding his condition. Two hypothetical responses to this clinical scenario are then outlined in sections with suitably grandiose titles designed to evoke the notion of a seismic temporal shift.

In 'The Way of the Past', the junior resident consults with the senior resident who, in turn, approaches the attending physician. In agreement that the risk of seizure recurrence is high, they inform the junior resident that the patient must be warned of this. The resident, with her path clearly charted by her superiors, tells the patient not to drive, to continue taking his medication and to follow up with his physician. The patient leaves with a sense of trepidation about the risk of subsequent seizure. This response is juxtaposed with 'The Way of the Future' – i.e., the way of evidence-based medicine:

> The resident asks herself whether she knows the prognosis of first seizure and realizes she does not. She proceeds to the library and . . . enters the Medical Subject Headings terms *epilepsy*, *prognosis*, and *recurrence*, and the program retrieves 25 relevant articles. Surveying the titles, one appears directly relevant. She reviews the paper, finds that it meets criteria she has previously learned for a valid investigation of prognosis, and determines that the results are applicable to her patient. The search costs the resident $2.68, and the entire process took half an hour. The results of the relevant study show that the patient risk of recurrence at 1 year is between 43 per cent and 51 per cent . . . After a seizure-free period of 18 months his risk of recurrence would likely be less than 20 per cent. She conveys this information to the

patient, along with a recommendation that he take his medication, see his family doctor regularly, and have a review of his need for medication if he remains seizure-free for 18 months. The patient leaves with a clear idea of his likely prognosis.

EBM Working Group 1992: 2420

Several core features of EBM are illustrated in this excerpt. First, in this envisioned future, the resident makes no appeals to higher authorities. Recognising her own fallibility, science (or 'evidence'), rather than gut instinct, becomes her guide. Second, her approach is cost effective ($2.68!) and efficient (30 minutes!). Third, patient care is improved; the patient is given clear – and presumably reassuring – advice.[3] These attributes of objectivity, scientificity, effectiveness and efficiency are the self-proclaimed hallmarks of evidence-based medicine, which is contrasted to 'intuition, unsystematic clinical experience, and pathophysiologic rationale' (EBM Working Group 1992: 2420). A series of truth claims is thus asserted not only about the nature of EBM itself, but the characteristics of prevailing medical practice (see Table 4.1). Although the term is never explicitly used in the article,[4] an underlying emphasis on rationality is evident throughout. In essence, its authors present EBM as a more *rational* kind of medicine, with its underlying implication that prevailing medical practice is *irrational* (as well as being non-evidence-based). As Michael Traynor (2000) notes, such foundational texts implicitly set up evidence-based medicine as a project of purification, one that asserts – and fundamentally relies on – a series of dualisms. This kind of framing evokes EBM as more than merely a 'new' epistemological approach to medicine; rather, it's an ontology that requires the shedding of old values and beliefs and the acquisition of new ones. The appropriate metaphor, as Traynor (2000) observes, is that of *conversion*.[5]

TABLE 4.1 The characteristics of EBM and standard medical practice according to its key proponents

Standard medical practice	Evidence-based medicine
Irrational	Rational
Unsystematic	Systematic
Guided by common sense and intuition	Guided by scientific knowledge
Values traditional scientific authority	Values new scientific developments
Biased	Objective
Maintains the status quo	Facilitates innovation
Inferior patient care	Superior patient care

Subsequent publications served to outline the topography of evidence-based medicine, (e.g., Hadorn *et al.* 1996; Sackett *et al.* 1996; Sackett *et al.* 2000), especially in terms of its evidence hierarchies, which were widely disseminated in the form of an 'EBM pyramid' (see Figure 4.2). In positing a singular hierarchy of evidence of effectiveness it introduced new kinds and meanings of 'evidence' (Adams 2013), with randomised controlled trials forming the 'gold standard' for individual studies and systematic reviews of such forming the pyramid's summit. I will be focusing intensively on the former in Chapter 5 and the latter in Chapter 6, but the point I want to emphasise here is the singularly narrow way in which EBM defined 'evidence'. As Jeremy Howick (2011: 4) notes, 'If EBM is something new, and its proponents insist it is, it must be a very specific view of what counts as (good) evidence'. In this framework, for evidence to speak in a valid way about how to prevent or treat health problems, it must use the language of statistics and epidemiology (Adams 2013).

Despite initial resistance among physicians, evidence-based medicine 'rapidly succeeded in displacing the traditional grounds of expert knowledge – in clinical expertise – in favour of a new regime of truth whose legitimate currency is statistical evidence' (Lambert 2009: 17). Indeed, the years directly following the publication of the 1992 paper saw a number of events that served to consolidate EBM as a transnational movement. In 1993, the UK-based Cochrane Collaboration was formed. A non-profit organisation devoted to conducting and disseminating systematic reviews of randomised controlled trials based on strict criteria, it has since become the 'gold standard' in appraisals of health care evidence. In 1995, *Evidence-Based Medicine*, a dedicated journal co-founded by David Sackett, was established. Its stated goal was to disseminate the findings of 'high quality' research (assessed according to EBM criteria) in the areas of diagnosis, prognosis, therapy, aetiology, quality of care and health economics (Sackett and Haynes 1995). Given the dramatic advances in information technology during this period, and the explosion of

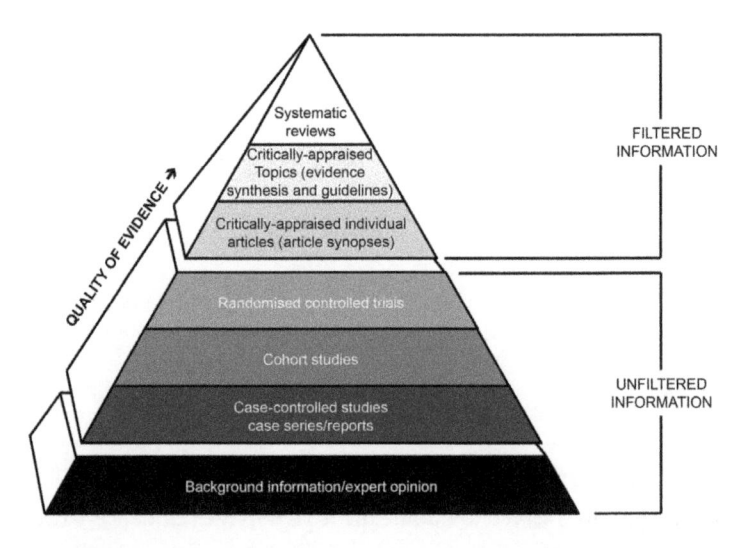

FIGURE 4.1 EBM evidence pyramid

Source: adapted from Sackett *et al.* 2000.

information relating to health care that accompanied it, it's not difficult to see why these organisations and publications – and the clear-cut orientation to 'evidence' they established – were so attractive to health care managers and policy makers (Wyer and Silva 2009).[6]

Various countries followed suit in developing bodies and agencies to appraise medical evidence and advise on the most effective health care tools and treatments (Mykhalovskiy and Weir 2004; Wahlberg and McGoey 2007). For example, in the UK, the National Institute for Clinical Excellence (now the National Institute for Health and Care Excellence) was created in 1999 to develop clinical guidelines for the National Health Service. In the USA, the embrace was similarly totalising, with EBM used to determine both the most effective clinical practices and the optimal insurance policies (Adams 2013). According to Vincanne Adams (2013: 58), today

> EBM approaches have become not just routine but rather tyrannical in the world of clinical health care in the industrialized nations . . . New regimes of accountability using EBM standards have emerged as a kind of 'audit' necessity in organizations far and wide from the Gates Foundation and Save the Children, to the NIH [National Institutes of Health] and the WHO.

In light of its far-reaching impacts on the organisation of health care policy and practice, we can begin to understand how EBM might be seen to constitute one of the most important (if contested) medical milestones of the twentieth century – although this was the result of a particular set of contextual processes as much as an effect of the active efforts undertaken to ensure its institutionalisation.

EBM and its conditions of possibility

While the uptake of evidence-based medicine occurred throughout the 1990s, in many respects this was the culmination of developments that began well before the term was coined – something acknowledged by proponents themselves, although primarily as a way of demonstrating its irrefutable logic and value. According to the originators of EBM, its foundations 'lie in developments in clinical research over the last 30 years' (EBM Working Group 1992: 2420); some accounts assert that its basic principles have been with us for centuries. For example, in their paper titled 'History and development of evidence-based medicine', Claridge and Fabian (2005) identify four EBM 'eras': ancient era EBM, Renaissance era EBM, the transitional era and modern era EBM, asserting a continuous thread in its basic principles across time and space – from the Bible, to blood letting practices in the Renaissance era, to David Sackett's clinical epidemiology programme at McMaster University.[7] In such accounts, which tend to veer more towards the hagiographic than the historiographic, evidence-based medicine is generally presented as the inevitable outcome of scientific progress.

There's little question that the basic principles underpinning EBM have been articulated from at least the 1960s. For example, the British physician and epidemiologist Archie Cochrane (from whom the Cochrane Collaboration takes its name) was a key figure in advocating for medical practice to be more directly informed by evidence. He is often characterised as the 'father' or 'founder' of evidence-based medicine for precisely this reason (Ashcroft 2007; Will 2007; Stavrou, Challoumas and Dimitrakakis 2014).[8] In his 1972 book *Effectiveness and Efficiency: Random Reflections on Health Services*, which I will discuss in more detail in Chapters 6 and 7, Cochrane argued that England's National Health Service was neither effective nor efficient, and that the incorporation of randomised controlled trials would facilitate the development of a more 'rational' service (Cochrane 1972).

Similar observations about the 'irrationality' of medical care were also made in the United States, although they were inflected by the specificities of the US context (namely, privatised health care in conjunction with publicly funded programmes such as Medicare and Medicaid). For example, concerns about 'unwarranted variation' figured heavily in the work of the clinical epidemiologist John Wennberg (Timmermans and Berg 2003). In 1967, Wennberg began analysing Medicare data to determine how well hospitals and doctors were serving their communities, finding evidence of 'tremendous variation in every aspect of healthcare delivery' (McCue 2003). He later noted of his initial study, 'The basic premise – that medicine was driven by science and by physicians capable of making clinical decisions based on well-established fact and theory – was simply incompatible with the data we saw' (McCue 2003). Wennberg went on to found the Dartmouth Atlas Project in 1988, which documents variations in how medical resources are used in the United States.

Given that its central tenets had been espoused for at least 30 years before the movement was widely taken up, its success in the 1990s can't merely be treated as an instance of 'scientific progress' finally trumping 'tradition' (a view that, in any case, is strongly at odds with the approach I take in this book). In contrast to such Whiggish narratives, various commentators have presented a rather different view of the emergence of EBM – one suggesting that it can't be divorced from a variety of concurrent and highly contextual developments. Without these 'conditions of possibility' (Foucault 1980: 116), it's unlikely that EBM could have emerged or attained anything approaching its present stature.

As Timmermans and Berg (2003) have illustrated, EBM's concern with standardisation is far from new, with the hospital standardisation movement of the early twentieth century forming an important precursor. In their words:

> Evidence-based medicine is part of a wider movement to generate uniformity and quality control by streamlining processes. In the broader historical context, standardization forms a powerful vestige of modernism lingering in an increasingly postmodern world. The notion that predictability, accountability, and objectivity will follow uniformity belongs to the Enlightenment master narratives promising progress through increased rationality and control.
>
> *Timmermans and Berg 2003: 8*

However, although efforts at standardisation substantially predate the rise of evidence-based medicine, Timmermans and Berg emphasise that its guidelines represent a distinctively far-reaching and direct attempt to prescribe the actions of health care professionals. In contrast to earlier standardisation efforts, which were restricted to the tools, skills and facilities required for the provision of health care, EBM advocates wanted to intervene at the *moment* of medical decision-making.

EBM's attempt to standardise processes of decision-making is frequently linked with the rise of 'audit society' (Power 1997; Strathern 2000) in the 1990s and the perceived need for increased accountability, transparency and cost effectiveness (e.g., Lambert 2006, 2009; Adams 2013; Storeng and Béhague 2014). In this period, the growing distrust in professional autonomy was accompanied by the rise of 'rituals of verification', which quickly became normalised across the public sector. According to Michael Power (1997), the new forms of public management that emerged in this period were themselves connected with the rise of neoliberal values that prioritised small government and reorganised it to mimic the presumed efficiency of the market, seeking to act on and through the interests and motivations of subjects and organisations themselves. Indeed, numerous observers have highlighted the ways in which EBM principles align with the neoliberal restructuring of the welfare state throughout the 1990s in a variety of countries and the rationalisation of services it engendered (see Mykhalovisky and Weir 2004 for further discussion). To quote Bruce Charlton (2009: 931):

> Whether EBM was self-consciously crafted to promote the interests of government and management, or whether this confluence of EBM theory and government need was merely fortuitous, is something I do not know. But the fact is that the EBM advocates were shoving at an open door.

However, while EBM can be linked with a broader drive towards standardisation and the convergence of a distinctive set of political and economic imperatives in the 1990s, it is also connected with a long history of ambivalence about the distinctive power physicians wield in matters of life and death. As should be clear, a particular view of the medical profession underpins evidence-based medicine. In some respects, the physician instantiated in EBM discourse bears a distinct resemblance to the infamous fictional surgeon Dr Jed Hill, immortalised in the 1993 film *Malice*. In what is unquestionably the film's most memorable scene, Hill (played by Alec Baldwin) has been sued for medical malpractice and is defending his actions during a deposition. Asked whether he has a God complex, he responds:

> I have an MD from Harvard. I am board certified in cardiothoracic medicine and trauma surgery. I have been awarded citations from seven different medical boards in New England. And I am never, ever sick at sea. So I ask you, when someone goes into that chapel and they fall on their knees and they pray to God that their wife doesn't miscarry, or that their daughter doesn't bleed to death, or that their mother doesn't suffer acute neural trauma from

> post-operative shock, who do you think they're praying to? . . . You go to your church and with any luck you might win the annual raffle, but if you're looking for God, he was in operating room #2 on November 17th and he doesn't like to be second-guessed. You ask me if I have a God complex? Let me tell you something. I *am* God.

A bloated caricature of 'the Way of the Old', Baldwin's character nevertheless exemplifies the kind of physicians the movement saw itself as working against: who, according to Charlton (2009: 931), were foundationally branded under EBM as 'prejudiced, conservative and irrational'. Thus, EBM accounts emphasise that it prioritises 'scientific evidence, rather than the views held by eminent practitioners, as the basis for clinical practice' (Daley 2005: 2), with medical practice repeatedly portrayed as dominated by 'authority, tradition, and the physician's personal experience' (Rodwin 2001: 439).[9]

As I will discuss in Part III, concerns about quackery were intimately bound up with attempts to professionalise medicine in the mid-nineteenth century and the development of formalised codes of medical ethics. Fears about medicine being driven by commercial influences and the vagaries of individual clinical opinion continued to be a preoccupation in the early twentieth century, with reformers in the USA making a series of attempts to introduce a more 'rational' therapeutics (see Marks 1997). Indeed, the 1960s and 1970s were a period in which the professional sovereignty of physicians noticeably waned in a variety of western countries, although, once again, the reasons for this erosion in autonomy were complex. For example, in the US context, Paul Starr (1978) pointed to an internal redistribution of power that increasingly favoured corporate organisations over medical societies. He also emphasised changing conceptions of citizenship and the concomitant sense of entitlement to health care. Accompanying the growing centrality of the state in financing health services (e.g., Medicare and Medicaid) was a breakdown of the assumption that more medical care would improve the nation's health. This, in turn, made changes in the organisation of medicine possible that had previously been inconceivable.

The birth of bioethics in this period was also critical to these changes in physician sovereignty (see Chapter 7). With its accusations of physician paternalism and emphasis on the need to nurture patient agency in the medical encounter, it legitimised a place in medicine and health care for voices from *outside* the medical profession. For different reasons, the same is also true of the field of epidemiology itself. As discussed in Chapter 1, the rise of the 'new epidemiology' in the period following the Second World War and its consolidation in the 1960s and 1970s as a legitimate player in the health and medical fields had important effects on the latter – serving to transform conceptions of disease causality and introducing new methods and approaches for studying medical problems. Thus, in some respects evidence-based medicine can be seen as the continuation of epidemiology's longer-standing challenge to biomedical conceptions of evidence – and a crucial means through which it advocated a place at the table. As Helen Lambert observes:

The branding as 'evidence-based' of an essentially social political strategy to unseat professors of medicine as sole arbiters of good practice rather effectively neutralised at the outset resistance from those occupying traditional positions of authority in the medical world. It simultaneously opened a pathway for the relatively young and – to conventional biomedical wisdom – relatively disrespectful fields of epidemiology and public health, to move into a more central position in biomedical education and practice.

Lambert 2006: 2639

With the rise of EBM, expertise was increasingly defined in epidemiological and biostatistical terms – knowledge that was seen to be more democratically available (Charlton 2009).

The ostensibly democratic potential of EBM is yet another reason why the movement was so avidly embraced upon its emergence – although, once again, this was the result of changes that occurred over the preceding decades, especially the growing consumer consciousness among patients from the 1960s and the transformation from 'patient' to 'consumer' models of care (see Chambré and Goldner 2008).[10] This shift became especially pronounced in the late 1980s with the development of AIDS and breast cancer activism (see Epstein 1996 and Klawiter 2008 respectively), although Sue Clegg (2005: 418) also points to the importance of the women's health movement more broadly, and the ways in which evidence 'was used to challenge the scientificity of medicine and expose its practices'. Patients welcomed the openness EBM promised and the attendant possibility of becoming more 'informed' partners in their interactions with physicians (Timmermans and Berg 2003). Indeed, proponents of evidence-based medicine clearly perceived it as a democratising force insofar as it was seen to disrupt the 'normal' power relations between professionals and patients, thereby liberating 'human rationality from the authority of tradition or the charisma of the healer and . . . detached from particular opinions, interests and attitudes' (Thorgaard 2014: 55).

In sum, although many of its central preoccupations were evident from the mid-twentieth century onwards, a variety of disparate and interconnected factors were responsible for the embrace of evidence-based medicine at the end of the twentieth century. These factors provided the social, cultural, political and economic conditions that enabled its claims to be seen as logical, self-evident and a kind of necessary intervention into medicine (at least in some quarters). However, as I have already hinted, the movement was not universally lauded and applauded.

EBM: challenges and incorporations

Despite the widespread embrace of evidence-based medicine, trenchant attacks of the movement and its underlying tenets have been launched within medicine and beyond it. Lambert (2006) provides a useful typology of six core criticisms that appeared in medical and public health journals. First, critics highlighted the incommensurability of population evidence and individual patient needs, pointing out that evidence deriving from RCTs can't just be straightforwardly 'read across' to the management of individual patients. A second criticism – levelled more by public health professionals than clinicians – was the constraining effects of EBM on what types of intervention were considered to be legitimate. A third and fourth set of critiques pointed respectively to the ways in which clinical experience and expertise were marginalised within EBM, and EBM's promotion of formulaic guidelines. These, in turn, were seen to be connected to the fifth major criticism of EBM: its tendency to ignore patient views and preferences. Finally, observers pointed to the difficulties of translating evidence into practice.

As should be evident, medical critics have varied in their degree of opposition to the fundamental tenets of EBM itself. For example, even those somewhat sceptical of the merits of evidence-based medicine recognise the problems with an over-reliance on individual clinical expertise, a tension that comes across in a spoof article titled 'Seven alternatives to evidence-based medicine', published by two Australian physicians in the *British Medical Journal* (Isaacs and Fitzgerald 1999). The authors' ambivalence about EBM is apparent in statements such as: 'clinical decisions should, as far as possible, be evidence based. *So runs the current clinical dogma*' (Isaacs and Fitzgerald 1999: 1618, emphasis added). Observing that there are a number of situations where evidence is lacking, they then proceed to document seven other potential bases for medicine, all of which take digs, to varying degrees, at stereotypical characteristics associated with physicians. For example, they identify 'eminence-based medicine', 'vehemence-based medicine' ('the substitution of volume for evidence'), and 'confidence-based medicine', although they note that one is 'restricted to surgeons' (Isaacs and Fitzgerald 1999: 1618).

Other parodies speak of a deeper underlying critique, such as one recently published in the *Journal of Evaluation in Clinical Practice*[11] under the title 'Maternal kisses are not effective in alleviating minor childhood injuries (boo-boos): a randomized, controlled and blinded study'. Set up to look like a research article published by the Study of Maternal and Child Kissing ('SMACK') Working Group, its proclaimed objective is to determine the efficacy of maternal kissing of 'boo-boos' in toddlers and concludes:

> Maternal kissing of boo-boos confers no benefit on children with minor traumatic injuries compared to both no intervention and sham kissing. In fact, children in the maternal kissing group were significantly more distressed at 5 minutes than were children in the no intervention group. The practice of maternal kissing of boo-boos is not supported by the evidence and we recommend a moratorium on the practice.
>
> *SMACK Working Group 2015: 1244*

The author's goal is clearly to demonstrate how potentially ludicrous the logic and methods of EBM are – although it's unclear whether the paper is intended to be taken as a commentary on the dubious value of EBM itself, or merely its expansion beyond the domain of clinical medicine.[12]

Even more pointedly, various publications in the same journal have highlighted that EBM, when measured against its own standards of evidence, is fundamentally lacking. Thus, Charlton (2009) points out that evidence-based medicine has never been required to prove itself superior to existing models of practice. In his words:

> Just think of it, for a moment. Here was a doctrine that advocated rejecting and replacing-with-itself the whole mode of medical science and practice of the past. It advocated a new model of health service provision, new principles for research funding, a new basis for medical education. And the evidence for this? Well . . . none. Not one particle. 'Evidence-based' medicine was based on zero evidence.
>
> *Charlton 2009: 932*

Likewise, Devisch and Murray (2009) have similarly noted that by EBM's own logic, there is no evidentiary basis for its distinction between admissible and inadmissible evidence: 'in practice, that which distinguishes the RCT from other forms of evidence ultimately comes down to a matter of belief, not evidence' (Devisch and Murray 2009: 950). They conclude that this paradigm relies on the very kinds of unquantified and unquantifiable judgments that it officially disavows.

Given the values they espouse, this is perhaps the most serious criticism from the perspective of EBM proponents themselves, but the lack of evidence *for* evidence-based medicine is something they acknowledged relatively early on. For example, in an overview of the movement published in 2002, Brian Haynes noted,

> We do not have convincing studies showing that patients whose clinicians practise EBM are better off than those whose clinicians do not practise EBM: no one has done a randomized controlled trial of EBM with patient outcomes as the measure of success.
>
> *Haynes 2002: 2*

This acknowledgment and incorporation of criticisms is typical of the movement and has arguably been an important factor in its success. As Lambert (2006) notes, a central characteristic of EBM is the way it has tended to assimilate objections as opposed to rejecting them.[13] In her words: 'As each type of putative objection has been identified in commentaries and papers, each has progressively been accommodated within the parameters of EBM itself . . . criticism has characteristically been countered not by rejection, contestation or entrenchment, but by incorporation' (Lambert 2006: 2636).

Stephen Buetow (2009) characterises three phases in the evolution of EBM as its chief architects responded to dissenters: its first iteration focused on determining and applying the best available evidence to clinical decisions; its second iteration recognised that clinical decisions were based on clinical expertise, patient preferences and research evidence; and its newest iteration advocates the use of clinical expertise as the means of integrating clinical circumstances, research evidence and patient preferences. However, despite these various accommodations – to clinical expertise, patient preferences and so on – it's questionable whether the movement has changed in fundamentals.[14] For example, efforts have been made to incorporate other forms of evidence (e.g., qualitative research) into EBM hierarchies, but the problem has been largely treated as a methodological as opposed to epistemological one (Lambert 2009; see also Clegg 2005; Dixon-Woods *et al.* 2006; Jensen 2007).[15] As Devisch and Murray (2009: 951) observe, EBM's conception of evidence has become naturalised 'to such an extent that it is now difficult to pose questions concerning evidence in terms other than those sanctioned by EBM itself'. Holmes and O'Byrne (2012: 45) characterise it as an 'imperial apparatus of capture' for precisely this reason.

However, as I've already alluded, a very particular notion of evidence operates within the movement. Thomas Csordas (2004: 475) observes that 'evidence has to be evidence of or for something'; thus, evidence is rather different from 'data', which have nothing to prove in themselves. Yet this difference is erased in EBM, as evidence is assumed to be the natural output of data. Indeed, in evidence-based medicine, findings themselves hold far less weight than the methods used to obtain them (Lambert 2006). This is one of the reasons why evidence-based medicine has been so powerful. As Timmermans and Berg (2003: 18) note, 'standards and guidelines can be discussed with regard to their scientific qualities or their technical adequacy, but to speak of their political nature seems almost to commit a category mistake'. After all, its proponents claim, EBM *counters* and *corrects* the political use of medicine (Rodwin 2001) and attempts to utilise it for such purposes are seen to constitute a 'misuse' or 'hijacking' of its principles and processes (Sackett *et al.* 1996: 72).

EBM expands

In light of its self-declared objective and apolitical nature, it is for precisely such reasons that EBM has been widely embraced among government agencies and health care organisations. As Maya Goldenberg (2005) notes, evidence-based medicine has a ring of obviousness to it; in principle it's almost impossible to challenge (who *wouldn't* want treatments based on the best available evidence?). This self-evident value has therefore enabled the expansion of 'evidence-based practice' (as the movement has become more broadly known) into domains outside of medicine proper. Importantly, proponents of EBM saw few issues with the application of its principles to fields beyond medicine. For example, Sackett *et al.* (1996) pointed approvingly to the rise of established and planned centres for 'evidence based practice' in 'medicine, child health, surgery, pathology, pharmacotherapy, nursing, general practice and dentistry'. Indeed, as we will see in Chapters 5 and 6, subsequent iterations of evidence-based medicine soon expanded its gaze to other aspects of health-related activity, including multilevel and complex behavioural interventions targeting whole communities (Carter *et al.* 2011). Likewise, 'evidence-based policy' is now a core concern in and beyond the field of public health (Lin and Gibson 2002; Smith 2013).[16]

The movement's central tenets have also 'colonized' (Howick 2011: 4) fields far removed from health and medicine, such as social work (see Webb 2001) and education (see Oakley 2002; Clegg 2005). As Ann Oakley (2002: 278) has noted: 'The example of the Cochrane Collaboration has made professionals and policymakers in other disciplines think hard about the parallels and differences between health care and other forms of professional intervention in people's lives'. This growing appetite for 'evidence-based practice' is epitomised in the work of the Campbell Collaboration, a sibling organisation to the Cochrane Collaboration founded in 2000 to disseminate systematic reviews of 'social interventions' in the areas of education, crime and justice and social welfare.

In consequence, evidence-based paradigms now shape the way that service providers, funding bodies, governments and policy makers view 'effectiveness', along with their willingness to fund and support interventions, practices and models of care (Broom and Adams 2012). As Saida Hodžić (2013) observes, drawing on the work of Vinh-Kim Nguyen, 'evidence' has become the lubricant that keeps resources flowing between donors, organisations and policy makers. Likewise, Vincanne Adams (2010: 49–50) points to the arrival of EBM as creating not only a language with which to evaluate programmes in global health but one that potential funders could use to 'ratchet up the surveillance that determined their support'.

The growing cachet of 'evidence' – and the dollar value attached – has therefore seen the rise of 'evidence-based advocacy', with advocacy organisations increasingly articulating their goals and agendas in terms of 'evidence' rather than explicit ideological or moral claims (Storeng and Béhague 2014). While evidence-based advocacy might be seen to run counter to the avowedly a-political nature of EBM itself, proponents frame it as the natural outgrowth of evidence-based medicine and health care. To quote Friedlaender and Winston (2004: 324), 'just as rigorous science builds the evidence base for change, rigorous efforts and their evaluation are necessary to ensure that this evidence will be translated into change'. In such framings, advocacy is redefined as 'the translation of research into action' (Friedlaender and Winston 2004: 324) and is transformed into an ethical responsibility – a topic I will elaborate on in Chapter 9.

Such developments speak to the ways in which 'evidence' is increasingly deployed as a 'powerful tool for political, moral, and economic negotiations' (Storeng and Béhague 2014: 5). However, as Adams (2010) points out, the language of evidence-based science has had very real effects on the ground, making public health efforts that *don't* produce these kinds of evidence seem 'non-scientific', and raising attendant questions about the value of the interventions themselves. In her words: 'Common sense about these interventions is displaced by a narrow rhetoric of scientific truth that makes all evidence that is not packaged in these terms seem like nonsense because its validity cannot be established' (Adams 2010: 52). Thus, Adams argues, claims about what counts as a legitimate health problem are reconfigured: to 'count', the problem must be countable.

Conclusion

The roots of evidence-based medicine are clearly complex, but there is little doubt that it has had a dramatic impact on the organisation of medicine and health care. The questions it posed (and ostensibly answered) about the nature of evidence and how it should be organised and incorporated into medicine had rippling effects that saw its epidemiological and statistical logic extended far beyond the context it was originally designed to address. However, EBM's commitment to the belief that evidence 'speaks for itself' disguises its fundamentally political attributes and effects on what kind of knowledge 'counts' (pun intended). In sum, evidence-based medicine, health care and practice *seem* benign 'until one considers the question of what constitutes "evidence" and how the technologies of capture, synthesis and dissemination imbue and exclude certain ideas about the importance of certain types of knowledge' (Broom and Adams 2012: 2). This is precisely my aim in the next two chapters, which consider in more detail the effects of evidence-based medicine on knowledge production through a closer examination of its particular technologies of capture and synthesis.

Notes

1 As I noted in the Introduction, in this chapter (and, indeed, the book more broadly) I use the term 'evidence-based medicine' not just to encapsulate the movement in its initial iteration, but to refer to the expansion of its core principles beyond medicine into public health and other fields. I use this term rather than 'evidence-based practice' because it highlights the medical underpinnings of what has since become the 'standard' model for conceptualising evidence, which the latter term tends to elide.

2 In some respects, the article can be read as a promotional piece for McMaster University's Internal Medicine Residency Program.

3 What I find most striking about this example is how underwhelming it is, given how *little* the proffered treatment differs in the two scenarios. In each case, the advice given to the patient ('take your medication, follow up with your doctor, and plan for the pos-sibility of a future seizure') looks virtually indistinguishable. While the future resident gives more specific information, it's doubtful whether the patient would be reassured by proclamations that he has a 43–51 per cent chance of another seizure in the next year. After all, he either will or he won't have a seizure.

4 Although it's worth noting that the paper was published in a section of the journal titled 'The rational clinical examination'.

5 Metaphors of conversion abound in discussions of evidence-based medicine. For exam-ple, in one biting critique, Charlton (2009: 932) notes, 'To know EBM was to love him; and to recognize him as the Messiah; and to anticipate his imminent coming'.

6 Several commentators have pointed to the emergence of biomedical informatics as an important precursor to evidence-based medicine (e.g., Dickersin and Manheimer 1998; Timmermans and Berg 2003; Wyer and Silva 2009). As Dickersin and Manheimer (1998: 327) observe: 'the actual practice of evidence-based healthcare may not have been possible before information systems technology advanced to its current state'.

7 David Sackett himself refers to the 'ancient roots' of EBM (Sackett *et al.* 1996: 72).

8 However, as Timmermans and Berg (2003) note, whether Cochrane is a 'true' predeces-sor of EBM is up for debate. For example, see Ashcroft (2007) for a discussion of some of the differences between Cochrane's views and those of EBM proponents.

9 This distrust of physicians is strongly evident in Cochrane's work. Although a trained physician himself, a degree of contempt for his counterparts came across strongly in *Evidence and Efficiency*. As one of the book's reviewers approvingly noted,

> The hero of the book is the randomized control trial, and the villains are the clinicians in the 'care' part of the National Health Service who either fail to carry out such trials or succeed in ignoring the results if they do not fit with their own pre-conceived ideas.
>
> *Dollery 1972: 56*

This negative view of physicians was also evident in Cochrane's self-penned obituary in which he wrote of himself: 'In 1957 he survived a professor of surgery's prognosis that he had only three months to live' (Cochrane 1988: 63). The message was clear: patients must be saved, not just from illness, but from physicians themselves.

10 This shift will be discussed in more detail in Chapter 7.

11 This journal has been consistently critical of EBM and has published scores of papers excoriating the movement.

12 As the author of the paper has subsequently been identified as Mark Tonelli, who has written previously about the philosophical limits of EBM (see Tonelli 1998), I suspect the former.

13 In many respects, this feature was evident from the outset. For example, the 1992 paper that ushered in the new 'era' of evidence-based medicine (EBM Working Group 1992) included a section titled 'Misapprehensions about evidence-based medicine', where the authors took pains to emphasise that the approach didn't ignore clinical experience or underlying pathophysiological mechanisms. Pre-empting subsequent characterisations of EBM as promoting slavish adherence to formulaic guidelines (i.e., 'cookbook medicine'), the authors implied that this was a more accurate identifier for the old paradigm because 'people like quick and easy answers', whereas 'critical appraisal involves additional time and effort' (EBM Working Group 1992: 2433).

14 Jeremy Howick (2011: 11) argues that in spite of evolving characterisations of EBM, its 'view that comparative clinical studies, preferably (systematic reviews of) randomized trials, provide more telling evidence for therapeutic effects than mechanistic reasoning and clinical expertise has remained constant'.

15 As Dixon-Woods *et al.* (2006: 31) note: 'whether conventional systematic review methodology is well suited to the incorporation of qualitative research is an important empirical and epistemological question, and one that has received surprisingly little attention'. Their own research suggests that the epistemological assumptions associated with qualitative research 'strain the epistemological and methodological assumptions that underwrite systematic review' (Dixon-Woods *et al.* 2006: 40).

16 The influence of the paradigm on public health is evident when we consider Kavanagh and colleagues' observation in 2002 that little intervention research was actually conducted in the field, despite the growing prominence of evidence-based practice. Fourteen years later, this is no longer true. As Adams (2013: 66) points out, 'contemporary journals of public health are chock full of publications with titles that include the phrase "a Randomized controlled study of [fill in the blank]"'.

References

Adams, V. (2010) Against global health? Arbitrating science, non-science, and nonsense through health. In J. Metzl and A. Kirkland (eds), *Against Health: How Health Became the New Morality*. New York: New York University Press, pp. 40–59.

Adams, V. (2013) Evidence-based global public health: Subjects, profits, erasures. In J. Biehl and A. Petryna (eds), *When People Come First: Critical Studies in Global Health*. Princeton, NJ: Princeton University Press, pp. 54–90.

Ashcroft, R. (2007) Review of Archie Cochrane's effectiveness and efficiency: Random reflections on health services. *BioSocieties*, 2: 141–145.

Broom, A. and Adams, J. (2012) A critical social science of evidence-based healthcare. In A. Broom and J. Adams (eds), *Evidence-Based Healthcare in Context: Critical Social Science Perspectives*. Surrey: Ashgate, pp. 1–22.

Buetow, S. (2009) EBM and the strawman. *Journal of Evaluation in Clinical Practice*, 15: 957–959.

Carter, S.M., Rychetnik, L., Lloyd, B., Kerridge, I. H., Baur, L., Bauman, A., Hooker, C. and Zask, A. (2011) Evidence, ethics and values: A framework for health promotion. *American Journal of Public Health*, 101(3): 465–472.

Chambré, S.M. and Goldner, M. (2008) Introduction: Patients, consumers and civil society. *Advances in Medical Sociology*, 10: xi–xix.

Charlton, B.G. (2009) The zombie science of evidence-based medicine: A personal retrospective. *Journal of Evaluation in Clinical Practice*, 15: 930–934.

Claridge, J. A. and Fabian, C. (2005) History and development of evidence-based medicine. *World Journal of Surgery*, 29(5): 547–553.

Clegg, S. (2005) Evidence-based practice in educational research: A critical realist critique of systematic review. *British Journal of Sociology of Education*, 26(3): 415–428.

Cochrane, A.L. (1972) *Effectiveness and Efficiency: Random Reflections on Health Services*. London: Nuffield Trust.

Cochrane, A.L. (1988) Obituary. *British Medical Journal*, 297: 63.

Cronje, R. and Fullan, A. (2003) Evidence-based medicine: Toward a new definition of 'rational' medicine. *Health*, 7(3): 353–369.

Csordas, T.J. (2004) Evidence of and for what? *Anthropological Theory*, 4(4): 473–480.

Daly, J. (2005) *Evidence-Based Medicine and the Search for a Science of Clinical Care*. Berkeley: University of California Press.

Devisch, I. and Murray, S.J. (2009) 'We hold these truths to be self-evident': Deconstructing 'evidence-based' medical practice. *Journal of Evaluation in Clinical Practice*, 15: 950–954.

Dickersin, K. and Manheimer, E. (1998) The Cochrane Collaboration: Evaluation of health care and services using systematic reviews of the results of randomized controlled trials. *Clinical Obstetrics and Gynaecology*, 41(2): 315–331.

Dixon-Woods, M., Bonas, S., Booth, A., Jones, D.R., Miller, T., Sutton, A.J., Shaw, R.L., Smith, J.A. and Young, B. (2006) How can systematic reviews incorporate qualitative research? A critical perspective. *Qualitative Research*, 6(1): 27–44.

Dollery, C.T. (1972) Constructive attack. *British Medical Journal*, 2(5804): 56.

EBM Working Group (1992) Evidence-based medicine: A new approach to teaching the practice of medicine. *Journal of the American Medical Association*, 268(17): 2420–2425.

Epstein, S. (1996) *Impure Science: AIDS, Activism, and the Politics of Knowledge*. Berkeley: University of California Press.

Ferriman, A. (2007) British Medical Journal readers choose the 'sanitary revolution' as greatest medical advance since 1840. *British Medical Journal*, 334: 111.

Foucault, M. (1980) *Power/Knowledge: Selected Interviews and Other Writings 1972–1977*. Edited by Colin Gordon. New York: Pantheon Books.

Friedlaender, E. and Winston, F. (2004) Evidence based advocacy. *Injury Prevention*, 10(6): 324–326.

Godlee, F. (2007) Milestones on the long road to knowledge. *British Medical Journal*, 334: S2.

Goldenberg, M.J. (2005) Evidence-based ethics? On evidence-based practice and the 'empirical turn' from normative bioethics. *BMC Medical Ethics*, 6: 11.

Guyatt, G.H. (1991) Evidence-based medicine. *Annals of Internal Medicine ACP Journal Club*, Suppl. 2: A–16.

Hadorn, D.C., Baker, D., Hodges, J.S. and Hicks, N. (1996) Rating the quality of evidence for clinical practice guidelines. *Journal of Clinical Epidemiology*, 49(7): 749–754.

Haynes, R.B. (2002) What kind of evidence is it that evidence-based medicine advocates want health care providers and consumers to pay attention to? *BMC Health Services Research*, 2:3.

Hodžić, S. (2013) Ascertaining deadly harms: Aesthetics and politics of global evidence. *Cultural Anthropology*, 28(1): 86–209.

Holmes, D. and O'Byrne, P. (2012) Resisting stratification: Imperialism, war machines and evidence-based practice. In A. Broom and J. Adams (eds), *Evidence-Based Healthcare in Context: Critical Social Science Perspectives*. Surrey: Ashgate, pp. 43–60.

Howick, J. (2011) *The Philosophy of Evidence-Based Medicine*. Chichester: Wiley Blackwell.

Isaacs, D. and Fitzgerald, D. (1999) Seven alternatives to evidence based medicine. *British Medical Journal*, 319: 1618.

Jensen, U.J. (2007) The struggle for clinical authority: Shifting ontologies and the politics of evidence. *BioSocieties*, 2: 101–114.

Kavanagh, A., Daly, J., Melder, A. and Jolley, D. (2002) 'Mind the gap': Assessing the quality of evidence for public health problems. In V. Lin and B. Gibson (eds), *Evidence-based Health Policy: Problems and Possibilities*. Melbourne: Oxford University Press, pp. 70–79.

Klawiter, M. (2008) *The Biopolitics of Breast Cancer: Changing Cultures of Disease and Activism*. Minneapolis: University of Minnesota Press.

Lambert, H. (2006) Accounting for EBM: Notions of evidence in medicine. *Social Science and Medicine*, 62(11): 2633–2645.

Lambert, H. (2009) Evidentiary truths? The evidence of anthropology through the anthropology of medical evidence. *Anthropology Today*, 25(1): 16–20.

Lin, V. and Gibson, B. (eds) (2002) *Evidence-Based Health Policy: Problems and Possibilities*. Melbourne: Oxford University Press.

McCue, M.T. (2003) Clamping down on variation. *Managed Healthcare Executive*, February 1. Available at: http://managedhealthcareexecutive.modernmedicine.com/managed-healthcare-executive/content/clamping-down-variation (accessed 4 March 2015).

Marks, H. M. (1997) *The Progress of Experiment: Science and Therapeutic Reform in the United States, 1900–1990*. Cambridge, MA: Cambridge University Press.

Mykhalovskiy, E. and Weir, L. (2004) The problem of evidence-based medicine: Directions for social science. *Social Science and Medicine*, 59: 1059–1069.

Oakley, A. (2002) Social science and evidence-based everything: The case of education. *Educational Review*, 54(3): 277–286.

Power, M. (1997) *The Audit Society: Rituals of Verification*. Oxford: Oxford University Press.

Rodwin, M.A. (2001) The politics of evidence-based medicine. *Journal of Health Politics, Policy and Law*, 26(2): 439–446.

Sackett, D.L. and Haynes, R.B. (1995) On the need for evidence-based medicine. *Evidence-Based Medicine*, 1(1): 5–6.

Sackett, D.L., Rosenberg, W.M.C., Gray, J.A.M., Haynes, R.B. and Richardson, W.S. (1996) Evidence based medicine: What it is and what it isn't. *British Medical Journal*, 312: 71–72.

Sackett, D.L., Straus, S.E., Richardson, W.S., Rosenberg, W. and Haynes, R.B. (2000) *Evidence-Based Medicine: How to Practice and Teach EBM*. Second edition. Edinburgh: Churchill Livingstone.

SMACK Working Group (2015) Maternal kisses are not effective in alleviating minor childhood injuries (boo-boos): A randomized, controlled and blinded study. *Journal of Evaluation in Clinical Practice*, 21(6): 1244–1246.

Smith, K. (2013) *Beyond Evidence-Based Policy in Public Health: The Interplay of Ideas*. Basingstoke: Palgrave Macmillan.

Solomon, M. (2015) *Making Medical Knowledge*. Oxford: Oxford University Press.

Starr, P. (1978) Medicine and the waning of professional sovereignty. *Daedalus*, 107(1): 175–193.

Stavrou, A., Challoumas, D. and Dimitrakakis, G. (2014) Archibald Cochrane (1909–1988): The father of evidence-based medicine. *Interactive Cardiovascular and Thoracic Surgery*, 18: 121–124.

Storeng, K.T. and Béhague, D.P. (2014) 'Playing the numbers game': Evidence-based advocacy and the technocratic narrowing of the Safe Motherhood Initiative. *Medical Anthropology Quarterly*, 28(2): 260–279.

Strathern, M. (ed.) (2000) *Audit Cultures*. London: Routledge.

Tonelli, M. R. (1998) The philosophical limits of evidence-based medicine. *Academic Medicine*, 73: 234–1240.

Thorgaard, K. (2014) Is evidence-based medicine about democratizing medical practice? *Outlines: Critical Practice Studies*, 15(1): 49–62.

Timmermans, S. and Berg, M. (2003) *The Gold Standard: The Challenge of Evidence-Based-Medicine and Standardization in Health Care*. Philadelphia, PA: Temple University Press.

Traynor, M. (2000) Purity, conversion and evidence based movements. *Health*, 4(2): 139–158.

Wahlberg, A. and McGoey, L. (2007) An elusive evidence-base: The construction and governance of randomized controlled trials. *BioSocieties*, 2: 1–10.

Webb, S.A. (2001) Some considerations of the validity of evidence-based practice in social work. *British Journal of Social Work*, 31: 57–79.

Will, C.M. (2007) The alchemy of clinical trials. *BioSocieties*, 2: 85–99.

Wyer, P.C. and Silva, S.A. (2009) Where is the wisdom? I – A conceptual history of evidence-based medicine. *Journal of Evaluation in Clinical Practice*, 15: 891–898.

5

RCTs AND THE UNENCUMBERED HUMAN

Introduction

In 2007, a new 'surgical vaccine' was added to the global arsenal of HIV/AIDS prevention initiatives: male circumcision. How did the 'oldest operation in the world' (Gollaher 2000) become its newest biomedical technology of prevention? The answer to this question is complicated, but the pre-eminence of the randomised controlled trial is critical to solving it. Two weeks following the publication of the results of two RCTs on male circumcision and HIV transmission in the same issue of *The Lancet*, UNAIDS and the World Health Organization officially endorsed the procedure. According to UNAIDS:

> Male circumcision is the most compelling evidence-based prevention strategy since the finding that antiretroviral medicine can reduce mother-to-child transmission of HIV. Governments, supported by non-governmental organizations, multilateral and bilateral development partners and others, need to take decisive action now to make this life-saving strategy affordable and safely available to relevant populations bearing the heaviest burden of HIV infection.
>
> *UNAIDS 2007: 2*

As this statement suggests, EBM notions of evidence were central to the embrace of male circumcision as an HIV prevention tool. Amidst a degree of scientific scepticism, and energetic criticism from various activist groups opposed to the procedure (widely known as 'intactivists'), proponents were able to 'prove' that male circumcision reduces HIV transmission. In consequence, numerous agencies have channelled funding into large-scale, countrywide projects, most notably the World Health Organization, USAID, the US President's Emergency Plan for

AIDS Relief (PEPFAR) and the Bill and Melinda Gates Foundation. According to the World Health Organization, 5.82 million males have been circumcised in east and southern Africa since 2008 through these and related funding programmes, and they aim to achieve 20.8 million circumcisions by 2016 (WHO 2014).

In this chapter I consider in more detail the emergence of the randomised controlled trial as the 'gold standard' evidence of effectiveness. As noted in Chapter 4, while critics have managed to broaden EBM hierarchies in terms of what is understood to constitute 'legitimate' evidence, they haven't displaced the special status of the RCT or disrupted EBM's underlying assumptions about how evidence should be produced and what it means. Following a broader discussion of the rise of the RCT and the set of assumptions upon which it relies, I return to male circumcision and HIV transmission. By focusing on this example, I aim to crystallise the ways in which EBM paradigms elide the fundamentally political nature of knowledge practices and produce a very narrow definition of efficacy based on a simplistic model that assumes the possibility of getting at the 'pure' effect of an intervention *regardless* of its context.

The rise of the RCT

Despite the evolution of evidence-based medicine that has occurred over the past 25 years, the randomised controlled trial remains the most privileged method within its evidence hierarchies and those of its intellectual offspring (e.g., evidence-based public health, evidence-based policy, evidence-based decision making and so on). In determining efficacy, RCTs are valued above all other study designs because of their unique means of dealing with potential bias: randomising participants to the intervention is seen to 'control' for confounding variables in a way that simply can't be replicated in any other context (Howick 2011; Solomon 2015). The intellectual weight placed on randomisation in the EBM paradigm cannot be overstated and is key to its proclaimed capacities to establish probabilistic causality.[1] Thus, the RCT doesn't 'rely directly on *how* the intervention might produce an outcome, and instead involves directly observing the putative outcome relative to the putative outcome produced by a control treatment' (Howick 2011: 16, emphasis in original). Indeed, as we saw in Chapter 4, mechanistic reasoning, along with clinical expertise, is somewhat denigrated within EBM – understood to be a useful adjunct to RCTs but 'hardly to be counted evidence at all' (Howick 2011: 123).

According to canonical public health accounts, the controlled clinical trial dates back to at least 1740, with James Lind's test on lemons for scurvy prevention in the British Navy (Marks 1997). Such histories typically provide a series of celebrated examples that culminate in the UK Medical Research Council's controlled trial of streptomycin for tuberculosis treatment in 1948[2] (Medical Research Council 1948). This is usually characterised as the first fully randomised controlled trial because of an innovation introduced by the epidemiologist Austin Bradford Hill: the use of sealed envelopes to ensure that the study investigators didn't know who received treatment and who received a placebo (Wessely 2007). However, Harry

Marks (1997) and Trudi Dehue (2010) point to the presentist dimensions of such accounts. To quote Dehue (2010: 55): 'Such histories apply present-day standards in deciding which former authors should be included in the story and which fragments should be selected out of these authors' writings.' Contra such narratives, she argues that various nineteenth- and early twentieth-century methodological experts explicitly *rejected* the notion of experimental group comparison as a suitable research method. Thus, the late twentieth-century prioritisation of the RCT required 'pivotal transitions in society at large . . . and in views of what it means to be an individual' (Dehue 2010: 106). In other words, while the value of randomisation is today seen to be so self-evident that we assume it has been with us since the advent of 'the experimental method' in the seventeenth century, it is actually a far more recent phenomenon (see also Hacking 1988, 1990).

Dehue shows that for philosophers such as David Hume, Adolphe Quetelet and John Stuart Mill, scientific experimentation involving wilful manipulation was deemed unsuitable for research with human beings. While such figures weren't against the notion of experimentation per se, human beings were deemed too complex to make experimental comparisons appropriate. Thus, George Lewis argued that experimentation was 'inapplicable to man as a sentient, and also as an intellectual and moral being' (in Dehue 2010: 107). Likewise, John Stuart Mill advocated systematic comparison of cases in which an effect did and did not occur, but he viewed it as 'unsuitable in research with humans because in that case true comparability could not be achieved' (Dehue 2010: 107). For example, he argued that national comparisons were unhelpful because such differences had no assignable limit – they impacted 'every . . . feature of their condition, in more ways than can be enumerated or imagined' (in Dehue 2010: 107). Accordingly, Mill also raised similar objections to the study of individual differences, because of the impossibility of isolating a single factor from others that might constitute an effect.

According to Dehue, while the notion of average effects has become thoroughly naturalised, nineteenth-century scientists strongly challenged its validity (see also Hacking 1988, 1990). One particularly vehement critic was the French physiologist Claude Bernard. Ridiculing a colleague who had collected samples from a railway station urinal for further study, Bernard argued that: 'anyone attributing value to the mean, apparently regards it as useful to study the average European urine!' This, he pronounced, produced 'a perfect analysis of non-existing urine' (in Dehue 2010: 108). For Bernard, an average success in, say, a medical procedure, didn't give any certainty about the next operation to come and probability statistics therefore meant 'literally nothing scientifically' (in Dehue 2010: 109). Dehue argues that this historical scepticism towards experimental comparison and the statistical mean was based on an organicist and determinist world view that made the notion of using chance to derive population values or allocate individuals to artificial groups utterly senseless. However, she suggests that changes began to occur in society in the second half of the nineteenth century – first in the USA and then European countries – including a shift from determinism to progressivism, which saw more interest in state-sponsored 'improvement' projects, from eugenicist programmes to child labour laws to unemployment insurance. This, in turn, was accompanied by fears that the government would squander public funds. The resultant rise of welfare capitalism saw the enshrinement of three maxims: individualism, efficiency and impersonal procedures for assessment.

These changes led to a growing focus on standardised methodological rules and population variability as a means of establishing what problems needed to be solved. Most importantly, chance was transformed into something that could be made good use of. Here we see the 'taming of chance' that Ian Hacking (1990) has explored at length. Randomly allocating people to groups resolved the problem of matching individuals to ensure their similarity – an approach that entailed obvious problems from the outset because 'the matching procedure . . . needed to be repeated for every thinkable factor that might create bias' (Dehue 2010: 113). However, this approach relies on the assumption that the problem to be solved lies within the individual (Dehue 2010). In other words, it requires an entity model of disease, as opposed to a holistic one. As De Vries and Lemmens (2006) note, testing 'A' against 'B' in such a fashion leaves various assumptions unchallenged: about the interchangeability of bodies, the efficacy of allopathic intervention and the randomness of error. I will return to these points below and in Chapter 6.

RCTs: 'as much alchemy as assay'

Although proponents of evidence-based medicine tout the 'elegant simplicity' of RCTs (e.g., Sackett 2013), a growing body of empirical research by anthropologists and sociologists has documented just how complex and messy such trials are – although research is weighted heavily towards the study of clinical drug trials (e.g., Walhberg and McGoey 2007; Petryna 2009; Will and Moreira 2010). As Catherine Will (2007) observes, RCTs lack the procedural objectivity they claim, as a variety of hidden work goes into conducting them (see also Heaven 2008). For this reason, she suggests that they are 'as much alchemy as assay' (Heaven 2008: 86).[3]

De Vries and Lemmens (2006) highlight the variety of assumptions built into RCTs around the choice of the object of randomisation and the measures used to determine effectiveness. These 'technical' elements fundamentally determine what sorts of questions get asked and how they get answered, as well as, obviously, what the answers are. The results of such trials are also the outcome of a variety of cleaning practices – practices that are far more extensive and multifaceted than is generally accounted for in formal discussions of trial methodology (Helgesson 2010). Where such work is recognised, it's generally read through the lexicon of 'bias', with its implicit assumption that an unbiased RCT is possible (Kaptchuk 2001). The problem with taking bias as a starting point is that it then forces any discussion about practice into a framework that could be called 'a sociology of error' (Helgesson 2010: 52). This, as we saw in Chapter 4, has been a broader characteristic of EBM itself, where epistemological criticisms are treated as methodological ones and dealt with accordingly. For RCT methodologists, such questions are therefore addressed exclusively through the lens of internal and external validity – i.e., the degree of confidence in the conduct of the study and the degree to which the results of the study are generalisable to other populations. Like internal validity, external validity is treated as a purely technical problem (Lather 1993: 675). However, the extent to which an RCT adequately represents the 'real world' is always subject to negotiation – and open to deconstruction (cf. Epstein 1996).

Although this is true of RCTs in general, external validity is recognised to pose a particular problem for complex interventions such as those conducted in primary care and public health settings – a topic I will explore in detail in Chapter 6. While the success of evidence-based medicine has encouraged the use of RCT designs in the fields of public health and health policy, their causal pathways 'involve not just biological but also behavioral steps that need to be understood and measured, to demonstrate a logical sequence between intervention and outcome' (Victora, Habicht and Bryce 2004: 401). These, in many cases, might not become visible until years after a controlled study would typically lapse (Adams 2013). However, as Vincanne Adams (2013) notes, while public health was thought to be capable of achieving only an approximate version of EBM, over time RCTs have come to take on a more central role in the field (a perfect illustration of the colonisation effect discussed in Chapter 4). In her words,

> granted, real-life public health scenarios did not look or feel like the laboratories or the clinics where EBM techniques were born, but, with effort, it was felt that they could be made to approximate these research spaces, conceptually and epistemologically.
>
> *Adams 2013: 64*

Indeed, a notable feature of RCTs conducted beyond clinical settings is the ways in which the potential distance between trial and reality (or internal and external validity) has increasingly been reinvented as an 'implementation gap' (Will 2007: 95). In other words, practice is seen as *lagging behind* the results of trials. Once the right resources are installed, once 'social' and 'cultural' barriers to implementation are removed and so on, practice (or 'reality') will catch up. In this way, we might think of RCT evidence as hyper-real – a kind of pure simulacrum[4] in Jean Baudrillard's (1996) sense. Yet, instead of challenging the hold of 'the real', it reinforces it in relation to itself – what Sue Clegg (2005: 420) terms 'the really real of the empirical'. In sum, despite the ways in which RCTs actively produce the world they aim to describe, their rhetorical authority is largely unquestioned within health circles (Wahlberg and McGoey 2007). As Wahlberg and McGoey note, RCTs are examples of 'clinchers': 'methods for warranting causal claims' (2007: 6).

Male circumcision and economies of credibility

The rise of male circumcision as an HIV prevention tool is a clear example of how RCTs are used to clinch causal claims, although there are several ways in which this story has been told. The narrative presented by proponents themselves is one where successively more conclusive evidence was mounted in support of the association and policy makers were ultimately persuaded to take action. An alternative story – the one most commonly recounted by anti-circumcision advocates – is about the role of vested interests in producing the evidence and promoting its uptake (e.g., Van Howe, Svoboda and Hodges 2005; Boyle and Hill 2011). In some of the more extreme accounts (most notably those promulgated on CircWatch[5]), the pro-circumcision 'agenda' reaches the status of a vast global conspiracy.

There's little question that the evidence on the relationship between male circumcision and HIV transmission was developed and received in what I'll call here, following Steven Shapin, a 'congenial credibility environment' (Shapin 1995: 264; see also Shapin 2010). The embrace of male circumcision in the context of HIV prevention was clearly affected to some extent by the culturally normalised status of the procedure as 'trivial and inconsequential . . . just a little snip' (Aggleton 2007: 15). For example, Laura Carpenter (2010) has shown that the remedicalisation of male circumcision has been more enthusiastically embraced in the USA than the UK, where both circumcision and HIV rates are substantially lower. Her research suggests that the prevalence of HIV/AIDS is an important factor in the willingness to pursue male circumcision as a viable response, but so too is the degree to which it is already practised.

The congenial credibility environment for male circumcision becomes starkly apparent when contrasted with evidence on the relationship between *female* circumcision and HIV transmission. Although it has long been argued that the procedure probably increases HIV transmission (see Bell 2005), epidemiological studies conducted in both Tanzania and Kenya have reported a 'surprising' inverse correlation between female circumcision and HIV status (Stallings and Karugendo 2001; Kinuthia 2010).[6] However, the topic is self-evidently a non-starter. Regardless of any evidence that might suggest an association, it's impossible to imagine a parallel research agenda solidifying around the procedure, because current political realities[7] work very strenuously against such claims.

Nevertheless, to suggest that this is the end of the story – as many intactivists are wont to do – is to assume that science is inimical to politics[8] (and vice versa). As I have previously argued (Bell 2015), this view has led to a situation of implacable oppositions between those in favour of and against the procedure. Without a trace of irony, each side simultaneously invokes what Bruno Latour (2004) has called the *fact* position and the *fairy* position. In essence, they present their own views as neutral scientific 'facts' and the opposition as fetishists (or 'fairies') who either demonise or valorise the foreskin (depending on the detractor's own position). In consequence, a fundamentally political dispute has been framed and debated in largely technical terms, with each party rallying its own experts, 'much like lawyers offering to the jury a parade of expert witnesses' (Epstein 1996: 6).

However, such attempts to disentangle science from politics are based on a simplistic understanding of the relationship between political interests and technical judgments – a point Shapin (1995, 2010) makes via a pertinent parallel illustration. Recounting his stint as a lab technician in a unit testing a range of chemicals and drugs for possible mutagenicity and carcinogenicity, he reports that three substances were singled out for study: tetrahydrocannabinol (the active component in marijuana), LSD (it was the 1960s, enough said) and caffeine. As the research progressed, evidence on the mutagenicity of caffeine appeared to be more persuasive than that pointing to the cellular risks posed by marijuana and LSD. However, given the unspoken agreement among the research team that the credibility environment for claims about the risks of marijuana and LSD was substantially greater than that for coffee, they ended up focusing on the risks posed by the former two substances. In characterising this decision, Shapin observes:

> At no stage in the formal discussions I witnessed leading to this outcome was anything unscientific said. Nor need it have been. For there was sufficient 'play' between the test situation and possible in vivo effects for relevant scepticism to be expressed about the caffeine metonymic relationship, and, of course, sufficient grounds of confidence in the pertinence of the marijuana and LSD systems. It is proper usage to say that the legitimacy of inductive inference from in vitro to in vivo was conceded or contested on scientific grounds and on political grounds, *yet no one was obliged to depart from a recognizably scientific idiom to give politics a grip.*
>
> *Shapin 1995: 264–265, emphasis added*

Similarly, the political context of knowledge production about HIV/AIDS doesn't make the technical claims fundamentally 'unscientific', although it does help to explain why the RCTs were conducted in the first place, and why their results were taken up.

Elsewhere I have highlighted various socio-political factors that facilitated an openness towards male circumcision as an HIV prevention tool, particularly emphasising the utility of male circumcision in navigating the complicated politics of HIV/AIDS (see Bell 2015). In brief, I argued that it was attractive to policy makers for three reasons. First, it transcended the debates about the respective merits of behavioural and structural approaches[9] – e.g., the ABC strategy (be Abstinent, Be faithful, use a Condom) versus calls to address the structural sources of inequality that facilitate and hasten HIV transmission. After all, the whole point of the RCTs was to isolate the impact of male circumcision on HIV transmission, *regardless* of individual sexual behaviour and *regardless* of the socio-economic context of the procedure. Second, it sidestepped the 'culture wars' between advocates of condoms and advocates of abstinence, with circumcision more politically palatable among conservatives than promoting condom use. Third, it also aligned with longstanding narratives about 'African sexuality', seen to be underpinned by promiscuity, gender violence and a lack of internalised moral restraints. The emphasis on an intractable 'cultural' pattern of behaviour made a physiological intervention that circumvented it entirely seem particularly attractive.

These disparate factors, in combination with the reality of an epidemic that continues unabated in many parts of sub-Saharan Africa, facilitated a policy environment in which there was a degree of receptivity to a 'new' biomedical approach to HIV prevention, one based on a 'more thoroughgoing engagement with the principles of "traditional" public health medicine' (Aggleton 2007: 20). As Richard Parker (2013) observes, faced with the difficulties of transforming structural factors and the limited success of behavioural approaches, there has been a rush to return to biomedical solutions driven by a variety of forces, from industry, research funders, biomedical and behavioural researchers themselves and the public health establishment. But the rise of evidence-based medicine was clearly crucial to the willingness to embrace the procedure at a policy level. Thus, in what follows I'm particularly interested in the ways that the evidence on male circumcision became enmeshed with EBM paradigms, how it transformed understandings of the issue and to what effect.

The evidence

The first person to posit an association between male circumcision and HIV transmission was Andrew Fink, an advocate of mass circumcision (see Fink 1988). In 1986 he published a letter in the *New England Journal of Medicine* speculating on a connection between the two. Although the letter focused on the potential link between male circumcision and HIV transmission, Fink's primary purpose in writing it seems to have been to push for the continued health care coverage of neonatal circumcision. This becomes clear in his closing statement: 'the fact that Blue Shield of Pennsylvania has recently elected to discontinue paying for newborn circumcision would be a monumental example of false economy' (Fink 1988: 1167).

The extent to which Fink's letter provided impetus for the subsequent series of publications reporting inverse relationships between HIV infection and male circumcision in sub-Saharan Africa is unclear, as some – but certainly not all – make reference to it.[10] The initial findings on the association were also generally reported in the context of studies focusing on the relationship between HIV and genital ulcers, rather than male circumcision specifically (see de Camargo Jr *et al.* 2013; Bell 2015). However, during this period, observational studies also began to map patterns of HIV transmission and male circumcision and documented an inverse correlation between the two. With some notable exceptions, studies throughout the 1990s continued to find inverse correlations between HIV infection rates and male circumcision, although they often advocated caution in interpreting this association, highlighting evidence of important confounders such as marital status, age, history of commercial sex encounters, and so on. Studies also found that the protective effect of male circumcision differed across populations and age groups.

The possibility of implementing male circumcision in the context of HIV prevention was raised in a 1994 literature review (de Vincenzi and Mertens 1994), although the authors concluded that the evidence wasn't compelling enough to warrant public health interventions without further study. Halperin and Bailey (1999) disagreed, arguing that 'It is time for the international health community to add male-circumcision services to the current limited armamentarium of AIDS prevention measures in countries with a high prevalence of heterosexually transmitted HIV and STDs' (p. 1813). As these varied assessments indicate, in the 1990s there were differing opinions on the strength of the available evidence and the wisdom of introducing the procedure into HIV initiatives. However, discussions changed notably in tone as EBM paradigms took hold.

The transformation in discourses on 'the evidence' is clearly illustrated through a comparison of de Vincenzi and Mertens' 1994 literature review and a meta-analysis published by Weiss, Quigley and Hayes in 2000. Importantly, the *amount* of evidence examined wasn't noticeably different between the two reviews (23 versus 27 studies); there was also a considerable degree of overlap between the studies reviewed. Instead, the contrasts relate to the way the evidence was presented and the conclusions drawn from it. While the 1994 review was relatively opaque about its methods, the 2000 review devoted considerable attention to discussing those studies that were included and excluded, how they were found, the criteria for inclusion and so on. A second difference is that the findings were presented in the form of a meta-analysis in the latter review; that is, data were systematically extracted from their context and relative risk ratios were compared across studies. Thus, while the differences between the study populations were prominently featured in the 1994 literature review (see Figure 5.1), in the 2000 review these differences were subsumed into two broad categories: population-based studies and studies of high-risk populations – and ultimately collapsed entirely, given that an overall effect of male circumcision was identified (see Figure 5.2).

These different approaches led, in turn, to strikingly different conclusions, as a comparison of the first two sentences of the concluding paragraphs of each review clearly reveal:

> The potential public-health benefits of male circumcision have been greatly discussed in the past 50 years, often in a passionate and emotional manner. However, relatively few studies have been carried out and those that have, present conflicting results.
>
> *de Vincenzi and Mertens 1994: 159*

> The data from observational studies provide compelling evidence of a substantial protective effect of male circumcision against HIV infection in sub-Saharan Africa, especially in populations at high risk of HIV/STD. The continuing rapid spread of HIV infection, especially in eastern and southern Africa, suggests that the potential public health benefit of introducing safe services for male circumcision on a wider scale should be explored.
>
> *Weiss, Quigley and Hayes 2000: 2369*

Another striking difference between the two reviews lay in the type of research they suggested was necessary to determine the efficacy of the procedure. RCTs were not explicitly referenced in the 1994 review; indeed, intervention studies were actively

Study Country, date (sample size)	Population	OR (95% CI) Univariate analysis	Adjustments
Study 1 Kenya, 1988 (n = 388)	Clients of prostitutes		Contact with prostitutes, travel
	History of urethritis	7.5 (2.2–27.2)*	5.2 (1.6–8.8)
	History of genital ulcers	0.8 (0.3–2.5)*	0.45*
Study 2 Kenya, 1989 (n = 293)	Follow-up of clients of prostitutes	10.2 (4.5–23.0)	
Study 3 Kenya, 1991 (n = 718)	Clients of prostitutes with genital ulcers or urethritis	5.0 (3.2–7.9)*	Not done
Study 4 Uganda, 1991 (n = 1977)	Men with STD	1.7 (1.3–2.0)	Not done
Study 5 Zambia, 1990 (n = 610)	STD clinic	2.4 (0.9–6.6)*	Not done
Study 6 Kenya, 1988 (n = 115)	Men with genital ulcers	3.6 (1.2–11.2)*	Age, number of partners, ethnic origin OR becomes not significant
Study 7 Rwanda, 1987 (n = 302)	All male workers in a factory	0.9 (0.3–2.6)	Not done
Study 8 Rwanda, 1988 (n = 274)	Husbands in HIV serologically concordant couples	1.1 (0.6–2.0)*	Not done
Study 9 Uganda, 1988 (n = 132)	Hospital ward	Not significantly different (NS)	Not done
Study 10 USA, 1989 (n = 167)	STD clinic heterosexual clients	8.4 (1.4–50.1)	Not done
Study 11 USA, 1989 (n = 32)	STD clinic	NS	Age, race, homosexuality, drug use, number of partners. Not significant
Study 12 USA, 1989 (n = 1374)	STD clinic	NS	Age, race, homosexuality, drug use, number of partners. Not significant
Study 13 USA, 1991 (n = 1389)	STD clinic (drug users and gay men excluded)	1.7 (0.9–3.4)*	Not done

FIGURE 5.1 Visual representation of key findings from the 1994 literature review

Source: adapted from de Vincenzi and Mertens 1994.

	Crude analysis				Adjusted analysis		
Study population	N	RR (CI)	P for heterogeneity	N	Relative risk (CI)	P for heterogeneity
All study designs						
All	27	0.52 (0.40–0.68)	< 0.001	15	0.42 (0.34–0.54)	< 0.001
Population-based	12	0.93 (0.71–1.21)	0.008	6	0.56 (0.44–0.70)	0.21
High-risk	12	0.27 (0.22–0.33)	0.09	7	0.29 (0.20–0.41)	0.03
Cross-sectional studies only						
All*	18	< 0.001	< 0.001	11	0.42 (0.32–0.55)	< 0.001
Population-based	7	0.003	0.003	5	0.55 (0.42–0.72)	0.17
High risk	8	0.48	0.48	4	0.24 (0.18–0.31)	0.49

FIGURE 5.2 Visual representation of key findings from the 2000 literature review

Source: adapted from Weiss, Quigley and Hayes 2000.

discouraged, with the reviewers highlighting their complexity and the problems with drawing definitive conclusions from their results. They stressed that 'research priorities might focus on a better understanding of the biological mechanisms through which the lack of circumcision could enhance STD and HIV transmission' (de Vincenzi and Mertens 1994: 158) and also pointed to the need for observational studies that better addressed the limitations of the available research.

In contrast, Weiss, Quigley and Hayes (2000) suggested that the main studies needed were those 'to examine the acceptability, feasibility and safety of introducing male circumcision', and RCTs that 'would overcome the inherent limitations of observational studies, and provide reliable empirical evidence on the overall impact of the introduction of male circumcision on HIV incidence' (p. 2369). Thus, between the two reviews there was a clear shift from prioritising studies on the biology of transmission to epidemiological studies that met the EBM 'gold standard' for evidence. Indeed, my suspicion is that RCTs weren't really thinkable in 1994 in the way they became in the EBM era; as de Vincenzi and Mertens' account suggests, the topic was considered too complex (and ethically fraught) to lend itself to RCT methodologies. However, as EBM paradigms took hold, the evidence was increasingly treated as *isolable* from the context in which it was generated, which, in turn, made RCTs look like the logical next step.

This trend continued in the Cochrane review published 5 years later (Siegfried *et al.* 2005). The authors elected not to conduct a meta-analysis, given the heterogeneity of the included studies, and their conclusions were more conservative than those of Weiss *et al.* (2000). However, they similarly chose to divide studies based on whether they focused on 'general' or 'high risk' populations and likewise emphasised the need for RCTs. To quote the authors: 'Although the positive results of these observational studies suggest that circumcision is an intervention worth evaluating in randomised controlled trials, the current quality of evidence is insufficient to consider implementation of circumcision as a public-health intervention' (Weiss *et al.* 2000: 172, emphasis added). Clearly, the Cochrane reviewers weren't prepared to take a firm position on the evidence without the results of RCTs – which were under way at the time of the review. As these publications suggest, as EBM paradigms began to infiltrate, there was a growing awareness that RCTs were necessary to clinch the debate.

The RCTs and the Cochrane review

In 2005, Auvert *et al.* published the findings of the first 'randomized, controlled, blindly evaluated intervention trial'. The study involved 3,274 uncircumcised men from Orange Farm and surrounding areas just outside of Johannesburg, South Africa. Men were randomly allocated to circumcision and followed longitudinally for 12 months. Beyond circumcision itself, the study procedures included face-to-face questionnaires about men's 'sexual behaviour',[11] blood samples to check their HIV status, a genital examination and an individual counselling session in which condoms were provided. The trial found that male circumcision conferred a 60 per cent protection against HIV and was stopped at the interim analysis because the findings were deemed so compelling that they were ethically bound to offer the treatment to men in the control arm of the study.[12]

In 2007, the findings of two further RCTs were published in the same issue of *The Lancet*. Gray *et al.*'s (2007) study took place near the Lake Victoria region in Rakai, Uganda, with 4,996 men. Also in the Lake Victoria region, Bailey *et al.*'s (2007) study took place in Kisumu, Kenya with 2,784 men, predominantly from the Luo tribe, who traditionally do not circumcise. The procedures in the trials were similar both to each other and Auvert *et al.*'s earlier study, and they were also stopped prematurely when male circumcision was found to have significant efficacy in interim analyses: treated efficacy was 55 per cent in Gray *et al.*'s study and 53 per cent in Bailey *et al.*'s study.

As previously stated, the three RCTs were critical to the willingness of international agencies to endorse male circumcision as an HIV prevention tool in sub-Saharan Africa. Although some social scientists urged the need to proceed with care and anti-circumcision advocates spoke out vociferously against the procedure, the RCTs effectively served to shut down debate.[13] The final seal of approval came from two subsequent systematic reviews analyzing the results of the RCTs. These reviews were crucial in providing independent verification of their findings – especially the Cochrane review published in 2009, titled 'Male circumcision for prevention of heterosexual acquisition of HIV in men' (Siegfried *et al.* 2009).

The Cochrane review has several features worth noting. First, in keeping with EBM hierarchies, the prior observational evidence was effaced and replaced – relegated to the background section and dismissed in a single sentence. These studies, and the complexity they highlighted around the impact of co-morbid STDs, ethnicity, age, marital status, history of commercial sex encounters and so on, became useful in explaining the impetus for the RCTs but essentially irrelevant once the 'real' evidence was in. Concluding that medical male circumcision reduces the acquisition of HIV by heterosexual men by 38 per cent – 66 per cent over 24 months, they argued that 'inclusion of male circumcision into current HIV prevention measures guidelines is warranted', although research to assess its feasibility, desirability and cost effectiveness in local contexts was necessary (Siegfried *et al.* 2009: 2). In other words, they endorsed studies exclusively on how to close the aforementioned 'implementation gap'.

Second, the Cochrane review served to verify both the internal *and* external validity of the RCT findings, warranting the broader effectiveness of the procedure irrespective of its geographic context. As the review's title indicates, its goal was to study the general efficacy of male circumcision in inhibiting heterosexually transmitted HIV. Thus, the fact that the trials were all conducted in the same region was of little note to the reviewers; indeed, the discussion of the RCT limitations was restricted to the question of their internal validity. The conclusions of the review were expressed in suitably global terms: 'Research on the effectiveness of male circumcision for preventing HIV acquisition is complete. No further trials are required to establish this fact' (Siegfried *et al.* 2009: 19).

The unencumbered human

In a 2001 discussion paper titled 'Male circumcision as an HIV control strategy: Not a "natural condom"', Kate Bonner observed that researchers didn't understand 'why and how circumcision is protective, exactly what the relationship is between circumcision status and other STIs, and whether the effect seen in high-risk populations is generalisable to other groups' (p. 152). Today, we still don't know the answers to these questions; however, the key difference is that these gaps in knowledge are deemed largely irrelevant.

As previously noted, although early reviews called for further research on the biology of transmission, this became increasingly de-prioritised as EBM paradigms took hold. This is clearly evident in the primary literature itself. For example, in most publications only one or two sentences are devoted to discussing the 'biological plausibility'[14] of male circumcision in preventing HIV and a handful of references are provided. Although a biological theory of transmission is often identified, this term covers various different hypotheses, including: 1) the greater likelihood of micro-traumatic abrasions or mini-ulcerations on the frenulum or foreskin; 2) a lack of keratinisation of the foreskin (either the epithelium, inner mucosa or both); and 3) the higher density of 'HIV target cells' (especially Langerhans' cells) in the foreskin. However, the number of studies directly examining such mechanisms is small and their findings are both contradictory and confusing.[15]

Although we understand very little about how or why male circumcision might directly inhibit HIV transmission at a biological level, the rise of evidence-based medicine made such questions largely irrelevant because the RCT evidence was seen to speak *for* biology, which, in turn, became a closed black box. As Timmermans and Berg (2003: 89) observe, because of its grounding in epidemiological and statistical reasoning, 'How the intervention works, physiologically, or how, for example, contradictory results from different diagnostic interventions on similar patients should be understood, is less relevant'. Again, this speaks to the extraordinary faith EBM places in randomisation as a means of enabling attributions of causality. As one EBM textbook extolling the virtues of RCTs states: 'random allocation balances the treatment groups for these and other prognostic factors, *even if we don't yet understand the disorder well enough to know what they are!*' (cited in Howick 2011: 49, emphasis added).

Although the rise of evidence-based medicine enabled the 'male circumcision effect' to be taken as given, can we assume that the operation would have the same effect globally? As Dehue (2010: 115) observes,

> taking individuals out of their normal context and studying them in newly created artificial groups can only make sense if we assume that the problem to be solved is not a contextual one and is fully located in the individual.

Clearly, the RCTs made precisely this assumption. As I have already stated, their goal was to isolate the effectiveness of male circumcision in reducing HIV transmission, *regardless* of the cultural context of the procedure and *regardless* of individual sexual 'behaviour'. Thus, the bodies of the men in the trials were treated as representative not only of the bodies of sub-Saharan African men in general, but men across the globe. It is precisely for this reason that researchers are now raising the possibility of incorporating male circumcision into HIV prevention initiatives in other geographically and culturally distant parts of the world, including Papua New Guinea, Thailand, the Dominican Republic and the Caribbean (Bell 2015).

In light of the unique contours of HIV/AIDS transmission in sub-Saharan Africa (e.g., pandemic levels of HIV and high rates of heterosexual transmission), the unquestioning transposition of the results of trials to the rest of the world seems surprising, to say the least. Pointing to important epidemiological differences between the HIV epidemic in sub-Saharan Africa and the USA, Sullivan and colleagues (2007) argue that a protective effect from circumcision is unlikely to be found in settings where HIV prevalence is lower. In their words, 'The results of any trial must be interpreted with the caution that inference not be extended to populations differing from the study participants in important ways' (Sullivan *et al.* 2007: 1162). However, as Adams (2013) observes, under the logic of EBM, the use of RCTs to evaluate and generalise results across vast differences in contexts of culture, geography, politics, economy, etc., is not understood to constitute a problem but an advantage; seemingly insurmountable differences in contexts and circumstances are seen as precisely the reason to rely on RCTs. Under its logic, trial subjects become effectively *unencumbered* – divested of their social, cultural, economic, political baggage through the randomisation process and related mechanisms for factoring out 'confounding variables'.

Conclusion

The assumption that the RCT provides the most definitive evidence of the efficacy of a procedure or intervention relies on a number of assumptions – about the utility of randomisation, the interchangeability of individual bodies and so on. These assumptions are surprisingly recent in origin, but they are integral to the logic of the RCT and its assertion of the possibility of isolating the 'pure' effect of an intervention. In some respects what we see here is a different sort of instantiation of the model of personhood introduced in Chapter 2: just as 'health behaviours' are treated appendages of the core person, 'context' is divestible in the same sort of way. But what is lost in the leap to the use of such methods is the recognition that sometimes *context* itself determines what methods can and can't be effective (Adams 2013: 62). As Adams (2013) argues, many different kinds of empirical realities may impinge on the ways that RCT data is produced, thereby conditioning its outcomes. This topic forms a central preoccupation in Chapter 6, which focuses specifically on what happens when RCTs are transposed to 'social' and 'behavioural' settings and the ways these issues are compounded in systematic reviews of such.

Notes

1 To quote one glowing account:

> It is not for nothing that RCTs come at the top of the hierarchy of knowledge – a position first accorded them nearly 30 years ago because of their unique ability to deal with bias. And because bias, in all its shapes and sizes, is the single biggest enemy of all attempts to determine if our treatment (as opposed to our charm, luck or the natural history of illness) really does work, then RCTs are indeed the King or Queen of assessment techniques.
>
> *Wessely 2007: 120*

2 As Armstrong (2007: 75) observes, this trial represents the 'celebrated point of origin of the method'.
3 The alchemy metaphor was originally used by De Vries and Lemmens (2006).
4 Devisch and Murray (2009) discuss evidence-based medicine as a simulacrum, but in a somewhat different sense to my employment of the term here. Their concern is the way that EBM fails to meet its own standards of evidence (as discussed in Chapter 4). In their words,

> EBM declares itself victorious through an appeal to intuition and to the emotions – an appeal that is dissimulated as scientific rigour and epistemological truth. In this respect, EBM is a scientific and epistemological simulacrum – something that appears only to the extent that its founding principles disappear.
>
> *Devisch and Murray 2009: 954*

5 This website was previously labelled CircLeaks, which gives some sense of its declared agenda to expose secret and not-so-secret circumcision 'promoters'.
6 Stallings and Karugendo's (2005) findings from Tanzania were presented at an International AIDS Society conference in 2005 and have never been published in a peer-reviewed journal. Kinuthia's (2010) findings on Kenya were presented in a Master of Public Health thesis. It is difficult to imagine any researcher or funding agency willing to entertain their respective calls for further research in this area.
7 The labelling of the procedure as female genital 'mutilation', the international efforts to eradicate it, its criminalisation as a form of 'child abuse' and so on.
8 As noted in Chapter 4, this view underwrites evidence-based medicine itself, with 'politics' and 'evidence' conceptualised as being in opposition. In this framing, politics is a 'barrier' to rational decision-making (Smith 2013).
9 These debates are a reflection of the broader debate discussed in Chapter 2 regarding the 'behavioural' versus social determinants of health.
10 That said, it's cited as the original source documenting a link between male circumcision and HIV transmission in the three papers on the findings of the RCTs.
11 The concept of 'sexual behaviour' is clearly another manifestation of the 'health behaviour' frame discussed in Chapter 2, and has similarly reductive effects on our understanding of what is an extraordinarily complex domain of human activity.
12 In essence, it was concluded that the requirement for clinical equipoise was no longer met. This is a key concept in medical ethics and relates to genuine uncertainty about whether a treatment will be beneficial. It is considered unethical to randomise patients to receive a treatment or placebo in contexts where the treatment is known to be more effective than the placebo. I will have to say more about the intersections between EBM and ethics in Chapter 7.
13 Perhaps more accurately, it didn't shut down the debate, but it enabled opponents – the majority of whom were vocal intactivists – to be derided as 'denialists'. This is a key theme in the work of Wamai and colleagues, who have responded aggressively to any detractors (e.g., Wamai et al. 2008, 2011, 2012, 2015). As de Camargo Jr et al. (2013) note, the paradigm

defending the causal relation between male circumcision and reduced HIV transmission has become essentially hegemonic in the academic literature. Interesting here is the ways in which challenges to the evidence are often framed on ethical grounds. To quote Banerjee and colleagues (2011: e111), 'Such denialism in the face of the ongoing pandemic are unethical and immoral'. This speaks to the ways in which conceptions of ethics and evidence are increasingly co-constituted – a topic I discuss in detail in Chapter 7.

14 As discussed in Chapter 1, the notion of 'plausibility' has particular cachet in epidemiology in establishing causality and is part of the Bradford Hill criteria.

15 For example, Hussain and Lehner (1995) found oral, foreskin and vaginal epithelium (surface tissue) to contain Langerhans' cells, and speculated that certain types of such cells common in both the foreskin and vaginal epithelium (CD4+) might provide the source of HIV infection (support for theory #3). Szabo and Short (2000) conducted histological examinations of the glans of circumcised and uncircumcised men and found the epithelia of subjects to be equally keratinised (evidence against theory #2). Patterson and colleagues (2002) examined foreskin and cervical tissue and found that foreskin mucosa was more susceptible to HIV infection than cervical mucosa or the external surface of the foreskin (support for theory #2). More recent empirical research directly challenges distinctions between the susceptibility of the inner and outer foreskin tissue in terms of both the number of Langerhans' cells and CD4+ cells (Fischetti *et al.* 2009; Qin *et al.* 2009) and their degree of keratinisation (Qin *et al.* 2009; Dinh *et al.* 2010), disputing theories #2 and #3. Other research, still, supports the idea of the greater infectivity of the inner foreskin (theory #2), *except* when seminal plasma and cervicovaginal secretions are mixed (Ganor and Bomsel 2011), which presumably occurs with some frequency.

References

Adams, V. (2013) Evidence-based global public health: Subjects, profits, erasures. In J. Biehl and A. Petryna (eds), *When People Come First: Critical Studies in Global Health*. Princeton, NJ: Princeton University Press, pp. 54–90.

Aggleton, P. (2007) 'Just a snip'? A social history of male circumcision. *Reproductive Health Matters*, 15(29): 15–21.

Armstrong, D. (2007) Professionalism, indeterminacy and the EBM project. *BioSocieties*, 2: 73–84.

Auvert, B., Taljaard, D., Lagarde, E., Sobngwi-Tambekou, J., *et al.* (2005) Randomized controlled intervention trial of male circumcision for reduction of HIV infection risk: The ANRS 1265 Trial. *PLoS Medicine*, 2(11): e298.

Bailey, R.C., Moses, S., Parker, C.B., Agot, K., *et al.* (2007) Male circumcision for HIV prevention in young men in Kisumu, Kenya: A randomized controlled trial. *The Lancet*, 369: 643–656.

Banerjee, J., Klausner, J.D., Halperin, D.T., Wamai, R., *et al.* (2011) Circumcision denialism unfounded and unscientific. *American Journal of Preventive Medicine*, 40(3): e11–e12.

Baudrillard, J. (1996) *Simulacra and Simulation*. Translated by Sheila Faria Glaser. Ann Arbor: University of Michigan Press.

Bell, K. (2005) Genital cutting and western discourses on sexuality. *Medical Anthropology Quarterly*, 19(2): 125–148.

Bell, K. (2015) HIV prevention: Making male circumcision the 'right' tool for the job. *Global Public Health*, 10(5–6): 552–572.

Bonner, K. (2001) Male circumcision as an HIV control strategy: Not a 'natural condom'. *Reproductive Health Matters*, 9(18): 143–155.

Boyle, G.J. and Hill, G. (2011) Sub-Saharan African randomised clinical trials into male circumcision and HIV transmission: Methodological, ethical and legal concerns. *Journal of Law and Medicine*, 19: 316–334.

de Camargo Jr, K.R., de Oliveira Mendonça, A.L., Perrey, C. and Giami, A. (2013) Male circumcision and HIV: A controversy study on facts and values. *Global Public Health*, 8(7): 769–783.

Carpenter, L.M. (2010) On remedicalisation: Male circumcision in the United States and Great Britain. *Sociology of Health and Illness*, 32(4): 613–630.

Clegg, S. (2005) Evidence-based practice in educational research: A critical realist critique of systemic review. *British Journal of Sociology of Education*, 26(3): 415–428.

Dehue, T. (2010) Comparing artificial groups: On the history and assumptions of the randomised controlled trial. In C. Will and T. Moreira (eds), *Medical Proofs, Social Experiments: Clinical Trials in Shifting Contexts*. Surrey: Ashgate, pp. 103–120.

Devisch, I. and Murray, S.J. (2009) 'We hold these truths to be self-evident': Deconstructing 'evidence-based' medical practice. *Journal of Evaluation in Clinical Practice*, 15: 950–954.

De Vries, R. and Lemmens, T. (2006) The social and cultural shaping of medical evidence: Case studies from pharmaceutical research and obstetric science. *Social Science and Medicine*, 62: 2694–2706.

Dinh, M.H., McRaven, M.D., Kelley, Z.L., Penugonda, S. and Hope, T.J. (2010) Keratinization of the adult male foreskin and implications for male circumcision. *AIDS*, 24(6): 899–906.

Epstein, S. (1996) *Impure Science: AIDS, Activism, and the Politics of Knowledge*. Berkeley: University of California Press.

Fink, A.J. (1986) A possible explanation for heterosexual male infection with AIDS. *New England Journal of Medicine*, 315(18): 1167.

Fink, A.J. (1988) *Circumcision: A Parent's Decision for Life*. Mountain View, CA: Kavanah Publishing.

Fischetti, L., Barry, S.M., Hope, T.J. and Shattock, R.J. (2009) HIV-1 infection of human penile explant tissue and protection by candidate microbicides. *AIDS*, 23(3): 319–328.

Ganor, Y. and Bomsel, M. (2011) HIV-1 transmission in the male genital tract. *American Journal of Reproductive Immunology*, 65: 284–291.

Gollaher, D.L. (2000) *Circumcision: A History of the World's Most Controversial Surgery*. New York: Basic Books.

Gray, R.H., Kigozi, G., Serwadda, D., Makumbi, F., et al. (2007) Male circumcision for HIV prevention in men in Rakai Uganda: A randomized trial. *The Lancet*, 369: 657–666.

Hacking, I. (1988) Origins of randomization in experimental design. *Isis*, 79(3): 427–451.

Hacking, I. (1990) *The Taming of Chance*. New York: Cambridge University Press.

Halperin, D.T. and Bailey, R.C. (1999) Male circumcision and HIV infection: 10 years and counting. *The Lancet*, 354: 1813–1815.

Heaven, B. (2008) *Epistemological Authority and Hidden Work: Negotiated Meaning in the Conduct of a Randomised Controlled Trial*. Doctoral Dissertation. Newcastle University.

Helgesson, C.-F. (2010) From dirty data to credible scientific evidence: Some practices used to clean data in large randomised clinical trials. In C. Will and T. Moreira (eds), *Medical Proofs, Social Experiments: Clinical Trials in Shifting Contexts*. Surrey: Ashgate, pp. 49–63.

Howick, J. (2011) *The Philosophy of Evidence-Based Medicine*. Chichester: Wiley Blackwell.

Hussain, L.A. and Lehner, T. (1995) Comparative investigation of Langerhans' cells and potential receptors for HIV in oral, genitourinary and rectal epithelia. *Immunology*, 85: 475–484.

Kinuthia, R.G. (2010) *The Association between Female Genital Mutilation (FGM) and the Risk of HIV/AIDS in Kenyan Girls and Women (15–49 years)*. Master of Public Health Dissertation. Atlanta: Georgia State University.

Kaptchuk, T.J. (2001) The double-blind, randomized, placebo-controlled trial: Gold standard or golden calf? *Journal of Clinical Epidemiology*, 54: 541–549.

Lather, P. (1993) Fertile obsession: Validity after poststructuralism. *The Sociological Quarterly*, 34(4): 673–693.

Latour, B. (2004) Why has critique run out of steam? From matters of fact to matters of concern. *Critical Inquiry*, 30(2): 225–248.

Marks, H. M. (1997) *The Progress of Experiment: Science and Therapeutic Reform in the United States, 1900–1990*. Cambridge, MA: Cambridge University Press.

Medical Research Council (1948) Streptomycin treatment of tuberculous meningitis. *The Lancet*, 251(6503): 582–596.

Parker, R. (2013) Shifting paradigms in HIV prevention and research. *Centers for AIDS Research Social and Behavioral Sciences Research Network 7th National Scientific Meeting Social, Behavioral, and Policy Perspectives on HIV/AIDS: the District of Columbia and Beyond*. Washington DC.

Patterson, B.K., Landay, A., Siegel, J.N., Flender, Z., Pessis, D., Chaviano, A. and Bailey, R.C. (2002) Susceptibilty to Human Immundeficiency Virus-1 infection of human foreskin and cervical tissue grown in explant culture. *American Journal of Pathology*, 161(3): 867–873.

Petryna, A. (2009) *When Experiments Travel: Clinical Trials and the Global Search for Human Subjects*. Princeton, NJ: Princeton University Press.

Qin, Q., Zheng, X.-Y., Wang, Y.-Y., Shen, H.-F., Sun, F. and Ding, W. (2009) Langerhans' cell density and degree of keratinization in foreskins of Chinese preschool boys and adults. *International Urology and Nephrology*, 41(4): 747–753.

Sackett, D.L. (2013) Six pairs of things to celebrate on International Trials Day. *Trials*, 14: 128.

Shapin, S. (1995) Cordelia's love: Credibility and the social studies of science. *Perspectives on Science*, 3(3): 255–275.

Shapin, S. (2010) *Never Pure: Historical Studies of Science as if It Was Produced by People with Bodies, Situated in Time, Space, Culture, and Society and Struggling for Credibility and Authority*. Baltimore, MD: Johns Hopkins University Press.

Siegfried, N., Muller, M., Deeks, J.J., Volmink, J., *et al.* (2005) HIV and male circumcision: A systematic review with assessment of the quality of studies. *Lancet Infectious Diseases*, 5(3): 165–173.

Siegfried, N., Muller, M., Deeks, J.J. and Volmink, J. (2009) Male circumcision for prevention of heterosexual acquisition of HIV in men. *Cochrane Database of Systematic Reviews*, 15(2): Art no.: CD003362.

Smith, K. (2013) *Beyond Evidence-Based Policy in Public Health: The Interplay of Ideas*. Basingstoke: Palgrave Macmillan.

Solomon, M. (2015) *Making Medical Knowledge*. Oxford: Oxford University Press.

Stallings, R.Y. and Karugendo, E. (2005) Female circumcision and HIV infection in Tanzania: For better or for worse? Third IAS Conference on HIV Pathogenesis and Treatment. Rio de Janeiro. Available at: www.tzonline.org/pdf/femalecircumcisionandHIVinfectionintanzania.pdf (accessed 27 December 2012).

Sullivan, P.S., Kilmarx, P.H., Peterman, T.A., Taylor, A.W. *et al.* (2007) Male circumcision for HIV transmission: What new data mean for HIV prevention in the United States. *PLoS Medicine*, 4(7): 1162–1166.

Szabo, R. and Short, R.V. (2000) How does male circumcision protect against HIV infection? *British Medical Journal*, 320: 1592–1594.

Timmermans, S. and Berg, M. (2003) *The Gold Standard: The Challenge of Evidence-Based Medicine and Standardization in Health Care*. Philadelphia, PA: Temple University Press.

UNAIDS (2007) *Male Circumcision: Africa's Unprecedented Opportunity*. Geneva, Switzerland: World Health Organization.

Van Howe, R.S., Svoboda, J.S. and Hodges, F.M. (2005) HIV infection and circumcision: Cutting through the hyperbole. *Journal of the Royal Society for the Promotion of Health*, 125(6): 259–265.

Victora, C.G., Habicht, J.P. and Bryce, J. (2004) Evidence-based public health: Moving beyond randomized trials. *American Journal of Public Health*, 94(3), 400–405.

de Vincenzi, I. and Mertens, T. (1994) Male circumcision: A role in HIV prevention? *AIDS*, 8: 153–160.

Wahlberg, A. and McGoey, L. (2007) An elusive evidence-base: The construction and governance of randomized controlled trials. *BioSocieties*, 2: 1–10.

Wamai, R.G., Weiss, H.A., Hankins, C., Agot, K. *et al.* (2008) Male circumcision is an efficacious, lasting and cost-effective strategy for combating HIV in high-prevalence AIDS epidemics. *Future HIV Therapies*, 2(5): 399–405.

Wamai, R.G., Morris, B.M., Bailis, S.A., Sokal, D., *et al.* (2011) Male circumcision for HIV prevention: Current evidence and implementation in sub-Saharan Africa. *Journal of the International AIDS Society*, 14: 49.

Wamai, R.G., Morris, B.J., Waskett, J.H., Green, E.C., *et al.* (2012) Criticisms of African trials fail to withstand scrutiny: Male circumcision does prevent HIV infection. *Journal of Law and Medicine*, 20: 93–123.

Wamai, R.G., Morris, B.J., Bailey, R.C., Klausner, J.D. and Boedicker, M.N. (2015) Male circumcision for protection against HIV infection in sub-Saharan Africa: The evidence in favour justifies the implementation now in progress. *Global Public Health*, 10(5–6): 639–666.

Weiss, H.A., Quigley, M.A. and Hayes, R.J. (2000) Male circumcision and risk of HIV infection in sub-Saharan Africa: A systematic review and meta-analysis. *AIDS*, 14(15): 2361–2370.

Wessely, S. (2007) Commentary: A defence of the randomized controlled trial in mental health. *BioSocieties*, 2: 115–127.

Will, C.M. (2007) The alchemy of clinical trials. *BioSocieties*, 2: 85–99.

Will, C. and Moreira, T. (eds) (2010) *Medical Proofs, Social Experiments: Clinical Trials in Shifting Contexts*. Surrey: Ashgate.

WHO (2014) WHO progress brief: Voluntary medical male circumcision for HIV prevention in priority countries of east and southern Africa. *World Health Organization*. Available at: www.who.int/hiv/topics/malecircumcision/male-circumcision-info-2014/en/ (accessed 17 April 2015).

6

SYSTEMATIC REVIEWS AND THE BEHAVIOURAL TURN

Introduction

In 1996, the Cochrane review 'The effectiveness of physician advice to aid smoking cessation' was published (Silagy and Ketteridge 1996).[1] Based on a meta-analysis of randomised controlled trials, it found that brief advice to stop smoking from a physician led to a slight increase in quit rates (between 1 and 2 per cent) at the population level. These findings were widely disseminated, with organisations such as the National Institute for Health Care Excellence in the United Kingdom, the Office of the Surgeon General in the USA, Australia's Department of Health and Ageing, and Health Canada all formally recommending such interventions as standard 'good practice' for physicians (Bell *et al.* 2012).

The review, which has been periodically updated since its initial publication, is part of a database that now contains 8,000 reviews (and counting!). It illustrates the ways in which analyses of the efficacy of surgical and pharmacological interventions were rapidly joined by reviews of interventions to modify 'risk behaviours' such as smoking, drug and alcohol use, dietary practices, physical inactivity, etc., assuming a relatively seamless transposition of principles and processes. Yet, although the conceptual framework has been carried over from the former to the latter, in grappling with 'the behavioural sphere' and attempting to encompass it within its legitimate domain of inquiry, evidence-based medicine has staked out a territory far beyond what was originally encompassed within its domain (cf. Mair 2011).

In this chapter I explore in detail the expansion of EBM paradigms from surgical and pharmacological interventions to social and behavioural settings. I demonstrate that evidence-based medicine isn't responsible for the idea that human 'behaviours' are amenable to experimental manipulation, but that such approaches have been significantly bolstered by its prioritisation of randomised trials – and especially by its emphasis on *synthesising* this knowledge. If RCTs are embedded in a metonymic relationship with reality (Shapin 1995, 2010), systematic reviews stand in metaphoric relationship with it – even more than RCTs, their point is to move beyond the local and particular to get at the broader mechanical nature of the universe. Using a Cochrane review on physician advice for smoking cessation as a case study, my goal is to show that EBM principles can't be transposed to such contexts without radically distorting the phenomena in question.

The rise of the 'behavioural' RCT

Although it is tempting to treat the rise of 'social' or 'behavioural' RCTs as an artefact of the cachet of evidence-based medicine, their roots are actually far older – and have traces in the growing importance placed on experimental comparisons in the late nineteenth and early twentieth century across a variety of fields (see Chapter 5). Indeed, psychology is often deemed to be the first discipline to embrace artificial randomisation (Hacking 1988, 1990; Stigler 1992; Dehue 1997, 2010). Thus, in the field of educational psychology, chance became used as a means of creating groups for comparison from the 1920s, with random allocation cited as an 'economical substitute' for matching (Dehue 2010: 113). Clearly then, the idea that human *behaviour* was amenable to artificial randomisation was in place long before the emergence of evidence-based medicine, although the rise of behaviourism and the attendant notion that 'behaviours' could be isolated and intervened into was a necessary precursor (see Chapter 2).

When Austin Bradford Hill (1952) first outlined the contours of the contemporary randomised controlled trial, various epidemiologists readily saw their potential for broader application – most notably, Archie Cochrane, the so-called 'father' of evidence-based medicine and a former student of Hill's. This is evident in Cochrane's account of Hill in *Effectiveness and Efficiency: Random Reflections on Health Services*, where he notes: 'his [Hill's] ideas have only penetrated in a small way into medicine, and they still have to revolutionize sociology, education, and penology' (Cochrane 1972: 22). However, Cochrane's view of the broader potential of RCTs becomes especially pronounced in his autobiography, which highlights how profoundly Hill's streptomycin trial influenced his thinking.[2] In Cochrane's words, 'Looking back, this is undoubtedly the point at which the immense potential of the randomised controlled trial began to dawn on me' (Cochrane with Blythe 1989: 158). Later in the book he continues: 'I found myself wondering increasingly how far randomised controlled trials and the kind of cross-sectional surveys in which we specialised might be of value in sociological research. This soon became an important preoccupation' (Cochrane with Blythe 1989: 191).

He convinced his employer, the Medical Research Council, to finance the addition of a sociologist to the unit's staff and developed an RCT on a topic that had interested him for some time: the effect of caning on boys caught smoking.[3] However, he wasn't able to follow through with an actual trial, grudgingly acknowledging that: 'randomised controlled trials of corporal punishment were almost certainly going to raise a lot of opposition' (Cochrane with Blythe 1989: 192). Instead, he developed an RCT to test punishments (detention or a talk from the head teacher) for lateness, although the trial was never completed. He also attempted to develop an RCT to test available 'treatments' for juvenile delinquency, although 'that was turned down at once' (Cochrane with Blythe 1989: 192). Indeed, Cochrane was never able to complete a single one of his social RCTs. 'I had never imagined that sociological research could prove so difficult', he later complained (Cochrane with Blythe 1989: 194).

As his autobiography makes clear, although Cochrane ardently prosyletised for the expanded use of RCTs beyond the confines of clinical medicine, his views met with strong resistance among his contemporaries. In an interview conducted with his biographer in the year before his death, Cochrane reflected on the negative response of German colleagues to a lecture he had given earlier in his career advocating the use of RCTs in organising the treatment of heart disease. (Just to be clear, his emphasis in the lecture was not the treatment of heart disease itself but determining the best place of treatment, the most appropriate length of stay and so on.) A vociferous debate ensued, with Cochrane noting:

> My god they were rude to me, in German. Fortunately I can fight back in German and we had a real battle. They considered me utterly unethical and I complained that they were unethical: they weren't checking that they were giving their patients the best treatment. It went on for nearly three-quarters of an hour. I got pretty tired. The real story comes at the end. The professor took me out and gave me dinner and on the way out in excellent English said, 'You know, Dr. Cochrane, you don't seem to understand about controlled trials. Controlled trials are done by the pharmaceutical industry. Gentlemen don't do them'.
>
> *cited in Wahlberg and McGoey 2007: 2*

We can imbue various meanings to the 'gentleman don't do them' statement, but clearly evident is its implication that RCTs are not suitable – in fact are highly unethical – when applied to the study of other types of phenomena beyond pharmaceuticals.[4]

Despite energetic opposition, by the 1970s RCTs were periodically conducted in the fields of health services, health education and health promotion; for example, the oldest studies included in the Cochrane review on physician advice for smoking cessation were published in the early to mid 1970s (see Porter and McCullough 1972; Burt *et al.* 1974). By the 1980s, they were used with growing frequency in and beyond these fields, although some observers advocated caution in their application. To provide one illustration, Kramer and Shapiro noted in 1984 that:

> In recent years, especially with the extension of RCT methodology to assessments of nondrug treatments, including health education, psychotherapy, and health care provision, new concerns have emerged that challenge our critical reliance upon the RCT as an automatic scientific 'gold standard' in clinical research.[5]
>
> *Kramer and Shapiro 1984: 2739*

Likewise, in a 1986 discussion of the role of RCTs in evaluating health education and health promotion interventions, Green and Lewis observed that: 'The bio-medical tradition of research tends to oversimplify the cause-and-effect relationships between (1) educational interventions and (2) health or medical outcomes expected to result from such interventions' (p. 267) and they characterised this tendency as the 'fallacy of underestimating the complexity of change processes' (p. 267).

A key criticism was that many of the core features of the classic RCT design couldn't be sustained beyond clinical settings (Kramer and Shapiro 1984). Another criticism was that even when such trials could be carried out under highly con-trolled conditions, their circumstances were typically so artificial that they had little external validity (Green and Lewis 1986). A third related criticism was that the 'causal chain in a community system is longer and harder to trace than in a clinical research study on volunteers – the classic application of a randomised control study design' (Nutbeam, Smith and Catford 1990: 85; see also Green and Lewis 1986). Such concerns have stimulated intensive discussion about the applicability of RCT methodologies to 'complex' interventions. Although some commentators have categorically rejected the status afforded to the randomised controlled trial in EBM paradigms, arguing that its experimental logic is incapable of dealing with com-plexity (e.g. Pawson and Tilley 1997; Pawson 2006, 2013), attempts to reconcile them are common.[6] Thus, discussions of the limitations of RCTs beyond clinical settings are generally made *within* the paradigm of evidence-based medicine itself. For example, observers have drawn on older distinctions between the 'efficacy' and 'effectiveness' of RCTs and those that are 'explanatory' versus 'pragmatic' in design to explain their applications when transposed to non-drug trials.[7] Others have advocated the cluster randomised controlled trial, where 'clusters' of related individuals are the object of randomisation instead of the individual him or herself, as a means of overcoming the limitations of RCTs beyond clinical settings (see Fuller and Potvin 2012). More recently, 'realist' randomised controlled trials have been proposed as a solution to the problem of complexity (e.g., Bonell *et al.* 2012).

'Context' and 'complexity' as black boxes

As discussed in Chapter 5, one of the core assumptions underpinning classic RCT designs is that the intervention effect can be isolated from its context.[8] Thus, despite the growing body of literature on 'complex' RCTs, and attendant efforts to accommodate and account for context and complexity, it is debatable whether they have dislodged this underlying assumption (and whether it is actually possible to do so while retaining an allegiance to the paradigm). Based on an analysis of the literature on health promotion interventions, McLaren and colleagues observed in 2007 that, 'the desire to adhere to a trial design is accompanied by an "efficacy" model of evidence, whereby a particular intervention, once it is confirmed to have "worked" in one context, may be applied in the same format elsewhere' (p. 415). More recent assessments of the literature suggest that little has changed in the past decade.

According to Cohn and colleagues (2013), while researchers agree that health interventions targeting practices and behaviours are inescapably complex, no consensus on what 'complexity' means has been forthcoming. Where attempts have been made to conceptualise it, complexity is often understood to consist of discrete but interacting components that can be effectively captured via processes of identification and enumeration. In their words,

> whilst this approach acknowledges the significance of the interactions between elements, the term 'components', coupled with an emphasis on measuring them as discrete elements (whether behaviours, variables, or outcomes etc.), produces a depiction of complexity that is essentially mechanical. Such an approach simply cannot accommodate the idea that together such elements form a dynamic and integrated system.
>
> *Cohn* et al. *2013: 41*

Their analysis suggests that in attempting to grapple with complexity, researchers are guilty of the fallacy of misplaced concreteness.[9] In other words, the problem is typically dealt with by attempting to develop more 'sensitive' strategies to capture data and by pursuing ever more sophisticated causal models to identify the 'active ingredients' that might drive a complex problem, rather than questioning the appropriateness of the RCT paradigm itself. In Cohn *et al.*'s (2013: 40) view, 'a richer appreciation of complexity and the commitment to the RCT as the "gold standard" of evidence are ultimately incompatible.'[10]

Likewise, 'context' is often dealt with in equally superficial ways in the literature. A recent examination of its treatment in population health intervention research (Shoveller *et al.* 2016) shows that it is typically employed as a catch-all category of unmeasured confounders or conceptualised as a set of barriers that prevent people from accessing the 'right' dose of an intervention.[11] In such accounts, context is something that can ideally be 'controlled' for, resulting (at best) in laundry lists of static features that relate primarily to the physical setting of the intervention. There are clear similarities here with the social determinants of health framework (see Chapter 2); indeed, in many respects they reflect the same underlying issue – each is conceptualised in ways that keep the assumptions of the prevailing paradigm intact. The notion of a 'pristine' intervention divorceable from its 'context' is thereby implicitly retained in much the same way that the 'social determinants of health' tend to preserve the delineated characteristics of the concept of individual 'health behaviour'.

Such assumptions are severely tested by ethnographic research exploring behavioural RCTs. In an illuminating study, Ben Heaven (2008, 2010) has examined the 'hidden work' of personnel involved in a pilot study for a behavioural change counselling intervention in northern England that was ultimately to be implemented as part of an RCT comparing the efficacy of medication versus lifestyle and dietary advice in treating a common chronic health condition. As his account illustrates, the ostensibly 'technical' training process – upon which the fidelity of the trial fundamentally relied – was in actuality a politically fraught clash between two social worlds: that of the trialists and that of the nurses delivering the intervention. Nurses resisted the training, some judging it to be pointless, and many resented the implication that their current practice was lacking. They also found the prescriptive nature of the approach to present a poor fit with the tacit knowledge they routinely employed in consultations with patients. In other words, the nurses saw their interactions with patients as intrinsically reliant on context for success; thus, this view was fundamentally incompatible with the underlying premise of the trialists that the efficacy of the intervention could be *divorced* from such and empirically tested.

In the end, the pilot study was deemed a failure, although the planned RCT proceeded based on the view that the problems were specific to the pilot site (Heaven 2008). However, as Heaven (2008) demonstrates, throughout the life of the trial the distinction drawn between 'the intervention' and 'standard practice' continued to pose problems – in part because 'standard practice' itself was a moving target (it was essentially defined as whatever the intervention was *not*) and because there was no universally agreed upon definition of what the intervention actually *was*. Thus,

> three years after the original meeting of the steering group, differences across the trial team still existed in regard to: what the interventions were, what the intended and appropriate knowledge claims were, and ultimately, what the science of the trial was.
>
> *Heaven 2008: 160*

The problems Heaven raises are compounded exponentially in systematic reviews of such studies. As we saw in Chapter 5, the *raison d'être* of the systematic review is to isolate the effectiveness of an intervention *across* different settings and populations.[12] Take, for example, an article defending the use of RCTs in mental health research by Simon Wessely (2007). Emphasising their value in evaluating pharmacological regimens,[13] he swiftly moves to a discussion of their efficacy in evaluating debriefing procedures – a process in which a mental health professional carries out an intervention shortly after individuals have been exposed to some form of adversity in the hopes of staving off post-traumatic stress disorder. Wessely asserts that despite the popularity of such procedures, meta-analyses of RCTs have shown that they don't work and that, in fact, such evidence suggests a significant *increase* in the risk of PTSD in those who have been debriefed. Apparent in such statements is the way in which systematic reviews are seen to speak definitively about 'the real', despite the fact that the interventions in question rely fundamentally on context for both their meaning and efficacy. First, 'trauma' and 'PTSD' are hardly the fixed and stable categories such accounts presume (see Young 1995; Fassin and Rechtman 2008). Second, even when examined within the specific contexts in which these concepts acquire meaning, surely the efficacy of a debriefing procedure is inextricably entangled with the specific 'adversity' that caused it, the individuals who experienced it, their relationship with the counsellor delivering the debriefing and the qualities of the individual counsellors themselves. Clearly, there is a very particular logic at work that enables systematic reviews of such interventions to be taken as definitive facts, one that relies on the assumption that the problem to be solved resides exclusively within the individual, that individual studies are substitutable and interchangeable, and that adding the results of one trial to another will yield a more complete picture of reality.

Systematic reviews: making apples into oranges

In much the same way that individual trials involve a variety of hidden work and cleaning practices that serve to strip data of context, a parallel process occurs within the systematic review itself. Such reviews create commensurability between the individual studies chosen for inclusion; thus, their aim is not to reproduce the evidence they examine but to *transform* it. This is clearly illustrated in the first meta-analysis of the evidence on relationship between male circumcision and HIV transmission: despite drawing on broadly the same evidence as a 1994 literature review, it was far more assertive in endorsing the efficacy of the procedure because of the ways data were systematically extracted from their context to posit an overall 'effect' (see Chapter 5).

In one of the few available ethnographic accounts of knowledge making in systematic reviews, Tiago Moreira (2007) argues that such reviews are structured around parallel attempts to: a) *disentangle* data from the milieus in which they are commonly found; and b) to *requalify* that data through comparisons across a variety of 'platforms'. Accordingly, papers are treated as both rhetorical devices and as repositories of hard 'data' that the reviewer needs to extract. In Moreira's words: 'As papers arrive at the systematic reviewers' office we observe a confrontation between these rhetorical forces incorporated in the articles and the data-mining aims of the reviewers' (2007: 187). Thus, although the constructedness of texts is recognised, the data are treated as separable from this context, through a process of voiding the authors' own interpretations of results.[14] The role of the template is integral in decontextualising data and getting at its 'real' meaning; as it constructs a 'screen' through which to read the paper, the reviewer can look for data without danger of becoming 'contaminated' by the authors' interpretations (Moreira 2007: 189).

Through this process, reviewers extract the 'same' data from each study, which is typically inputted into a single table including columns for various study characteristics (e.g., patient population, methodological quality, outcomes measured, etc.). However, in many respects, this sameness is actively produced by the extraction process itself, which involves a considerable amount of discretion on the part of the reviewer. As Moreira notes, items may be recalculated to fit the reviewer's template; they may also be extrapolated based on the information contained in the article. Thus, 'in a more than superficial way, they *rewrite* the paper; and such rewriting is an integral part of the work of re-calculation that is done while abstracting' (Moreira 2007: 189, emphasis in original). In consequence, the results of the studies appear within a set of relations that differ – potentially radically – from the claims of their original authors.

Ray Pawson (2002) describes this phenomenon through the language of 'compression',[15] highlighting the sorts of simplifications that are required to produce the 'grand summary of summaries' that systematic reviews generally aspire to (p. 162). Focusing on meta-analyses, he argues that the process of compression occurs at three points. First, it happens in the melding of programme mechanisms, where radically different interventions become treated as a comparison of 'like with like'. Second, it happens in the oversimplification of programme outcomes, with their intent to determine an overall 'mean effect'; here, we see the production of what are effectively 'means of means of means of means!' (Pawson 2002: 165). Third, it occurs in the concealment of programme contexts – i.e., the 'black box' problem noted above. In Pawson's words (2002: 166):

> any 'programme outcome' – single, pooled or mean – depends not merely upon 'the programme' but also on its subjects and its circumstances. These contextual variations are yet another feature that is squeezed out of the picture in the aggregation process of meta-analysis.

The effects of these compressions can be demonstrated through a return to the Cochrane review on physician advice for smoking cessation. The latest version of the review includes 42 randomised trials from 14 countries, although it draws much the same conclusion as its predecessors that: 'Simple advice has a small effect on cessation rates. Assuming an unassisted quit rate of 2 to 3 per cent, a brief advice intervention can increase quitting by a further 1 to 3 per cent' (Stead *et al.* 2013: 2). Given the array of studies included in the review, there's considerable heterogeneity in the study populations in terms of their geographic spread. Moreover, smokers themselves were recruited in markedly different contexts. The majority of the trials were conducted with smokers attending primary care clinics, but others recruited specific categories of smokers, such as those with medical conditions. Some focused on smokers in particular occupations (e.g., civil servants, naval shipyard workers); others exclusively targeted one gender (e.g., mothers or men). Yet, although many individual studies clearly found such differences to be important, this heterogeneity is erased in the review itself,[16] with results pooled in a meta-analysis to quantify the effects of physician smoking cessation advice on the generic or 'average' smoker (cf. Kravitz, Duan and Braslow 2004).

What is obviously lacking in descriptions of research evidence presented within this and other Cochrane reviews is any acknowledgement of 'social structural influences and social, cultural, political and economic dimensions, despite their critically important role in determining health status and outcomes' (Lambert 2006: 2642; see also Rogers 2004; McGuire 2005). Systematic review methodologies aggregate the results of studies varying widely across time and space based on a model of evidence where the trials are treated as simultaneously substitutable and additive. Yet, it's not clear that the studies included in such Cochrane reviews actually relate to one another in any coherent fashion (i.e., the 'like with like' issue that Pawson raises). We don't know whether the outcomes being compared were produced by the same or different mechanisms or whether the terms used to describe the interventions themselves were being drawn on with any consistency (Pawson 2002; Clegg 2005). However, as I noted in Chapter 5, this is a characteristic feature of the rise of evidence-based medicine itself, where the question of *how* an intervention works became irrelevant in the face of evidence that it *does* work.

These issues crystallise in a comparison of two of the studies included in the Cochrane review: Burt et al. (1974) and Schnoll et al. (2003). Burt et al.'s study was conducted in Scotland in the early 1970s and included 125 male survivors of acute myocardial infarction, who were randomised to either regular care or a detailed explanation of the health effects of smoking by a physician in the coronary care unit where they were being treated, followed by 'firm advice' to quit. In the authors' words: 'Each man was told dogmatically that he should never smoke again in any form as long as he lived' (Burt et al. 1974: 305). Those in the intervention arm were treated at a specialised clinic following discharge from hospital, where they continued to receive intensive advice and support. Sixty-two per cent of men in this arm were persuaded to quit, which the authors suggested was 'probably attributable to a forceful approach by the physician after he had established a personal relationship with the patient' (Burt et al. 1974: 306). The intensive follow-up support provided was also highlighted as an explanation for its success, although the authors speculated that patients who have had a heart attack are 'more strongly motivated to accept advice than apparently healthy individuals who feel well' (Burt et al. 1974: 306).[17] The researchers concluded: 'Even if addicted himself, it would be of value if every doctor, familiar with the dangers of smoking, were to make the facts known to those he meets' (Burt et al. 1974: 306).

Schnoll and colleagues' trial was conducted three decades later in the USA. It also focused on a particular sub-population with a serious medical condition: 432 smokers recruited at various cancer treatment centres. Participants were assigned to either usual care or a physician-based smoking cessation intervention, which included advice to quit and follow-up assistance if they expressed an interest in doing so (e.g., identification of a quit date, prescription for nicotine replacement therapy, provision of a self-help guide to quitting, etc.). For such smokers, an overview of progress occurred at follow-up visits. However, the research team found no difference between the control and intervention arms, although cancer site itself was a strong predictor of long-term quit rates (e.g., lung cancer versus testicular cancer).

Obviously, these studies differ dramatically in terms of their geographic and temporal location, their study population and the physicians who carried out the intervention – a feature clearly shared with other trials included in the review (see Figures 6.1 and 6.2). The validity of the comparison relies on the assumption that roughly the same intervention is being compared across time and space. However, can we, in fact, speak of 'the intervention' as if it can be disentangled from the context in which it was carried out? In other words, would the meaning of aggressive injunctions to quit given to male Scottish smokers in the 1970s who had recently suffered a heart attack bear any resemblance to the meaning of cessation advice given to smokers by their oncologist in the USA some 30 years later?

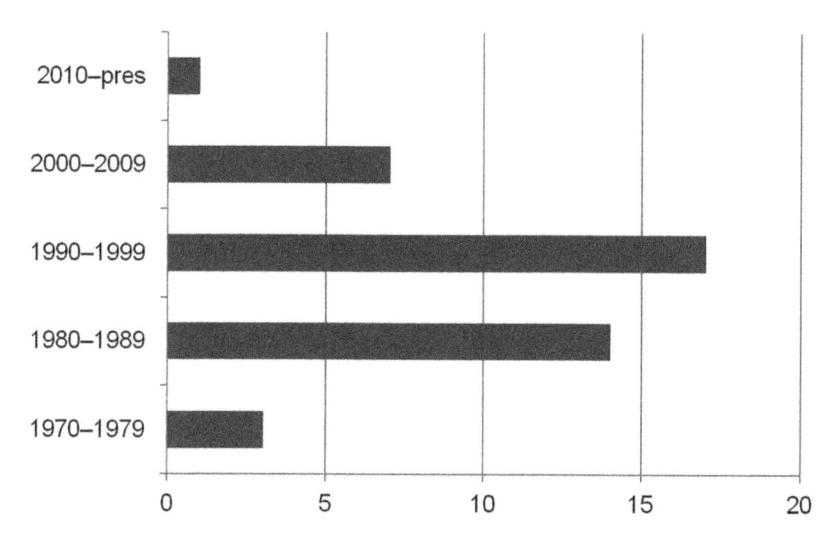

FIGURE 6.1 Distribution of Cochrane review studies across time

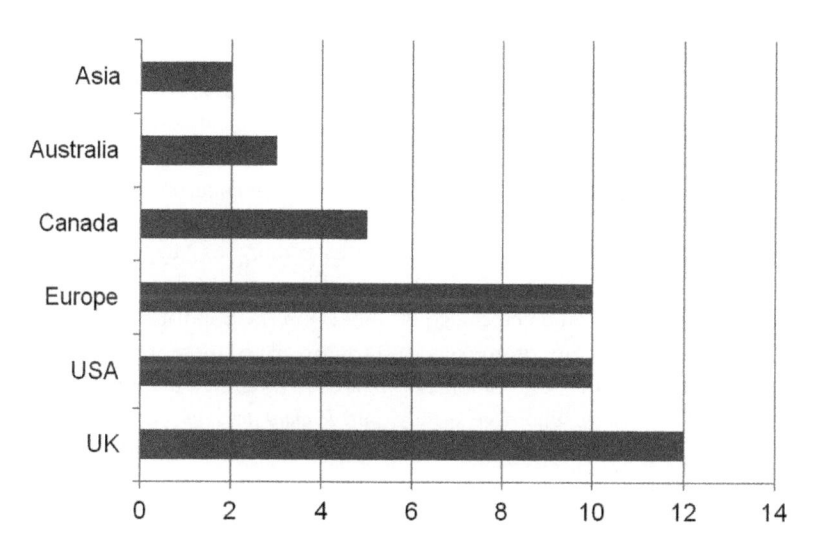

FIGURE 6.2 Geographic distribution of Cochrane review studies

Consider the radically different social, cultural and political context of smok-ing in these two studies. In one, the Surgeon General's report decisively linking smoking to cancer was barely 10 years old and half the male population smoked (including a high proportion of physicians themselves[18]). Cigarette taxes were low and smoking was pervasive – there were no smoking bans, no advertising bans and public awareness of the health effects of smoking was relatively limited. In the other, the overall prevalence of smoking has reduced dramatically, tobacco control measures are widespread and the health impacts of smoking are universally known. The differences don't end there. One intervention was conducted in a country with universal health care, the other in a country with a privatised system; one was conducted with people treated for a heart attack, the other with people diagnosed with cancer; one was delivered by a single physician with an extremely aggressive approach that included intensive follow-up care, the other by a cadre of physicians who would inevitably have differed in their style, even if they adhered to the specified intervention guidelines,[19] and so on. Viewed in such terms, what superficially looks like a 'constant' (the intervention itself) starts to unravel entirely and one starts to suspect that apples and oranges are being compared.

Precisely this observation was made almost 30 years ago, in response to the first meta-analysis ever conducted on the effectiveness of smoking cessation interventions in medical practice (Kottke *et al.* 1988b). The review is noteworthy insofar as it preceded the formal appearance of evidence-based medicine and the Cochrane Collaboration, although it was clearly driven by the same sorts of impulses and was conducted at the behest of the US Preventive Services Task Force to inform its recommendations for smoking cessation counselling.[20] It also takes a similar approach to evidence in terms of the amount of space devoted to an overview of the review methods and its prioritisation of controlled studies – although non-randomised trials were included in the review.

Like the later Cochrane review, the authors treated studies in an additive fashion, reporting an average difference of 5.8 per cent in smoking cessation rates between intervention and control groups.[21] However, some readers were sceptical of the results. In a letter to the editor published in the following issue, a reader noted:

> We need to be aware of the age of the studies examined. Only two of the studies examined were published after 1985 and over one third were published in 1980 or earlier. As the percentage of smokers in the population has dropped, the sex and racial mix of smokers has changed. Also, those who smoke now seem to be the hard-core[22] smokers who are less interested in quitting or more addicted than those who have already quit. *Perhaps the techniques most effective in earlier years will not be the techniques most effective with current smokers.*
>
> *O'Donnell 1998: 1552, emphasis added*

Clearly, the reader wasn't convinced that the 'same' thing was being measured in the included trials. The reviewers' rebuttal to the critique is instructive. They wrote:

> In response to the suggestion that the hard-core smokers of today may respond to different techniques than we found effective in the trials published, we can only speculate that the principles of effective intervention will remain the same because they are consistent with general behavioral theory, namely, the role of prolonged positive reinforcement in the maintenance of behavior change.
>
> *Kottke et al. 1998a: 1552*

Entangled evidence and the porphyroblast paradox

As highlighted in Chapter 2, the rise of behaviourism and the notion of 'health behaviours' it engendered has seen human actions treated as discrete, independently alterable phenomena or 'variables' that can be intervened into in much the same way as human physiology. However, by forcing behaviours into a natural science paradigm, epidemiological approaches tend to disguise the most significant parameters of social processes (Bourgois, Lettiere and Quesada 1997).

In describing a UK research centre's report on smoking 'behaviour' among 15- and 16-year-old school children, Michael Mair (2011) provides a useful illustration of what this paradigm makes visible and what it elides. The researchers found that smokers were more likely than non-smokers to live in deprived areas and to have certain individual attributes such as a parent who smokes, frequent consumption of alcohol, no hobbies or sporting activities, no club memberships and so on. These were, in turn, identified as key 'risk factors' for smoking. However, Mair points out that many of these individual 'attributes' are actually features of the youths' social environments. For example, in deprived areas, access to sporting facilities and youth clubs is often very limited, so 'what initially seemed to be a characteristic of individual smokers starts to look a great deal more like a reflection of the circumstances in which they live' (2011: 137).

The problem Mair identifies isn't merely a matter of confusing correlation with causation, but instead challenges the way that causality itself is constructed. Yet, this is generally how the problem is treated within EBM paradigms. For example, Egger, Schneider and Davey Smith (1998) have discussed the rise of meta-analyses of observational data and express concerns about the ways such data are typically interpreted. Their key argument is that without due care, meta-analyses of observational studies produce 'plausible but equally spurious findings' (p. 141) because of the inability of such studies to adequately account for confounding variables.[23] To illustrate their point they examine the relationship between suicide and smoking, noting that numerous cohort studies have shown a positive association between them. Mapping the relative risks for each study (see Figure 6.3), they demonstrate the highly precise and significant estimates of the increase in suicide risk associated with smoking different daily amounts of cigarettes. Their goal, of course, is to show that this relationship, which the meta-analysis makes appear convincingly causal, is obviously explained by other factors.

Egger, Schneider and Davey Smith explicitly exempt RCTs from their criticisms of meta-analysis, noting: 'the overall effect calculated from a group of sensibly combined and representative randomised trials will provide an essentially unbiased estimate of the treatment effect' (1988: 141). However, meta-analyses of the kind typified in the Cochrane review on physician advice for smoking cessation arguably suffer from the same limitations. This isn't because such reviews have failed to adequately account for 'confounding variables' or other sources of 'bias' but because these concepts misapprehend the nature of the phenomena in question. In other words, if the 'effectiveness' of a smoking cessation intervention is inextricably

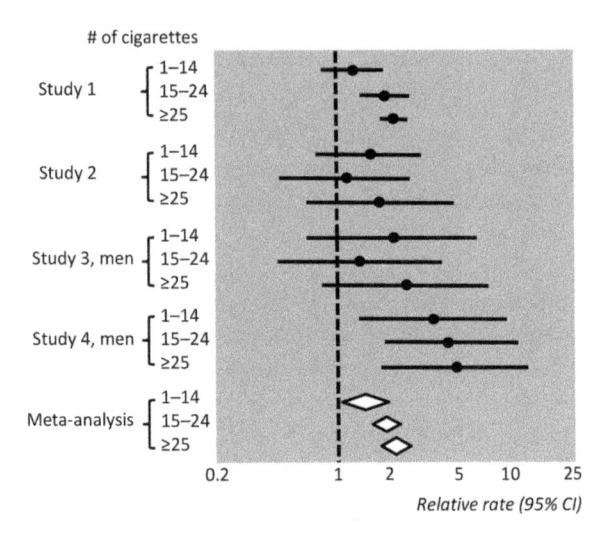

FIGURE 6.3 Results of meta-analysis of four cohort studies showing the adjusted relative rates of suicide among middle-aged male smokers compared with non-smokers based on daily cigarette consumption

Source: adapted from Egger, Schneider and Davey Smith 1998.

bound up with the social, cultural and political context in which it is carried out, then meta-analyses of RCTs produced in radically different environments are likely to produce equally spurious – and quite misleading – results, because the 'context' is not actually something external to the intervention; rather, the 'intervention' as a stable entity is an *illusion*.

The easiest way of illustrating this point is via an example taken from geology – what I will call here the porphyroblast paradox. A porphyroblast is a large crystal (garnets being the most common form) that grows in metamorphic rocks – rocks that metamorphose from one type to another and form under intense heat and pressure during mountain building. Structural geologists have long considered porphyroblasts to be important because as they grow they preserve deformation history – i.e., the physical strains or 'events' they have been subjected to over the course of millions of years. The prevailing view is that as deformation occurs, the porphyroblast rotates as it grows, kind of like a snowball that expands in girth as it rolls down a hill. However, a minority perspective is that porphyroblasts don't actually rotate at all, it just *looks* like they do because they are suspended in a matrix that itself is rotating. In other words, porphyroblast rotation is an illusion created not by what is happening in the porphyroblast itself, but the *context* in which it's embedded. This might seem like a minor difference, but its implications are substantial. To reuse the snowball analogy, under this view, it's the hill that's moving rather than the snowball.[24] Applied to the case at hand, the porphyroblast paradox suggests the possibility that what we *think* we are seeing: an 'intervention' that changes behaviour, is actually the result of what's happening around it rather than the intervention itself.

Vincanne Adams (2013) provides an excellent illustration of this phenomenon in her discussion of a hypothetical study in rural Nepal comparing two methods of condom distribution to determine what method works best to reduce sexually transmitted diseases. These alternative distribution methods are randomised across multiple villages, which are then compared to see which has lower STD rates (i.e., a cluster RCT is conducted). The problem, of course, is that while a study of this type could conceivably be carried out and might provide an answer to the question of which distribution method is more 'effective', the answer itself is likely to be spurious. To quote Adams:

> Questions about the social and infrastructural dynamics that get involved in managing the distribution, consumption, and use of condoms (to continue with the hypothetical case), and the meaning of cash versus gift transactions in relation to notions of sexuality in villages (based on religion, family pressure, sentiments of love, and the like) – and these are just examples – might, if pursued, lead one to the conclusion that reducing STDs has *nothing to do with how condoms are distributed*, but rather with things like the religion of the person distributing them, the color of the packaging, the commitment to healthy families over and above the cost of condoms, or the social and behavioral obligations that come along with receiving gifts from a health center. All of these considerations may be vital to explaining rates of STD reduction, or the lack thereof, but unless the RCT study is designed to include them all, there will be no way to know this, and assuming that the RCT has captured the essential variables that matter *may lead to misleading claims*.
>
> *Adams 2013: 63, emphasis added*

Indeed, even if all these so-called 'confounding variables' could be adequately captured, the problem wouldn't be resolved because they aren't just mechanical components but dynamic elements that come together to produce the system, becoming meaningful and changing in the process of interaction (cf. Cohn *et al.* 2013).[25]

Conclusion

Although the idea that human *behaviour* is amenable to artificial randomisation was in place long before the emergence of evidence-based medicine, it has cemented the status of RCTs as the most effective means of establishing causality – not just for physiological interventions but 'behavioural' ones as well. As EBM principles and processes expanded from clinical studies to public health and other allied fields, the problems of 'context' and 'complexity' have been periodically addressed, but mostly via the logic of the paradigm itself. However, if RCTs conducted in these settings are ill equipped to deal with complexity, this is even more true of systematic reviews, which subject evidence to a series of compressions that make it speak in ways that – by design – eradicate context entirely. The resultant 'facts' are not only limited in their capacity to speak meaningfully about health problems and solutions (among other things), they run the risk of misrepresenting them entirely. In the final section of the book I will be turning my focus from the production of 'facts' to the production of 'values' (i.e., the ethical turn in medicine and public health), but this issue will continue to figure as a prominent theme.

Notes

1 As I will discuss, this is not the first systematic review on this topic, although it is the first one focusing specifically on randomised controlled trials.
2 Cochrane's unwavering faith in RCTs was so great that in the introduction to his auto-biography Dick Cohen describes him as an agnostic 'whose final spiritual home was to be the randomised controlled trial' (Cochrane with Blythe 1989: xii).
3 This topic comes up in passing in *Effectiveness and Efficiency* when Cochrane discusses the potential value of RCTs in ascertaining the efficacy of caning in discouraging cigarette consumption among high school boys and his attempts to convince a school principal to test this.
4 These clashing views on ethics, and the ways evidence-based medicine has served to transform them, will be discussed in more detail in Chapter 7.
5 Given its date of publication, this quote demonstrates that many of the features of evidence-based medicine in terms of its conceptions of 'good' evidence were in wider circulation well before the movement formally emerged in the 1990s.
6 See, for example, Rychetnik *et al.* (2002), Kavanagh *et al.* (2002), Hawe, Shiel and Riley (2004) and Green and Glasgow (2006). Although each is critical of the over-emphasis on the 'classic' RCT in evaluating complex interventions, none advocates displacing it entirely. Instead, they suggest the need to broaden conceptions of the RCT to better account for fidelity and external validity issues (Rychetnick *et al.* 2002; Hawe, Shiel and Riley 2004) and expand EBM paradigms to more clearly acknowledge the value of additional kinds of evidence (Kavanagh *et al.* 2002; Green and Glasgow 2006).
7 These distinctions were initially drawn in the context of clinical trials (see Schwartz and Lellouch 1967; Charlton 1994) but they provided a ready-made way of conceptualising the applicability of RCTs to non-drug settings and the attendant problem of external validity, which 'pragmatic' RCTs were seen to address.
8 Bonell *et al.* (2012) argue that this is a misunderstanding of RCT design and that the use of control groups aims to illustrate how interventions interact with contextual factors in order to bring about an outcome. However, as Marchal *et al.* (2013) note in their commentary on the paper, Bonell and colleagues don't actually explain *how* the use of control groups allows researchers to take context into account rather than merely controlling for it – a criticism that I think also holds true for Bonell *et al.*'s response (see Bonell *et al.* 2013).
9 This is my interpretation of their argument rather than their own framing.
10 As Marchal *et al.* (2013) note, a 'realist RCT' is an oxymoron.
11 See also Chapter 5 for similar points.
12 Like RCTs themselves, there have been some efforts to expand the systematic review paradigm; for example, an Equity Methods Group has been formed within the Cochrane Collaboration that aims to encourage authors of reviews to consider intervention effects *beyond* those exhibited at a population level. However, the Group hasn't had a substantive impact on the overarching methodologies for conducting such reviews, or the prevailing assumptions about what the results of such reviews mean.
13 It's worth noting that such drug trials differ in very important ways from those testing the efficacy of other kinds of drugs. As Andrew Lakoff (2007: 58) points out, RCTs of novel psychiatric medications rely on symptom rating scales that require

agreement on what the salient characteristics of the illness are, which has been a struggle in the case of mental illnesses – in part because of the inaccessibility of these illness to physiological measures, and in part because of competing epistemologies among experts in the field.

14 As I discussed in Chapter 4, this assumption that data speak for themselves is integral to EBM paradigms.

15 Pawson is specifically talking about meta-analyses in the area of evidence-based policy, but I think his points apply more broadly.

16 Heterogeneity is considered in the review only insofar as it pertains to the overall results of individual trials. Thus, the authors note that 'The general absence of substantial heterogeneity between trials when relative risks are compared makes for reliable estimates of relative effect' (Stead *et al.* 2013: 9).

17 Here we see an early invocation of what later became more formally conceptualised as a 'teachable moment' (see Chapter 3).

18 See Adriaanse and Van Reek (1989) for a historical overview of physicians' smoking patterns in the UK and numerous other countries.

19 The authors assure the reader that trained data coordinators 'assisted physicians with standardizing intervention components at each site' (Schnoll *et al.* 2003: 356), and emphasise their interchangeability through the use of the singular term 'the physician'. However, a degree of fuzziness regarding what constituted 'the intervention' and 'standard' practice was clearly evident in the study, much along the lines that Heaven (2008, 2010) has highlighted, given that many patients in the usual care condition had the benefits of quitting discussed with them and 19 per cent received nicotine replacement therapy.

20 This speaks to the ways in which the growing demand for 'evidence' in many respects culminated in the emergence of evidence-based medicine rather than being precipitated by it.

21 However, they provide the following caveat: 'These results suggest that smoking might be described as a social habit manifested as individual behavior; change of social behavior is best achieved through change in the social environment' (Kottke *et al.* 1988b: 2889).

22 The legitimacy of the concept of the 'hard-core' smoker is contested in the field of tobacco control (see Burns and Warner 2002; Chapman 2007); however, it does speak to a recognition of the dramatic ways in which the social composition of smoking has changed over the past three decades – especially in terms of its growing concentration among those of lower socio-economic status.

23 Despite these early criticisms, Egger has since been involved in various meta-analyses of observational studies, including an extremely influential meta-analysis on the relationship between body mass index and cancer (Renehan *et al.* 2008).

24 Actually, it's more complicated than this; the more accurate analogy would be that the snow is rotating around the snowball.

25 For this reason, Fuller and Potvin (2012) argue that the 'constant effect' assumption can't be met in cluster RCTs and that the interactions between the treatment and its social context effectively become the primary object of study. However, given that the whole point of the RCT is to remove the effect of context, this assumption is typically embedded into cluster RCT designs and is precisely why they tend to be conducted in the first place.

References

Adams, V. (2013) Evidence-based global public health: Subjects, profits, erasures. In J. Biehl and A. Petryna (eds), *When People Come First: Critical Studies in Global Health*. Princeton, NJ: Princeton University Press, pp. 54–90.

Adriaanse, H. and Van Reek, J. (1989) Physicians' smoking and its exemplary effect. *Scandinavian Journal of Primary Health Care*, 7: 193–196.

Bell, K., Bowers, M., McCullough, L. and Bell, J. (2012) Physician advice for smoking cessation in primary care: Time for a paradigm shift? *Critical Public Health*, 22(1): 9–24.

Bonell, C., Fletcher, A., Morton, M., Lorenc, T. and Moore, L. (2012) Realist randomised controlled trials: A new approach to evaluating complex public health interventions. *Social Science and Medicine*, 75: 2299–2306.

Bonell, C., Fletcher, A., Morton, M., Lorenc, T. and Moore, L. (2013) Methods don't make assumptions, researchers do: A response to Marchal *et al. Social Science and Medicine*, 94: 81–82.

Bourgois, P., Lettiere, M. and Quesada, J. (1997) Social misery and the sanctions of substance abuse: Confronting HIV risk among homeless heroin addicts in San Francisco. *Social Problems*, 44(2): 155–173.

Burns, D.M. and Warner, K.E. (2003) Smokers who have not quit: Is cessation more difficult and should we change our strategies? In S.E. Marcus (ed.), *Smoking and Tobacco Control Monograph No. 15*. Bethesda, MD: US Department of Health and Human Services, pp. 11–32.

Burt, A., Illingworth, D., Shaw, T., Thornley, P., White, P. and Turner, R. (1974) Stopping smoking after myocardial infarction. *The Lancet*, 1(7852): 304–306.

Chapman, S. (2007) *Public Health Advocacy and Tobacco Control: Making Smoking History*. Oxford: Blackwell.

Charlton, B.G. (1994) Understanding randomized controlled trials: Explanatory or pragmatic? *Family Practice*, 11(3): 243–244.

Clegg, S. (2005) Evidence-based practice in educational research: A critical realist critique of systemic review. *British Journal of Sociology of Education*, 26(3): 415–428.

Cochrane, A.L. (1972) *Effectiveness and Efficiency: Random Reflections on Health Services*. London: Nuffield Trust.

Cochrane, A.L. and Blythe, M. (1989) *One Man's Medicine: An Autobiography of Professor Archie Cochrane*. The Memoir Club. London: British Medical Journal.

Cohn, D., Clinch, M., Bunn, C. and Stronge, P. (2013) Entangled complexity: Why complex interventions are just not complicated enough. *Journal of Health Services Research and Policy*, 18(1): 40–43.

Dehue, T. (1997) Deception, efficiency, and random groups: Psychology and the gradual origination of the random group design. *Isis*, 88(4): 653–673.

Dehue, T. (2010) Comparing artificial groups: On the history and assumptions of the randomised controlled trial. In C. Will and T. Moreira (eds), *Medical Proofs, Social Experiments: Clinical Trials in Shifting Contexts*. Surrey: Ashgate, pp. 103–120.

Egger, M., Schneider, M. and Davey Smith, G. (1998) Spurious precision? Meta-analysis of observational studies. *British Medical Journal*, 316: 140–144.

Fassin, D. and Rechtman, R. (2008) *The Empire of Trauma: An Inquiry Into the Condition of Victimhood*. Princeton, NJ: Princeton University Press.

Fuller, D. and Potvin, L. (2012) Context by treatment interactions as the primary object of study in cluster randomized controlled trials of population health interventions. *International Journal of Public Health*, 57: 633–636.

Green, L.W. and Glasgow, R.E. (2006) Evaluating the relevance, generalization, and applicability of research: Issues in external validation and translation methodology. *Evaluation and the Health Professions*, 29(1): 126–153.

Green, L.W. and Lewis, F.M. (1986) *Measurement and Evaluation in Health Education and Health Promotion*. Palo Alto, CA: Mayfield.

Hacking, I. (1988) Origins of randomization in experimental design. *Isis*, 79(3): 427–451.

Hacking, I. (1990) *The Taming of Chance*. New York: Cambridge University Press.

Hawe, P., Shiell, A. and Riley, T. (2004) Complex interventions: How 'out of control' can a randomised controlled trial be? *British Medical Journal*, 328: 1561–1563.

Heaven, B. (2008) *Epistemological Authority and Hidden Work: Negotiated Meaning in the Conduct of a Randomised Controlled Trial*. Doctoral Dissertation. Newcastle University.

Heaven, B. (2010) Bridging the ontological divide: Different social worlds in the conduct of a pilot study. In C. Will and T. Moreira (eds), *Medical Proofs, Social Experiments: Clinical Trials in Shifting Contexts*. Surrey: Ashgate, pp. 33–48.

Hill, A.B. (1952) The clinical trial. *New England Journal of Medicine*, 247: 113–119.

Kavanagh, A., Daly, J., Melder, A. and Jolley, D. (2002) 'Mind the gap': Assessing the quality of evidence for public health problems. In V. Lin and B. Gibson (eds), *Evidence-based Health Policy: Problems and Possibilities*. Melbourne: Oxford University Press, pp. 70–79.

Kottke, T.E., Battista, R.N., DeFriese, G.H. and Brekke, M.L. (1988a) Attributes of interventions that stop smoking: In reply. *Journal of the American Medical Association*, 260(11): 1552.

Kottke, T.E., Battista, R.N., DeFriese, G.H. and Brekke, M.L. (1988b) Attributes of successful smoking cessation interventions in medical practice. *Journal of the American Medical Association*, 259(19): 2883–2889.

Kramer, M.S. and Shapiro, S.H. (1984) Scientific challenges in the application of randomized trials. *Journal of the American Medical Association*, 252(19): 2739–2745.

Kravitz, R. L., Duan, H. and Braslow, J. (2004) Evidence-based medicine, heterogeneity of treatment effects, and the trouble with averages. *Milbank Quarterly,* : *82*(4): 661–687.

Lakoff, A. (2007) The right patients for the drug: Managing the placebo effect in antidepressant trials. *BioSocieties*, 2: 57–71.

Lambert, H. (2006) Accounting for EBM: Notions of evidence in medicine. *Social Science and Medicine*, 62: 2633–2645.

McGuire, W. (2005) Beyond EBM: New directions for evidence-based public health. *Perspectives in Biology and Medicine*, 48(4): 557–569.

McLaren, L., Ghali, L.M., Lorenzetti, D. and Rock, M. (2007) Out of context? Translating evidence from the North Karelia project over place and time. *Health Education Research*, 22(3): 414–424.

Mair, M. (2011) Deconstructing behavioural classifications: Tobacco control, 'professional vision' and the tobacco user as a site of governmental intervention. *Critical Public Health*, 21(2): 129–140.

Marchal, B., Westhorp, G., Wong, G., Van Belle, S., Greenhalgh, T., Kegels, G. and Pawson, R. (2013) Realist RCTs of complex interventions: An oxymoron. *Social Science and Medicine*, 94: 124–128.

Moreira, T. (2007) Entangled evidence: Knowledge making in systematic reviews in healthcare. *Sociology of Health and Illness*, 29(2): 180–197.

Nutbeam, D., Smith, C. and Catford, J. (1990) Evaluation in health education: A review of progress, possibilities and problems. *Journal of Epidemiology and Community Health*, 44: 83–89.

O'Donnell, M.P. (1988) Attributes of interventions that stop smoking: To the editor. *Journal of the American Medical Association*, 260(11): 1552.

Pawson, R. (2002) Evidence-based policy: In search of a method. *Evaluation*, 8(2): 157–181.

Pawson, R. (2006) *Evidence-Based Policy. A Realist Perspective*. London: Sage.

Pawson, R. (2013) *The Science of Evaluation: A Realist Manifesto*. London: Sage.

Pawson, R. and Tilley, N. (1997) *Realistic Evaluation*. London: Sage.

Porter, A.M. and McCullough, D.M. (1972) Counselling against cigarette smoking: A controlled study from a general practice. *Practitioner*, 209: 686–689.

Renehan, A.G., Tyson, M., Egger, M., Heller, R.F. and Zwahlen, M. (2008) Body-mass index and incidence of cancer: A systematic review and meta-analysis of prospective observational studies. *The Lancet*, 371: 569–578.

Rogers, W. (2004) Evidence-based medicine and women: Do the principles and practices of EBM further women's health? *Bioethics*, 18(1): 50–71.

Rychetnik, L., Frommer, M., Hawe, P. and Shiell, A. (2002) Criteria for evaluating evidence on public health interventions. *Journal of Epidemiology and Community Health*, 56: 119–127.

Schnoll, R.A., Zhang, B., Rue, M., Krook, J.E., Spears, W.T., Marcus, A.C. and Engstrom, P.F. (2003) Brief physician-initiated quit-smoking strategies for clinical oncology settings: A trial coordinated by the Eastern Cooperative Oncology Group. *Journal of Clinical Oncology*, 21(2): 355–365.

Schwartz, D. and Lellouch, J. (1967) Explanatory and pragmatic attitudes in therapeutic trials. *Journal of Chronic Disease*, 20: 637–648.

Shapin, S. (1995) Cordelia's love: Credibility and the social studies of science. *Perspectives on Science*, 3(3): 255–275.

Shapin, S. (2010) *Never Pure: Historical Studies of Science as if It Was Produced by People with Bodies, Situated in Time, Space, Culture, and Society and Struggling for Credibility and Authority*. Baltimore, MD: Johns Hopkins University Press.

Shoveller, J., Viehbeck, S., Di Ruggiero, E., Greyson, D., Thomson, K. and Knight. R. (2016) A critical examination of representations of context within research on population health interventions. *Critical Public Health*, DOI: 10.1080/09581596.2015.1117577.

Silagy, C. and Ketteridge, S. (1996) Physician advice for smoking cessation. *Cochrane Database of Systematic Reviews*, 1. Art no.: CD000165.

Stead, L. F., Buitrago, D., Preciado, N., Sanchez, G., Harmann-Boyce, J. and Lancaster, T. (2013) Physician advice for smoking cessation. *Cochrane Database of Systematic Reviews*, 2. Art no.: CD000165.

Stigler, S.M. (1992) A historical view of statistical concepts in psychology and educational research. *American Journal of Evaluation*, 101(1): 60–70.

Wahlberg, A. and McGoey, L. (2007) An elusive evidence-base: The construction and governance of randomized controlled trials. *BioSocieties*, 2: 1–10.

Wessely, S. (2007) Commentary: A defence of the randomized controlled trial in mental health. *BioSocieties*, 2: 115–127.

Young, A. (1995) *The Harmony of Illusions: Inventing Post-Traumatic Stress Disorder*. Princeton, NJ: Princeton University Press.

PART III
Ethics

7

MEDICINE ACQUIRES ETHICS

Introduction

In 1975, the *Journal of Medical Ethics* published its inaugural issue. The aim of the journal, as its editors described it, was to 'provide a forum for the reasoned discussion of moral issues arising from the provision of medical care' (JME Editors 1975: 1). They made it clear that medical ethics depends on 'the resources of the disciplines of law, philosophy and theology, as well as on the whole range of medical and paramedical specialties' (JME Editors 1975: 1). In other words, medical ethics was not considered to be the sole province of physicians themselves, but was instead characterised as a multi-disciplinary endeavour – one that extended far beyond the scope of individual clinical decision-making. Thus, papers on euthanasia, artificial insemination, cryo-banking, abortion and research ethics committees sat side-by-side with ones on patient communication.

This new emphasis on medical ethics as a field independent from medical practitioners themselves and with a scope well beyond the clinician-patient encounter is today referred to by the term 'bioethics' – and is an area that has witnessed extraordinary growth over the past 40 years. Some 20 years after the *Journal of Medical Ethics* was founded, Paul Komesaroff (1995a) commented that bioethics constituted a major academic industry – an observation that holds even more true today. Sixteen years into the twenty-first century, bioethics is increasingly called upon to provide moral direction both inside and outside of the domains of health care and medicine (Bosk 2008; Fox and Swazey 2008; Murray and Holmes 2009; Petersen 2011; Pickersgill 2012). Today, professional ethicists are in demand in a variety of settings (Bosk 1999): hospitals in many countries are required to have a mechanism in place for resolving ethical conflicts, ethicists are mandatory on research ethics committees, and they have a prominent voice in health care policy and the media. As Charles Bosk (2008: 9) has observed, the extraordinary rise of bioethics over the past four decades speaks to the broader approval attached to the notion that 'what is wrong with health care is somehow connected to ethics and that such problems are best fixed by ethicists'.

In the final section of the book, my focus is on the ethical turn in medicine and public health. The field of bioethics naturally forms a central focus, although my interest is in 'ethics' more broadly, a term I treat as encompassing related concepts such as 'human rights' – which forms the focus of Chapter 9. Indeed, bioethics itself isn't a stable or easily definable field (De Vries *et al.* 2006; Murray and Holmes 2009; Petersen 2011).[1] Instead, it traverses a range of distinct but intersecting areas variously known as 'medical ethics', 'clinical ethics', 'biomedical ethics', 'research ethics', 'public health ethics' and 'global bioethics'. In this chapter, I focus on ways in which ethics came to be forefronted in discussions of health and medicine and to what effect. Following a discussion of the rise of bioethics and its connection with changing conceptions of health and medicine, I consider its intersections with contemporary notions of evidence and its more recent expansion into the fields of public and global health. My primary goal is to lay the groundwork for the final two chapters of the book, as well as to tie some of the threads of the prior two sections together. As I aim to show, one can't really understand the rise of epidemiology and its attendant notions of 'evidence' in health and medicine without also considering the rise of 'ethics' as an explicit orienting principle, for the three are bound tightly together.

Medical ethics in historical context

According to David Armstrong (2006), conventional histories of medical ethics typically ascribe its roots to the distant medical past, emphasising continuities over time. Histories presented under the banner of 'bioethics', however, are more likely to represent it as a radical break with the past. Fox and Swazey (2008) characterise these as 'big bang' narratives, with the emergence of bioethics understood 'as a response to specific advances in biomedical technologies, to particular sets of issues, or certain pivotal events' (pp. 22–23). As they observe, for many of its key chroniclers, the birth of bioethics is intimately tied up with technological progress and advances in biomedicine such as organ transplants, developments in fertility control and so on. Alan Petersen (2011) points out that in such accounts, 'technology' is generally conceived as outside 'society': it's presumed to be pre-social and unaffected by politics and power. These depictions also tend to present a 'teleological view of history in that the present is portrayed as somehow an inevitable outcome of a series of antecedent events or circumstances' (Petersen 2011: 8). In this respect, such histories share much in common with accounts of the rise of evidence-based medicine – and, indeed, epidemiology itself – where, as noted in Chapters 1 and 4, the past is typically understood through the lens of the present, and the movements are treated as a natural and inevitable response.

Contra such accounts, Armstrong (2006) points to important differences between conceptions of ethics as manifested in the first code of medical ethics in 1847 versus the arrival of bioethics as a distinct field in the latter part of the twentieth century. According to Armstrong, the Code of Ethics published by the newly formed American Medical Association in 1847 was closely bound up with the professionalisation of the discipline and its associated processes of 'occupational closure' (2006: 867).[2] Thus, the Code focused primarily on reciprocal obligations between doctors and their patients and between the profession and the public. Accordingly, it stressed that doctors had a duty to give due attention and considera- tion to the sick so as to 'inspire the minds of their patients with gratitude, respect and confidence' (cited in Armstrong 2006: 867). Patients, in turn, had a duty to restrict their interactions to *qualified* practitioners as opposed to 'self-constituted doctors and doctresses, who are so frequently met with, and who pretend to possess infallible remedies for the cure of every disease' (cited in Armstrong 2006: 867).

Armstrong (2006) highlights a number of parallels between medical ethics as it was formulated at this time and the project of public health (see Chapter 1). Just as the mid-nineteenth century strategies of sanitary science drew a line of separation around the human body and policed its boundaries, medicine during this period was similarly concerned with 'delineating and monitoring the boundaries of a new medical body' – with the quack seen to constitute the equivalent threat to the medical profession that 'dirt' (bodily effluvia) posed to public health (Armstrong 2006: 869). In essence, Armstrong argues that this period saw the materialisation of two new bodies that would form the bedrock of clinical encounters over the fol- lowing century: the patient as anatomical body (as a site for diagnosis of pathology and an object for observation and examination) and the newly professionalised body of the physician that crystallised out of the mass of heterodox healers.

In the second half of the twentieth century, however, medical ethics under- went a fundamental change – one reflected in the 1958 revision of the American Medical Association's ethical code (which by this stage had been reformulated as 'Principles of Medical Ethics'). Although the document continued to emphasise the importance of professional etiquette, it now included a new feature: the poten- tial dangers physicians posed to their patients. According to the new code, 'The medical profession should safeguard the public and itself against physicians deficient in moral character and professional competence' (cited in Armstrong 2006: 874). As Armstrong (2006) observes, this focus on the dangers of the medical profession to patient well-being was consolidated in the following decades under the banner of 'bioethics'. Thus, 'the problem was no longer the medical profession and its internal relationships but the potential threats that the medical profession posed for the patient. The new task of ethics was to protect the patient *from medicine itself*' (p. 874, emphasis added). However, bioethics not only aimed to safeguard patients, but to provide a political framework in which patient agency could be legitimately and safely nurtured (Armstrong 2014a). Indeed, it's this emphasis on the moral agency of the patient that arguably constitutes the core dividing line between bio- ethics and the form of medical ethics that preceded it (Wolpe 1998).

In many respects, this new emphasis on patient agency was connected with changing conceptions of health that occurred in the first half of the twentieth century. In 1936, the French surgeon René Leriche wrote that 'health is life lived in the silence of the organs' (Canguilheim 1989: 149). In this conceptualisation, health is essentially a negative rather than positive state insofar as it's something we can only know it by its absence (Osborne 1997).[3] However, when the World Health Organization was founded in 1948, it presented a definition of health that was distinctively different from what had preceded it. According to the preamble of its Constitution (which has changed little in subsequent iterations), health is defined as 'a state of complete physical, mental and social well-being and not merely the absence of disease and infirmity'. Here we see an articulation of health characterised not merely by its absences but its attributes – as a state (a *complete* state, no less![4]) of physical, mental and social well-being. Moreover, it asserted that everyone had a *right* to this state, which governments had a responsibility to protect.

As discussed in Chapter 1, this new conception of health was connected with the emergence of chronic disease as a core preoccupation in the fields of medicine and public health in the first half of the twentieth century. As a form of morbidity based less on pathology and more on the patient's sense of well-being and capacity to function, it legitimised new technologies such as the population survey (Armstrong 2014b). In this framework, the *subjective* dimension of health became necessarily forefronted – an emphasis clearly reflected in the WHO definition. However, this view of health had a number of flow-on effects. First, health became essentially indeterminate; thus, while claims regarding a 'right' to health accompanied the new definition, the definition itself made such claims necessarily aspirational rather than concrete, because they couldn't readily be operationalised in the form of corresponding obligations (Osborne 1997; Greco 2004; O'Neill 2005).[5] Second, if health is conceptualised primarily in positive rather than negative terms, then it becomes the province of specialists *other than* physicians, legitimising a space for disciplines such as epidemiology and psychology. Finally, by forefronting the individual's subjective sense of health, it concomitantly emphasised the importance of individual *agency*.[6] This emphasis becomes particularly evident in the Constitution's statement that: 'Informed opinion and active cooperation on the part of the public are of the utmost importance in the improvement of the health of the people' (WHO 1946).

Thus, the explicit roots of the contemporary ethical turn in medicine can be traced to the post-Second World War era and the assertion of humanist universalism that accompanied it (Ashcroft 2010). The principles outlined in documents such as the WHO Constitution and the 1947 Nuremberg Code of Medical Research[7] helped to establish the languages of both bioethics and human rights (Reubi and Mold 2013) – two fields that responded to the same set of social and historical events, although they developed into largely distinct assemblages (Ashcroft 2010).

The consolidation of bioethics

There is general agreement that bioethics developed first in the United States and subsequently spread to other countries around the globe, with the 1970s typically identified as the period in which the field began to professionalise (Fox and Swazey 2008). It was in this era that the term 'bioethics' was coined (Reich 1994) and it saw the emergence of specialised institutes and the inaugural issues of the first bioethics journals, such as the *Journal of Medical Ethics*. The topic also entered medical school curricula via texts such as Beauchamp and Childress's *The Principles of Biomedical Ethics* (1979). Now in its seventh edition, the book is generally considered a core – perhaps *the* core – textbook in the field. To quote one account: 'it seems fair to say that it has served as groundwork for the training of countless students and professionals in medicine and biomedical ethics worldwide' (Rauprich and Vollman 2011: 582; see also Clouser and Gert 1990; Brody 1997; Baker 2002; Zielinska 2015 for similar observations).

Beauchamp and Childress's goal was to develop a 'systematic analysis of the moral principles that should apply to biomedicine' (1979: vii) and they identified four key principles at its core: respect for autonomy (the patient's right to self-determination); non-maleficence ('do no harm'); beneficence (balancing the risks and benefits of treatment); and justice (distributing benefits, risks and costs fairly). The principle-based approach Beauchamp and Childress advocated, which has remained the core of the textbook in subsequent iterations, was central to the ways bioethics unfolded as a discipline (K. Walker 2009; Wolpe 1998). However, although four foundational principles were identified, the first, 'respect for autonomy', is arguably the most important, primarily because it serves as bioethicists' answer to *paternalism*. As David Reubi (2012) notes, paternalism is a core rhetorical device used in the bioethical literature to characterise physician practice prior to its arrival and explain the primary reason for its emergence. According to Bosk (2008: 9), 'The claim is often advanced that with its emphasis on patient autonomy, bioethics played a large role in overturning a regime of physician paternalism and replacing it with one that was patient centered'. Bosk points out that this view is based on the assumption that once the right values are installed in the doctor–patient relationship, the problems disappear – an assumption I will explore in more detail in Chapter 8.

Yet, almost from its inception, bioethics was subject to intensive criticisms from commentators both inside and outside of medicine. In light of bioethicists' core message that 'training in medicine did not necessarily qualify them [physicians] to make good ethical decisions' (Callahan 1973: 67), it should come as little surprise that physicians responded in kind to such criticisms. In 1973, Daniel Callahan, the co-founder of the Hastings Center (an influential bioethics institute), recounted a variety of attacks he had received from physicians relating primarily to the abstraction of bioethics and its inability to be of practical use to medicine. This and other criticisms continued apace into the 1990s, as the influence of bioethics dramatically intensified.[8]

Mainstream (or 'principlist') approaches to bioethics were criticised for encouraging a checklist mentality that, at best, merely names issues worth remembering and, at worst, obscures and confuses moral reasoning (Clouser and Gert 1990). Under this framework, critics argued that bioethics essentially becomes a set of principles already in hand that are slavishly applied to individual cases (Clouser and Gert 1990; Chambers 1999; K. Walker 2009; M.U. Walker 2009).[9] In the words of Paul Redding,

> [E]thics itself sometimes sounds like a branch of modern science – a discipline that is capable of being 'applied' in concrete situations and which claims a particular place within the complex division of labor of the scientific edifice. One gains the impression of the professional 'ethicist' as yet another specialist member of the modern medical 'team': the philosophical analogue of the biophysicist or the micropathologist.
>
> *Redding 1995: 92*

Related criticisms focused on the inability of bioethics to recognise its cultural and social embeddedness (e.g., Komesaroff 1995b; Brody 1997; De Vries and Subedi 1998; De Vries *et al.* 2006; Bosk 2008; Fox and Swazey 2008). For example, Raymond De Vries and colleagues (2006) have pointed to a kind of trained incapacity on the part of bioethicists that renders them unable to view the world from anything except their own perspective. This, it is argued, has led to a hegemonic thrust in the way that US bioethics has been exported to other countries (Fox and Swazey 2008) – a phenomenon Howard Brody (1997: 280) has labelled 'bioethical imperialism'.

Finally, as previously noted, bioethics was also criticised because of its abstractness and disconnect from the 'real' concerns of doctors and patients. Observers have repeatedly questioned whether it can offer any substantive guidance for medical practice because of its inability to provide an adequate account of day-to-day decision-making (e.g., Komesaroff 1995a). To quote one pointed critique:

> [W]hat is worthy of our attention is how naïve the idea that ethical analysis leads effectively to ethical practice seems when stated plainly. After all, there are not many areas where we equate theoretical and practical wisdom. We have cultural myths about lawyers dying intestate, cobblers' children running around unshod, and mental-health professionals whose entire being screams for a few effective therapeutic interventions.
>
> *Bosk 2008: 10*

Bioethics has therefore been accused of lacking empirical evidence that it has produced a beneficial impact on medical decision-making (Komesaroff 1995a).

Striking about these criticisms is their degree of overlap with the concerns raised about evidence-based medicine. As I detailed in Chapter 4, EBM was similarly castigated for its production of formulaic guidelines, its irrelevance for individual clinical encounters, its presumed universalism, the lack of evidentiary basis that it works and so on. The similarities in physicians' responses to both movements are largely a product of the parallels between the critiques each levelled. Just as evidence-based medicine later challenged the *evidentiary* basis upon which the medical profession made decisions, bioethicists challenged the *ethical* basis of its decision-making.

Indeed, many of the same factors that precipitated the later uptake of evidence-based medicine facilitated the emergence and embrace of bioethics. In other words, their different interventions into medicine resulted from the same conditions of possibility (see Chapter 4). Beyond the obvious desire to check physician power and growing concerns about the hazards the medical profession posed to patients, the patient advocacy movement was clearly important to the rise of ethics as a field distinct from the medical profession, and its new emphasis on the moral agency of patients (Wolpe 1998). The shift from medical 'patient' to 'consumer' that began in the 1970s saw a growing emphasis on the values of informed consent, personal responsibility, rationality and proactive choice (Sulik and Eich-Krohm 2008) – values that became codified in the bioethical principle of 'autonomy'.

The emphasis on autonomy that accompanied the rise of bioethics arguably suited corporate interests as well as patient ones, which some have suggested was an important factor in its embrace. For example, Jeanne Guillemin (1998) asserts that in standardising the physician–patient relationship, bioethics was crucial to the rise of medical services as commodities on the national market and the free-market takeover of health care in the USA. Likewise, Bruce Jennings (1998) and Paul Roote Wolpe (1998) have pointed to the ways in which the focus on patient autonomy served to minimise the perceived need for government regulation of the content of medical care (Jennings 1998; Wolpe 1998). As Wolpe notes (1998: 53), 'If patients make individual, informed decisions about their care, presumably with knowledge of the risks and potential benefits, then the government itself can assume a lesser role in monitoring and regulating the content of care.' Pharmaceutical firms were quick to capitalise on this cultural shift within health care, which facilitated the rise of direct-to-consumer advertising from the late 1980s (Donohue 2006).

According to Annemarie Mol (2008), the 'autonomous choosing subject' instantiated in bioethics thus operates according to the 'logic of choice'. She argues that there are two distinct variants that underwrite the logic of choice: the patient as consumer and the patient as citizen.[10] In the former variant, patients are customers buying products in a market; in the latter, they are defined primarily in relation to the state and their relationships are framed in terms of contracts – contracts that entail rights and responsibilities for both parties. The key motif in the consumer model is that of the *active* patient/consumer who chooses a product to her liking; the key motif in the citizen model is that of the *emancipated* patient/citizen freed from the shackles of physician paternalism. Together, they serve to legitimate the individual's sense of autonomy as something objective, a point I will elaborate on in Chapter 8.

The relationship between 'ethics' and 'evidence'

Although the concept of autonomy clearly forms the centrepiece of mainstream bioethics, the success of the field cannot just be understood in terms of the ways it served to further corporate and technical interests. Under the principlist framework Beauchamp and Childress advocated, efficiency and effectiveness were also important values: the former via the emphasis on justice and the need to distribute benefits, risks and costs fairly, and the latter in the emphasis on non-maleficence and beneficence and the need to ensure that treatments were beneficial rather than harmful. Bioethics thus provided a means of answering thorny ethical questions about how to best distribute scarce medical resources.[11] As Bosk (2008) notes, prior to the arrival of bioethics, to signal an issue as 'ethical' was to imply that it wasn't resolvable – that there was no gold standard against which to measure responses and credit some as 'right' and others as 'wrong'. Bioethical principlism therefore held considerable allure for medical managers and administrators, promising, as it did, 'consistency, efficiency, and ready implementation' (Murray and Holmes 2009: 1).

Here we see yet further intersections between bioethics and the EBM movement, which, as I discussed in Chapter 4, was founded on similar concerns about the need to make medicine more effective and efficient. This was the explicit impetus for the 1972 book *Effectiveness and Efficiency: Random Reflections on Health Services* by Archie Cochrane, the so-called 'founder' of EBM. Although not framed in such terms, in many respects the book can be read as an argument for a new form of ethical practice in health care, one in which the values of effectiveness and efficiency are paramount. Likewise, the first formal articulations of EBM in the 1990s implicitly asserted its ethical superiority to prior practice, which it characterised as irrational, unsystematic, biased and resulting in inferior patient care (see Chapter 4). Although bioethics enshrined other values as well, there is clearly basic agreement between the two movements that evidence forms a crucial aspect of medical decision-making.

In fact, I'm not convinced that the randomised controlled trial could have achieved its contemporary prominence without the bioethical insistence on the principles of beneficence and non-maleficence and the way they enabled new *ethical* arguments for the trial design. As I discussed in Chapters 5 and 6, RCTs conducted beyond drug settings were initially seen as ethically problematic; however, bioethics presented a clear ethical logic for such trials. To quote the *Cambridge Textbook of Bioethics*: 'The ethical importance of clinical[12] trials is sometimes underestimated. Yet the need to evaluate treatments for their safety and efficacy, so as to minimize harm to patients, reduce clinical uncertainty, and improve the efficiency of resource allocation, is great' (Ashcroft and Viens 2008: 203). This, in point of fact, was precisely Cochrane's original defence of them. In his words:

> It can be argued that it is ethically questionable to use on patients a procedure whose value is unknown, but the answer is that it is unethical not to do so if the patient will otherwise die or suffer severe disability and there is no alternative therapy.
>
> *Cochrane 1972: 23*

Here we see an early insistence on the idea that treatments must be *effective* to be *ethical* – a view essentially echoed (albeit in a different language) in Beauchamp and Childress's *The Principles of Biomedical Ethics*, published 7 years later.

However, while bioethics clearly emphasised the importance of evidence as an underlying principle, it simultaneously transformed the ways that such evidence was produced. This new relationship between ethics and evidence solidified in the 1979 Belmont Report (HHS 1979) developed by the National Commission for the Protection of Human Subjects of Biomedical and Behavioral Research, which was set up in the wake of the widespread public outcry over the Tuskegee Syphilis study.[13] The Commission was charged with identifying 'the basic ethical principles that should underlie the conduct of biomedical and behavioural research involving human subjects and to develop guidelines which should be followed to assure that such research is conducted in accordance with those principles' (HHS 1979). Three principles were outlined, along with a discussion of their applications: 1) respect for persons – manifested in the requirement for informed consent; 2) beneficence – manifested in an assessment of risks and benefits; and 3) justice – manifested in the fair selection of subjects. If they sound familiar, it's because Beauchamp was one of the co-authors of the report, as well as co-authoring the *Principles of Biomedical Ethics* during the same period. The degree of crossover between the two documents is widely recognised, with Beauchamp later noting that: 'these projects grew up and matured together' (cited in Fox and Swazey 2008: 129).

The principles espoused in the Belmont Report now form the basis of institutional research ethics review requirements in a number of national settings,[14] where questions of ethics and evidence are brought together on a daily basis at countless research ethics committee meetings around the world. As Martyn Pickersgill (2012) observes, scientific evidence production is today is an 'ethical' business, and 'formal and informal ethical discourses and practices – what might be called "regimes of normativity" – structure scientific work and the meanings it is ascribed' (p. 579). Although all forms of research are subject to such requirements,[15] bioethicists have, for obvious reasons, taken a particular interest in medical experiments. Although RCTs were seen to raise a host of ethical issues that became the source of some of bioethicists' core concepts (clinical equipoise! therapeutic misconception![16]), they served to further legitimise bioethics as a field with a distinctive contribution to make to medical care and research. Bioethics, in turn, helped to legitimise RCTs, not only by providing a clear ethical justification for them, but by creating a very narrow lens through which their ethical dilemmas were conceptualised and ostensibly resolved.

However, the relationship between bioethics and evidence-based medicine hasn't just been unidirectional, with the former dictating the grounds of the latter; instead, it can be understood more in terms of mutual enablement and elaboration. In much the same way that bioethics has shaped the 'evidence' prioritised in evidence-based medicine, EBM techniques also increasingly shape bioethics.

The empirical turn in bioethics – 'evidence-based ethics' as it has been labelled – speaks to this influence (see Goldenberg 2005). In this framing, evidence-based ethics becomes the bioethical analogue to evidence-based medicine. According to one proponent:

> As in medical decisions based on evidence-based medicine, ethical decisions based on evidence-based ethics would involve conscientious and judicious use of the best evidence relevant to the care and prognosis of the patient to promote better informed and better justified ethical decision-making.
>
> *cited in Goldenberg 2005: 3*

Indeed, a growing number of Cochrane reviews[17] are dedicated to just such 'ethical' questions. For example, there are now systematic reviews devoted to examining the effectiveness of audio-visual materials in enhancing informed consent procedures for clinical trials (Synnot et al. 2014), and planned reviews on the effectiveness of 'extended discussion' of informed consent information for trial comprehension and participation (Hon, Narayan and Goh 2012). Thus, just as bioethical discourses structure scientific knowledge production, discourses on evidence simultaneously shape bioethics itself. Clearly evident is the ways in which 'science and ethics – or, more opaquely, but also more specifically, the normative per se – articulate with one another' (Pickersgill 2012: 597).

Yet, the relationship isn't always a seamless one, with each bolstering the values and principles of the other. In particular, the enshrinement of 'autonomy' as the core of bioethics often conflicts with the enshrinement of 'evidence' as the core of evidence-based medicine. After all, while EBM presents RCTs as a means to an end – i.e., a tool that physicians and patients can use to inform their decision making, it simultaneously tends to cast patient choice as superfluous. 'For if trials show which treatments are more effective and efficient than their alternatives, there is no further need to make decisions. Just go for the treatments the trials show to be best!' (Mol 2008: 54). Thus, in some respects EBM and the bioethical emphasis on patient-centredness can be seen as competing strategies (Armstrong 2007). That said, in many respects, this ambivalence is encoded into each movement itself: the tension between autonomy and beneficence/non-maleficence in one context (what happens if a patient doesn't want a treatment that will save his life or campaigns for one with no proven efficacy?) and the tension between scientific facts and patient values in the other.

As Mol (2008: 48) observes, under this framework, 'facts' are intrinsically separable from 'values'. This view assumes the existence of professionals who limit themselves to presenting facts and using instruments and tools. In the unfolding of a consultation, which is seen to progress in a linear fashion, the health professional is supposed to give information, after which the patient assesses his or her own values and comes to a decision. This ideal therefore presumes that choice occurs at a discrete moment in time, one embedded in the following sequence: physician presents (neutral) facts → patient makes (value-laden) choice → (technical) action results (Mol 2008: 62). Moreover, under the consumer/citizen model, while patients have the *right* to make *choices*, the *right choices* should be made – something I will discuss in further detail in Chapters 8 and 9.

Bioethics expands its gaze

Increasingly, however, bioethics has expanded its gaze *beyond* the individual patient–doctor relationship. Just as the principles of evidence-based medicine were taken up in allied health fields such as public health, bioethics too has increasingly turned its attention from the domain of patient–physician interactions to public and population health more broadly under the guise of 'public health ethics' (see Holland 2015).

In some respects, this can be partially understood as an effect of the expansion of evidence-based medicine itself. As its principles were exported into public and global health, RCTs became increasingly common in those fields and raised new ethical issues that bioethicists claimed a stake in solving. However, it is also an effect of a growing interest among bioethicists in the ethics of public health interventions. The AIDS epidemic was central to broadening the scope of bioethics, with core aspects of the field of public health ethics formulated in the context of concerns raised about practices such as compulsory HIV testing, mandatory reporting and quarantining (e.g., Mann 1997; Childress *et al.* 2002; Bayer and Fairchild 2004).

Although public health ethics is essentially a branch of bioethics, the field presents its mandate as distinct from that of medical ethics, based on the premise that the former deals with the *individual* and the latter with *populations* (see Mann 1997; Kass 2001; Childress *et al.* 2002; Bayer and Fairchild 2004; Bayer *et al.* 2007; Holland 2015). Indeed, a key assertion of public health ethics as it has solidified in the twenty-first century is that traditional bioethics is ill-equipped to deal with the ethical issues raised by public health, primarily because of the emphasis it places on individual autonomy (e.g., Kass 2001; Bayer and Fairchild 2004; Holland 2015). Nevertheless, the conceptual framework of public health ethics arguably reflects the core principles of bioethics itself; the difference is primarily in how the principles are weighted.[18]

In their influential article outlining the foundations of public health ethics, Childress[19] and colleagues (2002) discuss nine moral considerations for the field, including: producing benefits; avoiding, preventing and removing harms; producing the maximal balance of benefits over harms and other costs; distributing benefits and burdens fairly; respecting autonomous choices and actions; protecting privacy and confidentiality; keeping promises and commitments; disclosing information in a transparent fashion; and building and maintaining trust. These are essentially an elaboration of the principles Beauchamp and Childress initially outlined, although noteworthy is the relegated position of autonomy with respect to questions of efficacy. Indeed, the field has primarily been oriented to the question of when individual autonomy can be overridden in the name of public health.[20] In the words of Childress *et al.* (2002: 175): 'The ethical question then is, when can paternalistic interventions (defined as interventions designed to protect or benefit individuals themselves against their express wishes) be ethically justified if they infringe general moral considerations such as respect for autonomy, including liberty of action?'

However, some have argued that the language of bioethics is fundamentally inadequate for conceptualising the ethical issues inhering in public health. An early voice making this argument was Jonathan Mann (1997), who posited that 'human rights is a language most useful for guiding societal level analysis and work, while ethics is a language most useful for guiding individual behavior' (p. 10). In his view, the failure of public health to consider human rights was so entrenched that all public health policies and programmes should be assumed to be discriminatory until it could be proven otherwise (Mann 1997). Following Mann's lead, the concept of human rights is increasingly invoked as means of facilitating a more justice-oriented form of public and global health ethics (e.g., Mann 1997; Farmer and Campos 2004; Annas 2010).

Today the two fields are formally linked together in UNESCO's Universal Declaration on Bioethics and Human Rights (UNESCO 2005). Throughout the Declaration, 'human dignity' and 'human rights' are discussed in tandem and the traditional concerns of bioethics (benefit and harm, autonomy, consent, etc.) are combined with those of human rights (equality, justice and equity, non-discrimination, etc.). Indeed, some commentators argue that human rights will ultimately supersede bioethics, because it's better equipped to create binding global norms and uphold them (see Ashcroft 2010 for a discussion). Thus, in some respects we appear to have come full circle, with the languages of bioethics and human rights merging back together. However, as I discuss in Chapter 9, human rights is not necessarily the panacea such accounts suggest and assertions of its ability to remedy the limitations of bioethics are often based on a presumed opposition between freedom and power that deserves to be treated with some caution.

Conclusion

The explicit ethical turn in health and medicine can be traced to the era following the Second World War, when the principles later formalised in the fields of bioethics and human rights were first outlined. Although bioethical principlism was intensively criticised for its reductiveness, arguably this was also its primary attraction and a core reason why it was so widely taken up – both in medicine and ultimately beyond it. After all, here was a field that promised to provide answers to heretofore irresolvable ethical dilemmas. The values it espoused also aligned with a variety of disparate interests – from patient advocates and health care administrators to corporate entities. Importantly, although it enshrined 'autonomy' as its core orienting value, it also drew evidence into the realm of ethics, not just in terms of concepts such as maleficence and beneficence, but via the ways it directly inserted itself into the knowledge production process. Over the next two chapters I will consider these intersections between ethics and evidence, primarily through the lens of 'choice', focusing first on the ways in which it plays out in the context of informed consent and patient care and then on its invocation in relation to human rights and public health.

Notes

1 For this reason, attempting to delineate the field or isolate its central preoccupations in the way I'm attempting here is a challenging enterprise, one that can result in mischaracterisations and overgeneralisations (De Vries *et al.* 2006).
2 This is typically acknowledged by bioethicists themselves (see Faden and Beauchamp 1986).
3 Thomas Osborne presents this as Canguilheim's interpretation, but based on my reading of Canguilheim, this seems to be Osborne's particular gloss.
4 This aspect of the WHO definition has come under heavy fire ever since it was espoused, although the many critics have not succeeded to date in revising it (see Huber *et al.* 2011).
5 After all, declarations and covenants that promote human rights don't just set out noble aspirations, but theoretically enable claims and entitlements (O'Neill 2005).
6 Observers tend to point to the 1947 Nuremberg Code of Medical Research as providing the foundations of bioethics; however, I think this document is also important in establishing its central preoccupations. Moreover, while the World Health Organization was established in 1948, the Constitution was pre-circulated in the *American Journal of Public Health* in 1946, so it actually predates the Nuremberg Code.
7 The Nuremberg Code was created in the wake of the Nazi war crimes trials and contains 10 principles that should inform the conduct of medical experiments, most notably the principle of informed consent, which I will discuss in detail in Chapter 8.
8 Komesaroff (1995a) argues that in the 1990s there was an explosion of interest in medical ethics in the popular media and society at large. Likewise, Fox and Swazey (2008) highlight events in the 1990s – such as the cloning of 'Dolly' the sheep – as dramatically increasing the visibility and influence of bioethics.
9 I should also make it clear that these criticisms aren't restricted to bioethics, but have frequently been made of the larger field of ethics itself (e.g., Dancy 2004).
10 See also Clarke *et al.* (2007) for an extended discussion of the citizen–consumer model beyond the specific context of health care. Petersen and Lupton (1996) also discuss the logic of choice under the rubric of the 'healthy' citizen (see Chapter 3).
11 As Farmer and Campos (2004) note, the topic of medical rationing, with its implications of scarcity, is a staple in the bioethics literature.
12 Ashcroft and Viens are using the term 'clinical trial' as a synonym for RCTs more broadly. In their words, 'While clinical trials are most often used to test therapeutic pharmaceutical products, they can also be utilized to evaluate medical devices or surgical produces, plus other preventive, screening, detection, and non-pharmacological therapeutic products/methods' (Ashcroft and Viens 2008: 201).
13 The Tuskegee Syphilis Study was funded by the US Public Health Service between 1932 and 1972, when it was shut down following a newspaper exposé and the resultant public outcry. In the study, poor black sharecroppers in Alabama, 399 of whom had (or developed) syphilis, were followed over time to study the natural course of the disease. They were not explicitly told they had syphilis or treated for the disease, although penicillin was endorsed as being effective in the 1940s. In conjunction with the Nazi concentration camp experiments, the study forms part of the 'obligatory history' section of virtually all texts about research ethics (Fitzgerald 2004) and is typically used to explain why institutional ethics oversight of research involving humans is a natural and necessary response to the issues it poses. As Melissa McCullough (2010: 60) observes,

> Atrocities such as were perpetuated by the Nazi regime, [and] the today unthinkable Tuskegee syphilis experiment . . . have proven time and again to be quick

reminders to those who dare complain about the heavy regulation they are subjected to when undertaking a research project today.

14 For example, the Canadian human research ethics guidelines list three core principles: respect for persons, concern for welfare and justice (CIHR, NSERC, SSHRC 2014); and the Australian human research ethics guidelines list four: research merit and integrity, justice, beneficence and respect for persons (NHMRC, ARC, AV-CC 2015). These are clearly minor reworkings of the Belmont principles.

15 Although the Belmont Report had an underlying biomedical orientation, the principles it espoused were generalised to social science and psychological as well as medical research (see Schrag 2010). I don't have space to elaborate on what I suspect are some paradigmatic connections, but there are interesting parallels with the ways that the scope of evidence-based medicine expanded to encompass complex social phenomena (see Chapter 6). That said, I think it does speak to the *unassailability* of evidence and ethics, such that certain versions of both exerted a kind of irresistible pull that led to successive expansions in their scope.

16 See Chapter 5, note 12 for a discussion of clinical equipoise and the Conclusion for a discussion of therapeutic misconception.

17 These reviews are primarily conducted by the Cochrane Consumers and Communication Group, whose slogan is 'Trusted Evidence. Informed decisions. Better Health'. Apparent here is the way in which notions of evidence have become strongly tied up with the notion of the agentic patient-consumer who makes informed health care choices. These themes will be discussed in detail in Chapter 8.

18 For example, Nancy Kass (2001) argues that the founders of bioethics articulated principles equally relevant for public health, but 'the more specific action guides and codes of health care ethics that have followed are an imperfect fit for public health' (p. 1776).

19 Childress was the second author of the *Principles of Biomedical Ethics* (1979).

20 This question is also frequently discussed with reference to the much older philosophical frameworks of 'consequentialism' and 'deontology'. In essence, the former philosophy judges moral value based on consequences and the latter asserts that moral value is independent of such. Public health ethicists typically advocate a mixture of both philosophical frameworks, although heavier weight has traditionally been placed upon consequentialism as a means of determining the ethics of public health interventions (as the framing of the question itself suggests).

References

Annas, G.J. (2010) Human rights and American bioethics: Resistance is futile. *Cambridge Quarterly of Healthcare Ethics*, 19: 133–141.

Armstrong, D. (2006) Embodiment and ethics: Constructing medicine's two bodies. *Sociology of Health and Illness*, 28(6): 866–881.

Armstrong, D. (2007) Professionalism, indeterminacy and the EBM project. *BioSocieties*, 2: 73–84.

Armstrong, D. (2014a) Actors, patients and agency: A recent history. *Sociology of Health and Illness*, 36(2): 163–174.

Armstrong, D. (2014b) Chronic illness: A revisionist account. *Sociology of Health and Illness*, 36(1): 15–27.

Ashcroft, R.E. (2010) Could human rights supersede bioethics? *Human Rights Law Review*, 10(4): 639–660.

Ashcroft, R.E. and Viens, A.M. (2008) Clinical trials. In P.A. Singer and A.M. Viens (eds), *The Cambridge Textbook of Bioethics*. Cambridge, MA: Cambridge University Press, pp. 201–206.

Baker, R. (2002) Bioethics and history. *Journal of Medicine and Philosophy*, 27(4): 447–474.

Bayer, R. and Fairchild, A. (2004) The genesis of public health ethics. *Bioethics*, 18(6): 473–492.

Bayer, R., Gostin, L.O., Jennings, B. and Steinbock, B. (2007) Introduction: Ethical theory and public health. In R. Bayer, L.O. Gostin, B. Jennings and B. Steinbock (eds), *Public Health Ethics: Theory, Policy, and Practice*. Oxford: Oxford University Press, pp. 1–24.

Beauchamp, T.L. and Childress, J.F. (1979) *Principles of Biomedical Ethics*. New York: Oxford University Press.

Bosk, C.L. (1999) Professional ethicist available: Logical, secular, friendly. *Daedalus*, 128(4): 47–68.

Bosk, C.L. (2008) *What Would You Do? Juggling Bioethics and Ethnography*. Chicago, IL: University of Chicago Press.

Brody, H. (1997) Biomedical ethics and cultural diversity. *Indian Journal of Pediatrics*, 64(3): 277–284.

Callahan, D. (1973) Bioethics as a discipline. *Hastings Center Studies*, 1(1): 66–73.

Canguilhem, G. (1989) *On the Normal and the Pathological*. Dordrecht: D. Reidel Publishing Company.

Chambers, T. (1999) *The Fiction of Bioethics: Cases as Literary Texts*. London: Routledge.

Childress, J.F., Faden, R.R., Gaare, R.D., Gostin, L.O., Kahn, J., Bonnie, R.J., Kass, N.E., Mastroianni, A.C., Moreno, J.D. and Nieburg, P. (2002) Public health ethics: Mapping the terrain. *Journal of Law, Medicine and Ethics*, 30: 170–178.

CIHR, NSERC, SSHRC (2014) *Tri-Council Policy Statement: Ethical Conduct for Research Involving Humans*. Ottawa: Canadian Institutes of Health Research, National Science and Engineering Research Council and Social Sciences and Humanities Research Council.

Clarke, J., Newman, J.E., Smith, N., Vidler, E. and Westmarland, L. (2007) *Creating Citizen-Consumers: Changing Publics and Changing Public Services*. London: Sage.

Clouser, K.D. and Gert, B. (1990) A critique of principlism. *Journal of Medicine and Philosophy*, 15: 219–236.

Cochrane, A.L. (1972) *Effectiveness and Efficiency: Random Reflections on Health Services*. London: Nuffield Trust.

Dancy, J. (2004) *Ethics Without Principles*. Oxford: Oxford University Press.

De Vries, R. and Subedi, J. (eds) (1998) *Bioethics and Society: Constructing the Ethical Enterprise*. Upper Saddle River, NJ: Prentice Hall.

De Vries, R., Turner, L., Orfali, K. and Bosk, C. (2006) Social science and bioethics: The way forward. *Sociology of Health and Illness*, 28(6): 665–677.

Donohue, J. (2006) A history of drug advertising: The evolving roles of consumers and consumer protection. *Milbank Quarterly*, 84(4): 659–699.

Faden, R.R. and Beauchamp, T.L. (1986) *A History and Theory of Informed Consent*. New York: Oxford University Press.

Farmer, P. and Campos, N.G. (2004) Rethinking medical ethics: A view from below. *Developing World Bioethics*, 4(1): 17–41.

Fitzgerald, M.H. (2004) Punctuated equilibrium, moral panics and the ethics review process. *Journal of Academic Ethics*, 2: 315–338.

Fox, R.C. and Swazey, J.P. (2008) *Observing Bioethics*. New York: Oxford University Press.

Goldenberg, M.J. (2005) Evidence-based ethics? On evidence-based practice and the 'empirical turn' from normative bioethics. *BMC Medical Ethics*, 6: 11.

Greco, M. (2004) The politics of indeterminacy and the right to health. *Theory, Culture and Society*, 21(6): 1–22.

Guillemin, J. (1998) Bioethics and the coming of the corporation in medicine. In R. De Vries and J. Subedi (eds), *Bioethics and Society: Constructing the Ethical Enterprise*. Upper Saddle River, NJ: Prentice Hall, pp. 60–77.

HHS (1979) *The Belmont Report: Ethical Principles and Guidelines for the Protection of Human Subjects of Research*. US Department of Health and Human Services. Available at: www. hhs.gov/ohrp/humansubjects/guidance/belmont.html (accessed 15 May 2010).

Hon, Y.K., Narayanan, P. and Goh, P.P. (2012) Extended discussion of information for informed consent for participation in clinical trials. *Cochrane Database of Systematic Reviews*, 5. Art no.: CD009835.

Holland, S. (2015) *Public Health Ethics*. Second edition. Cambridge: Polity Press.

Huber, M., Knottnerus, A., Green, L., van der Horst, H., *et al.* (2011) How should we define health? *British Medical Journal*, 343: d4163.

Jennings, B. (1998) Autonomy and difference: The travails of liberalism in bioethics. In R. De Vries and J. Subedi (eds), *Bioethics and Society: Constructing the Ethical Enterprise*. Upper Saddle River, NJ: Prentice Hall, pp. 258–269.

JME Editors (1975) Editorial. *Journal of Medical Ethics*, 1(1): 1.

Kass, N.E. (2001) An ethics framework for public health. *American Journal of Public Health*, 91(11): 1776–1782.

Komesaroff, P.A. (1995a) From bioethics to microethics: Ethical debate and clinical medicine. In P. Komesaroff (ed.), *Troubled Bodies: Critical Perspectives of Postmodernism, Medical Ethics, and the Body*. Melbourne: Melbourne University Press, pp. 62–86.

Komesaroff, P.A. (ed.) (1995b) *Troubled Bodies: Critical Perspectives of Postmodernism, Medical Ethics, and the Body*. Melbourne: Melbourne University Press.

McCullough, M. (2010) One size does not fit all: The ethical imperative to limit the concept of research exceptionalism. *American Journal of Bioethics*, 10(8): 60–61.

Mann, J.M. (1997) Medicine and public health, ethics and human rights. *Hastings Center Report*, May–June: 6–13.

Mol, A. (2008) *The Logic of Care: Health and the Problem of Patient Choice*. London: Routledge.

Murray, S.J. and Holmes, D. (2009) Introduction: Towards a critical bioethics. In S.J. Murray and D. Holmes (eds), *Critical Interventions in the Ethics of Healthcare: Challenging the Principle of Autonomy in Bioethics*. Farnham: Ashgate, pp. 1–14.

NHMRC, ARC, AV-CC (2015) *National Statement on Ethical Conduct in Human Research*. Canberra: National Health and Medical Research Council, Australian Research Council, Australian Vice-Chancellors' Committee.

O'Neill, O. (2005) The dark side of human rights. *International Affairs*, 81: 427–439.

Osborne, T. (1997) Of health and statecraft. In A. Petersen and R. Bunton (eds), *Foucault, Health and Medicine*. London: Routledge, pp. 173–188.

Petersen, A. (2011) *The Politics of Bioethics*. London: Routledge.

Petersen, A. and Lupton, D. (1996) *The New Public Health: Health and Self in the Age of Risk*. London: Sage.

Pickersgill, M. (2012) The co-production of science, ethics, and emotion. *Science, Technology, and Human Values*, 37(6): 579–603.

Rauprich, O. and Vollmann, J. (2011) 30 years of *Principles of Biomedical Ethics*: Introduction to a symposium on the sixth edition of Tom L Beauchamp and James F. Childress' seminal work. *Journal of Medical Ethics*, 37(10): 582–583.

Redding, P. (1995) Science, medicine, and illness: Rediscovering the patient as a person. In P.A. Komesaroff (ed.), *Troubled Bodies: Critical Perspectives of Postmodernism, Medical Ethics, and the Body*. Melbourne: Melbourne University Press, pp. 87–102.

Reich, W.T. (1994) The word 'bioethics': Its birth and the legacies of those who shaped it. *Kennedy Institute of Ethics Journal*, 4(5): 319–335.

Reubi, D. (2012) The human capacity to reflect and decide: Bioethics and the reconfiguration of the research subject in the British biomedical sciences. *Social Studies of Science*, 42(3): 348–368.

Reubi, D. and Mold, A. (2013) Introduction: Global assemblages of virtue and vitality: Genealogies and anthropologies of rights and health. In A. Mold and D. Reubi (eds), *Assembling Health Rights in Global Context: Geneaologies and Anthropologies*. London: Routledge, pp. 1–19.

Schrag, Z.M. (2010) *Ethical Imperialism: Institutional Review Boards and the Social Sciences, 1965–2009*. Baltimore, MD: Johns Hopkins University Press.

Sulik, G.A. and Eich-Krohm, A. (2008) No longer a patient: The social construction of the medical consumer. In S.M. Chambré and M. Goldner (eds), *Patients, Consumers and Civil Society* (Advances in Medical Sociology, Volume 10). Emerald Group Publishing, pp. 3–28.

Synnot, A., Ryan, R., Prictor, M., Fetherstonhaugh, D. and Parker, B. (2014) Audio-visual presentation of information for informed consent for participation in clinical trials. *Cochrane Database of Systematic Reviews*, 5. Art. no.: CD003717.

UNESCO (2005) Universal Declaration on Bioethics and Human Rights. *United Nations Educational, Scientific and Cultural Organization*. Available at: www.unesco.org/new/en/social-and-human-sciences/themes/bioethics/bioethics-and-human-rights/ (accessed 21 February 2016).

Walker, K. (2009) My life? My choice? Ethics, autonomy, and evidence-based practice in contemporary clinical care. In S.J. Murray and D. Holmes (eds), *Critical Interventions in the Ethics of Healthcare: Challenging the Principle of Autonomy in Bioethics*. Farnham: Ashgate, pp. 15–32.

Walker, M.U. (2009) Introduction: Groningen naturalism in bioethics. In H. Lindemann, M. Verkerk, and M.U. Walker (eds), *Naturalized Bioethics: Toward Responsible Knowing and Practice*. New York: Cambridge University Press, pp. 1–20.

Wolpe, P.R. (1998) The triumph of autonomy in American bioethics: A sociological view. In R. De Vries and J. Subedi (eds), *Bioethics and Society: Constructing the Ethical Enterprise*. Upper Saddle River, NJ: Prentice Hall, pp. 38–59.

World Health Organization (WHO) (1946) *Constitution of the World Health Organization*. New York: International Health Conference.

Zielinska, A.C. (2015) Moral principles and ethics committees: A case against bioethical theories. *Ethics and Social Welfare*, 9(3): 269–279.

8

CONSENT AND THE INFORMED PATIENT

Introduction

The prostate specific antigen (PSA) test is the most common cancer-screening tool given to men in Canada today (Beaulac, Fry and Onysko 2006; CPAC 2009). Men often seek it out and many prostate cancer support organisations strongly endorse it. For example, Prostate Cancer Canada, a patient advocacy organisation, through their 'Know Your Number' campaign, recommends that Canadian men first start getting PSA tests in their forties and urges men at high risk for cancer to discuss getting tested even earlier. Yet, despite its popularity, the test is marred by controversy. In a 2010 op-ed piece in the *New York Times*, Richard Ablin, the researcher who discovered the test, condemned its use as a screening tool, labelling it a 'hugely expensive public health disaster' (see also Ablin and Piana 2014). Quite simply, Ablin argued, the evidence is clear that the test is not effective in this context – 'hardly more effective than a coin toss'. Quoting a recent study, Ablin (2010) observed that it

> showed a small decline in death rates, but also found that 48 men would need to be treated to save one life. That's 47 men who, in all likelihood, can no longer function sexually or stay out of the bathroom for long.

Although not a bioethicist, the structure of his argument takes a classic ethical form:[1] is one life saved worth 47 lives dramatically – and unnecessarily – compromised?

A recent Cochrane review on prostate cancer presents us with an answer to the dilemma Ablin raises (a dilemma, it must be said, founded in the distinctive epidemiological reasoning of evidence-based medicine). To quote from the review:

> Pooled data currently demonstrates no significant reduction in prostate cancer-specific and overall mortality. Harms associated with PSA-based

screening and subsequent diagnostic evaluations are frequent, and moderate in severity. Men should be informed of this and the demonstrated adverse effects when they are deciding whether or not to undertake screening for prostate cancer.

Ilic et al. *2013: 2*

Based on this logic, once patients are *informed*, they can then decide for themselves whether to proceed with the test.

In this chapter I focus on 'informed consent' and its corollary: the 'informed patient'. The former represents the primary means through which the bioethical principle of autonomy is operationalised in health care and is arguably its most important contribution to medical practice. I begin with a discussion of the emergence of informed consent and how it differed from the notions of consent that preceded it before turning to its relationship with 'evidence-based' decision-making. This, I suggest, has served to inflect it in particular ways that reinforce the assumption that there are 'right' and 'wrong' choices to be made. I then return to the topic of cancer screening as a means of illustrating the assumptions underpinning the concept of informed consent and the problems with its conception of individual agency.

The emergence of 'informed consent'

As I discussed in Chapter 7, 'respect for autonomy' is perhaps the most cherished principle in mainstream bioethics. Although the term 'autonomy' has various meanings in the literature (e.g., self mastery, the freedom to choose, accepting responsibility for one's own decisions), it's most concretely operationalised in the doctrine of 'informed consent'. In essence, informed consent is the 'regulatory mechanism of autonomy' (Wolpe 1998: 47).

According to Faden and Beauchamp (1986), informed consent contains three elements: 1) the patient (or research subject) must agree to an intervention based on an understanding of relevant information; 2) consent must not be controlled by influences that engineer the outcome from the outset; and 3) the consent must involve the intentional and explicit granting of permission for an intervention.[2] While acknowledging the debate over the extent to which informed consent existed prior to the twentieth century, Faden and Beauchamp argue that twentieth-century articulations of the concept are substantively different from those that preceded them. The crux of the change, they suggest, lies in a shift from beneficence to autonomy as an underlying principle. Thus, disclosure was no longer determined exclusively by the physician's goal of providing medical benefits (which, in some circumstances, might be deemed to preclude disclosure) but became instead seen as a means of respecting autonomy. According to Faden and Beauchamp, the notion of educating patients did become more important in medicine in the late eighteenth century – as evidenced in the writings of the physician and social reformer Benjamin Rush – but this was primarily to increase patient compliance with physician advice. In their words, 'Rush was not advocating informed consent; he wanted patients to be sufficiently educated so that they could understand physicians' recommendations and therefore be motivated to *comply*' (Faden and Beauchamp 1986: 65, emphasis in original).

Faden and Beauchamp argue that the right of informed consent as it is currently conceptualised didn't become apparent until the 1950s and 1960s, attributing it to the issues raised by the civil rights, women's rights and consumer rights movements. In their words,

> these urgent societal concerns helped reinforce public acceptance of the notion of rights as applied to health care. At the same time, the Nazi atrocities and the celebrated cases of abuse of research subjects in the United States raised suspicions about the general trustworthiness of the medical profession.
> *Faden and Beauchamp 1986: 87*

In this account, the rise of informed consent, as with the emergence of bioethics more broadly, is framed as a natural outcome of social progress.

There is little question that the 1947 Nuremberg Code articulates a view of 'voluntary consent' that closely resembles the later formal definitions of 'informed consent'.[3] According to the Code:

> The voluntary consent of the human subject is absolutely essential. This means that the person involved should have legal capacity to give consent; should be so situated as to be able to exercise free power of choice, without the intervention of any element of force, fraud, deceit, duress, over-reaching, or other ulterior form of constraint or coercion; and should have sufficient knowledge and comprehension of the elements of the subject matter involved, as to enable him to make an understanding and enlightened decision.
> *US Military Tribunal 1949*

Here, we clearly see traces of what later became the trinity of elements constituting informed consent: information, comprehension and voluntariness. However, Fox and Swazey (2008) point out that the Code was infrequently cited in medical journals prior to the 1970s.

There is general agreement that the 1979 Belmont Report (HHS 1979) placed the concept of 'informed consent' at the centre of the bioethical apparatus (see Chapter 7). As Fox and Swazey (2008: 128) note, the Report has since attained 'venerated status' in the field of bioethics, and its influence has extended well beyond the context of research into medical practice and health care more broadly. Although the report espoused three core principles: respect for persons, beneficence and justice, the first, manifested in the requirement for informed consent, was arguably the most important. Today, formal informed consent requirements are conceptualised as technologies of dialogue and respect (Reubi 2012) and govern research involving human subjects and health care itself (Faden and

Beauchamp 1986). Moreover, as a broader value, informed consent is expected to underpin encounters between physicians and patients. Patients, in this framing, have the right (and responsibility, but we'll get to that) to make an *informed decision* about their health care.

Producing informed consent

Numerous scholars have observed that the notion of informed consent is based on a particular view of the clinical (and research) encounter, and what constitutes decision-making in this context. As noted in Chapter 7, bioethics was framed in terms of rejecting paternalistic attitudes in order to create a new, more ethical, relationship between doctor and patient; in doing so, a space was opened up for intervention and reform (Reubi 2012). The core narrative thread in such accounts is as follows:

> As patients we are treated as objects and made passive. This is a bad practice that should be stopped. Patients deserve to be heard. They should be respected as subjects who have the right to make the crucial choices about their own lives for themselves.
>
> *Mol 2008: 7*

This, in turn, produces an accompanying narrative: that it's the duty of health care professionals to provide patients with information and then ask them what they want; that they can only act after the various available options have been explained to the patients and they have provided their explicit consent (Mol 2008: 234).

Underlying the notion of informed consent is the assumption that responsibility for decision-making has an objective, finite quality and that increasing one party's responsibility correspondingly reduces the other's. In this account, decision-making is a zero-sum game (Mendrick *et al.* 2010). In light of this framework, the literature on treatment decision-making generally relies on a dichotomy between the paternalistic physician and the one committed to patient autonomy (Sinding *et al.* 2010). Thus, recommendations for decision-making stress that patients should receive information about the various available options, reflect on it, weigh up the alternatives and then come to a decision (Mendrick *et al.* 2010). In this framework, the physician's role is perceived as essentially passive – or rather 'activating' (see Chapter 3); it's the patient who is active. As Sinding *et al.* (2010: 195) observe, the key institutional messages transmitted to patients in health care settings are: 'patients have options, medical knowledge is available to them, and decisions are theirs to make'.[4]

A certain kind of person is imagined in conceptions of informed consent: a *rational* person with the capacity to think, decide and act (Reubi 2012). In this framework, the patient also has a *responsibility* to make choices. As David Reubi (2012: 357) points out, under such conceptions, they are not allowed to remain in ignorance; 'they have no right to "choose not to choose"'.[5] After all, choice is what transforms the patient from an *object* into a *subject* (Mol 2008). It therefore becomes an unassailable ethical good, even if, in some instances, choice may need to be forced upon people (Reubi 2012) and is thus experienced as a kind of violence (cf. Murray and Holmes 2009). Here we see a crystallisation of the 'militaristic and melodramatic view of individual agency' that Lauren Berlant (2011) has written about, where the human is cast as 'most fully itself when assuming the spectacular posture of performative action' (p. 96).

A certain kind of physician is also imagined. This new, more ethical, physician is one who presents options to the patient rather than telling them what to do. As Doug White (1995: 23) notes, 'current ideas of autonomy inhibit people from using their authority directly. Authority has to pretend it doesn't exist'. Importantly, this new physician not only presents options, she presents *evidence-based* ones. Sinding and colleagues (2010) argue that evidence-based medicine has activated new forms of physician–patient interactions – relations increasingly mediated by scientific evidence. In this framework (as Chapters 4 and 7 highlight), it's ideally[6] the physician's role to render a *neutral* accounting of statistical likely-to-happens that the patient can use to make an 'informed' decision. Based on research with women diagnosed with breast cancer, they illustrate the underground economy of advice and direction generated by the discourses and practices of patient empowerment and evidence-based medicine, as patients and physicians attempt to work with – and around – these expectations.

Another effect of the insertion of evidence-based medicine into the physician–patient relationship is the way it reinforces the notion that there are right and wrong choices to be made. As Sanders and Skevington (2004: 676) observe, 'if a well-informed patient expresses a preference that is in conflict with the research evidence, their choice may be considered to be irrational'. In other words, the rise of evidence-based decision-making inflects the notion of autonomy in a particular way, such that making the 'wrong' choice, by definition, becomes seen as the result of an information failure, and therefore not a *true* expression of autonomy at all. This is clearly illustrated in a Cochrane review titled 'Personalized risk communication for informed decision-making about taking screening tests' (Edwards *et al.* 2013). Naturally, only randomised controlled trials were included in the review and an examination of the outcome measures used for determining whether an 'informed' decision had been made is instructive. The primary outcome measure was individual scores on instruments such as the 'Multidimensional Measure of Informed Choice'; secondary measures included cognitive outcomes such as the accuracy of risk perception and behavioural outcomes such as the uptake of tests and – most tellingly – 'appropriate uptake' (Edwards *et al.* 2013: 12).

Cancer screening and questions of life and death

In what follows I want to return to the PSA test and a second cancer-screening technology: the cancer antigen 125 (CA125) test, as a means of exploring the assumptions underpinning notions of 'informed decision-making'. PSA and CA125 are proteins found in the blood that are respectively associated with possible or established prostate and ovarian cancer. Nevertheless, these tests are incorporated differently into cancer screening and monitoring. As noted at the outset, the PSA test is widely – if controversially – used as a screening tool for prostate cancer in asymptomatic men, despite the fact that arbiters of evidence-based medicine, such as the Cochrane Collaboration, advise against its use as a population-level screening tool. It's also a standard means of monitoring men treated for prostate cancer, although there are debates about the threshold for determining biochemical recurrence, whether biochemical recurrence accurately predicts clinical recurrence and when to embark on therapy after PSA levels have begun to rise (McLeod 2005; Lilja, Ulmert and Vickers 2008).

Unlike the PSA test, the CA125 test is not used in primary care settings as a screening tool unless women present with symptoms that suggest ovarian cancer or are otherwise deemed to be at high risk for the disease, such as those with mutations in the so-called breast cancer (BRCA) genes. Here, practice largely coheres with the evidence base,[7] with a variety of systematic reviews concluding that there is insufficient evidence to support population-level screening for ovarian cancer using the CA125 test because the harms associated with such screening outweigh any benefits (e.g., Fung *et al.* 2004; US Preventive Services Task Force 2004; Moyer and US Preventive Services Task Force 2012). Instead, the test is most widely used to monitor women treated for ovarian cancer, where it is typically incorporated into routine surveillance. However, a large randomised controlled trial (Rustin *et al.* 2010) has found that those patients treated once they were symptomatic, as opposed to when molecular signs of recurrence manifested (measured via a doubling of serum marker levels), fared no worse – suggesting no survival advantage from intensive CA125 surveillance. This has generated intensive debate about the utility of the test in monitoring women treated for the disease.

In both instances, the response to these controversies has been markedly similar. In much the same way that patients in primary care settings who request the PSA test are expected to be told of its limitations so they can make an 'informed choice' about whether to proceed with screening, recent reviews have concluded that CA125 monitoring in tertiary care settings should be individualised rather than routinely performed, based on patient preference (Marcus *et al.* 2014; Pepin *et al.* 2014). To quote Karam and Karlan (2010: 338),

> women who have completed their first-line chemotherapy for ovarian cancer and show no clinical evidence of disease should be informed about the usefulness and drawbacks of CA125 measurements and offered the choice to pursue periodic measurements as well as other surveillance.

In both instances we can clearly see the ways in which the notion of 'informed choice' mediates the gap between the population-level EBM assessments of effectiveness and the individual patient. Here, the responsibility is placed entirely on patient-choosers: equipped with the knowledge of the benefits and limitations of screening, they just have to decide what to do with this information (cf. Mol 2008: xii).

Clearly, there is much that is assumed in this framework. First, it is assumed that evidence-based medicine has provided us with the answers to questions about the efficacy of screening – a view that we have good reason to be suspicious of. Are RCTs an appropriate means of exploring the efficacy of screening? This would suggest that a clear cause–effect relationship between screening and cancer can be established, an assumption that deserves to be treated with some caution (see Chapters 3 and 5). It also assumes that we have a solid grasp of cancer itself and what exactly screening is detecting. However, as discussed in Chapter 3, the sum total of what we don't know about cancer vastly exceeds what we do. In the words of Lochlann Jain:

> Too wily to be tethered to a solid noun, the conundrums of cancer match its craftiness. Despite news articles promising a cure . . . scientists continue to furiously debate how cancer arises, whether it should be studied as one disease or hundreds, whether mice provide adequate research models, and who might benefit from the arsenal of commonplace, if dangerous, cancer treatments such as chemotherapy and radiation.
>
> *Jain 2013: 2*

Although there are definite social patterns in who gets cancer and who is more likely to die from it, it is popularly seen to be an equal opportunity disease – one that strikes rich and poor, young and old, and black and white alike. Moreover, people carrying malignant tumours often remain relatively asymptomatic until the disease is at an advanced stage; indeed, it's the *treatments* rather than cancer itself that cause many of the negative images we typically associate with it – bald heads, scarred bodies and so on (Bell 2009). Thus, much of the dread associated with the disease stems from the fact that it 'fills the role of an illness experienced as a ruthless, secret invasion' (Sontag 1990: 5).

Faced with a disease that continues to largely defy scientific attempts to understand how it grows and spreads, and the intense fear a diagnosis of cancer generates, cancer screening has arisen as a perceived partial answer. By and large, cancer prevention campaigns throughout the twentieth century have been highly successful in promoting the idea that early detection is the next best thing to prevention itself (Jain 2013). And, of course, this assumption isn't entirely wrong. As Jain (2013: 153) observes, 'Find a tumor early when it's small, and cut it out. This isn't just magical thinking: screening policies do correlate to stage-based survival data.'

It is also worth bearing in mind that epidemiology and evidence-based medicine, with their population-level statistics and cost-benefit analyses, say nothing about a particular person's individual destiny (see Chapters 1 and 4). Recall the equation presented by Richard Ablin, the founder of the PSA test, that '48 men would need to be treated to save one life. That's 47 men who, in all likelihood, can no longer function sexually or stay out of the bathroom for long.' Moreover, as Jain notes, while these sorts of tidy equations proliferate in discussions of cancer screening, comparisons of this kind require similar entities to be meaningful. Is a life ended (or saved) equivalent to a life impaired? Jain also points out that when human motivations confront cancer data, the objectivity of cost-benefit equations is called into question. What cost is worth what benefit? To whom? In what circumstances?

A perfect illustration of this point can be found in the 2006 film *Stranger than Fiction*, when the protagonist, Harold (Will Farrell) has just been told by Professor Jules Hilbert (played by Dustin Hoffman) that he is probably going to die shortly.[8] Harold is naturally distraught to hear this news, but Professor Hilbert encourages him to try and make the best of a bad situation. 'Hell, Harold,' he points out, 'you could just eat nothing but pancakes if you want.' Harold is not appeased. 'What's wrong with you?' he cries. 'Hey! I don't want to eat nothing but pancakes; I want to *live*. I'm mean, who in their right mind who had a choice between pancakes and living chooses pancakes?' Hilbert responds: 'Harold, if you paused to think I believe you'd realise that that answer is inextricably contingent upon the type of life being led and, of course, the quality of the pancakes.' His point is that such a question simply cannot be answered in the abstract; it depends entirely on *context*. Or, to return to the case at hand:

> It may matter if you've seen someone die of cancer. It may matter if you have a family history of cancer. It may matter if you think you are saving yourself or someone else. It may matter if you have a religious or ethical commitment to altruism.
>
> *Jain 2013: 175*

As soon as we examine personal accounts of the experience of these tests, the model of the autonomous patient rationally weighing up risks and benefits to come to a decision (facts → choice → action) flies out the window.

PSA screening: Richard's story

I met Richard[9] in 2008 at a Canadian prostate cancer support group where I was conducting fieldwork. A gay black man in his early fifties, he immediately stood out in a group that was predominantly white, heterosexual and over the age of 65 (a fact he was acutely aware of). Richard had a strong family history of prostate cancer on his mother's side. Indeed, when I asked him about his diagnosis with cancer three years earlier, this was where he started: not with his *own* story, but that of his *family*. In his words,

> a number of her uncles and first cousins of hers have dealt with it and passed away with [it] or whatever. And so, it's in my family. Being within the Black community as well, there seems to be a higher incidence of prostate cancer in North America in particular, I guess.

According to Richard, because of his family history, his physician had been proactive about doing annual digital rectal exams, but at the age of 49 Richard himself broached the possibility of a PSA test. He distinctly recalled making the request himself, reflecting:

> I'm trying to remember why at 49 I decided to do a PSA test, because I'm not one for needles and all that sort of stuff, and I would prefer to wait until I was 50 to start this. And so, for whatever reason at 49 I went in for a PSA test.

Clearly, although Richard presented his request to undergo PSA screening as a self-initiated decision, it was intimately bound up with his sense of personal anxiety about prostate cancer. For Richard, the odds were stacked against him from the outset because of his family history and ethnic background. Indeed, later in our conversation it became clear that the death of his mother's first cousin, Simon, from prostate cancer was instrumental to his decision to seek out the PSA test, as Simon's brother had 'made it aware to all family males – get checked . . . Because after watching what Simon went through and how he died, it's a horrible disease, you want to be catching this early'.

Richard wasn't immediately diagnosed with prostate cancer after being screened. He recounted that his reading came in at 2.6, a score his physician told him was slightly above the cut off for his age. However, because of his family history, the physician sent him to a urologist 'just to see'. According to Richard, he had another PSA test before his scheduled appointment with the urologist, and the urologist did a check up and assured him that his prostate was fine. He recalled asking the urologist what his PSA reading had been, noting:

> he flipped his charts and he came back and he said it was 3.0. Well, I started to panic. Not knowing very much about it at the time, I thought 'okay, why in three months has it gone from 2.6 to 3.0?'

His doctor reassured him that it was a very small rise, but offered to do a biopsy to ease Richard's mind. Richard decided to think about it and sought advice from family and friends about whether to proceed with the biopsy, recounting that his partner's brother emphatically counselled him to go ahead with it: 'He said, "You'd rather catch this early than late. Do it"'.

When I queried him about whether he was seriously concerned about cancer at this point, he thought about it and responded:

> No, I hadn't got there yet. Because I just felt, you know, I think I'm the type of person who knows their body and trusts their intuition and stuff like that, and I felt there really wasn't nothing wrong with me. But then, you know, I didn't know that much about prostate cancer at the time, and I guess with most cancers you don't really know you have a problem until it's too late, do you know what I mean?

With this awareness at the forefront, Richard decided to proceed with the biopsy, although he recounted his extreme anxiety in its lead up, and the pain of the procedure itself. Three weeks later he got the results: he didn't have prostate cancer, but was diagnosed with prostatic intraepithelial neoplasia, a condition that is thought to increase the risk of developing prostate cancer. This initiated a process wherein Richard's PSA levels were monitored every six months. His level at his next visit was lower, but a year later his PSA levels had returned to 3.0. At this point he decided to proceed with a second biopsy.

He had the second biopsy under similar circumstances to the first and, as he recounted it, found himself back in the urologist's office three weeks later: 'It was on a Wednesday, in October, October 6th I believe . . . I went on my way from work; it was about 4.30–5pm'. In the conversation that followed, Richard tearfully described both his shock and devastation upon being told that he had early-stage prostate cancer. Now, three years following treatment (at great personal expense he elected to have proton therapy in the United States), he was in generally good health, and informed me that he wasn't experiencing any treatment side effects – although 'my erections aren't what they used to be'. He continued to receive PSA tests every six months. In his words,

> my PSA is going down – as long as it goes down to like zero – my most recent reading was 0.48, so it's been steadily going down. At one time there was a slight bump up, nothing to be concerned about, but it's going down.

Richard considered himself to be one of the lucky ones; as he saw it, he had made a decision to have the PSA test based on his personal circumstances, and the test had saved his life.

CA125 monitoring: Anneke's story

Anneke was a member of a local ovarian cancer support group who got in touch in 2013 when she found out about my interest in talking to people about their experiences of cancer 'survivorship'. A white 55-year-old with three adult children, Anneke had previously worked in a high-level administrative position, although she was now on a disability allowance. Unlike Richard, Anneke recounted the circumstances of her diagnosis in a very matter-of-fact fashion, indicating that she had been diagnosed with ovarian cancer two years previously, after she had felt a 'very large lump' in her pelvic region. Concerned, she made a trip to see her family doctor, who performed a pelvic exam. According to Anneke, her doctor at this stage suspected ovarian cancer, but reassured her that it was probably just fibroids. She was given an ultrasound and a CA125 test, both of which indicated abnormalities, and was referred to the Vancouver Cancer Centre. She reported that she was then scheduled for a hysterectomy and ovarian cancer was confirmed at this stage. Following a bout of chemotherapy she was declared in remission, but, as is all-too-common with ovarian cancer, it recurred the following year.

At the time of the interview she had just completed a second round of chemotherapy, and the cancer was once again in remission, although she had resigned herself to a future marked by periods of remission and recurrence. In her words,

> The first time after I finished chemo I was quite cocky and I thought, 'oh, I've beat it!', you know. 'The chemo worked and, you know, I'm so great and I'm strong'. And I used to tell people, 'well, you know, it's good I was in pretty good shape before I got cancer, because, you know, I was able to get through it really well'. Well then, you know, a year goes by and then you're sick again and then you think 'oh, I didn't beat it', you know. 'It's back and I'm just like everybody else', you know, in my group, that gets it again and, you know, it makes you think 'oh, God, I'm going to get it a few times and then I'm going to die!'

In recounting her initial optimism that she could 'beat' cancer (which, from the vantage point of her subsequent recurrence, she clearly thought was naïve), she noted that her oncologist had reminded her that it was only a matter of when, not if, her cancer would recur. In Anneke's words, 'In fact, one Resident said at one point, he says, "Well, your CA125 is still, you know, below the level," and I said, "Not still, it's again!"'. Still implies that it's, you know, eventually going to go bad, right.'

When quizzed about her CA125 levels and how much attention she paid to them, Anneke noted that her oncologist

> is not too concerned about what the level is. And what they say is, you know, they look at the direction if it's increasing, but that they don't treat you unless there is, you know, clinical evidence, you know, that you have a pain, or you know, on the x-ray they can see a tumour; so in terms of that.

Indeed, as the conversation continued it became clear that a member of her health care team had recently raised the issue of whether she should continue to be monitored via the CA125 test now that she was once again in remission. As Anneke described it:

> She [the Resident] said: 'What do you want to do?' and I said: 'What do you mean?' And she said 'Well, in terms of follow-up?' And I said 'Well, I'd like to see the, you know, Dr. Marks [her primary oncologist] in three months and I'd like to have, you know, the blood check and the blood test [CA125]'. And she said, 'Well, it's not necessary'. And I said: 'Like, well, I want to be followed. I want to know what's going on in my body'. And she said 'Well, it's up to you'. And I thought that was very rude. So I don't know if that was her or if that's a change in how the Cancer Agency is dealing with their patients, or what.

Evident here is a clear disjuncture between the perspective of Anneke and that of her physician. From the physician's point of view, she was facilitating Anneke's informed decision about whether to proceed with the CA125 test, but Anneke clearly didn't see it in these terms.

Rethinking the autonomous patient

Clearly, although there are a number of differences between Richard and Anneke's cases, in both contexts, their health care providers arguably acted in accordance with the ideal of the autonomous patient. Although Richard didn't discuss whether the limitations of the PSA test were disclosed to him, it's likely that he was given a standard brochure on its benefits and limitations.[10] In any case, the decision to have the test was clearly his, and his physician complied with Richard's wishes. Likewise, Anneke's health care providers asked her whether she wanted to be monitored via the CA125 test after the completion of treatment, and she was informed of its limitations as a tool; the decision to continue with CA125 monitoring was clearly hers.

Yet, closer examination reveals the flaws in this view of the autonomous patient. Richard had already decided upon the test prior to seeing his physician – *compelled*, in large part, by the recent death of a family member and at the urging of the deceased's brother. While he didn't have any symptoms of prostate cancer, Richard was looking for a sign that would enable him to access the inner workings of his body, well aware that 'with most cancers you don't really know you have a problem until it's too late' – a refrain he repeated throughout the interview. Understood in this light, there was no real choice to be made. The perception of a lack of choice in this context isn't something that Richard can be emancipated from (cf. Mol 2008). After all, he either will or he won't get cancer; as Jain (2013: 167) observes, 'Meaningful individual prediction can't be definitively calculated for an individual until after one has, or has not, had cancer, at which point the chance will have been either 100 per cent or 0 per cent'. Here, we see the irresolvable gap between the statistics produced by evidence-based medicine and the individual patient. Anneke, on the other hand, was given the CA125 test as a diagnostic tool and her CA125 levels were regularly monitored during treatment. She witnessed them go down when the treatment worked; she witnessed them go back up when the cancer recurred. Like Richard, for Anneke the test provided access to the inner workings of her body: 'I want to know what's going on in my body,' she declared. Suddenly confronted with a situation where a test that she had come to rely on was potentially going to be taken away, she didn't perceive this as a choice but as a *punishment*[11] – as evidence that the Centre didn't care about her as an individual patient.

In many respects, these accounts both speak to the unruly nature of technologies. As Annemarie Mol (2008: 56) observes, 'Technologies do more than is expected of them. What is more: they also change expectations.' Thus, these technologies are far more fluid than the logic of choice assumes, while 'will and wishes are more constrained' (Mol 2008: 61). For Richard, the PSA test undoubtedly contributed to his perception of himself as being 'at risk' of cancer – something Chris Gillespie (2012, 2015) has explored at length. Indeed, the literature on PSA testing frequently highlights the paradoxical nature of the test: men seek it out to reduce their anxiety about prostate cancer (i.e., for 'peace of mind') but the test itself is anxiety-inducing, especially when men are waiting for results or their results indicate an elevated PSA level (Dale *et al.* 2005; see also Gillespie 2012). Implicit recognition of the fear the test generates is evident in the medical joke that PSA actually stands for 'patient-scaring antigen' (McLeod 2005: S29). Indeed, the social effects of screening are such that it arguably becomes a 'proto-illness' that significantly impacts the ordinary and mundane aspects of individual daily life (Gillespie 2015).

CA125 similarly comes to take on a marked significance for many women treated for ovarian cancer and I have previously explored the ways in which it becomes seen as an index of cancer itself (see Bell 2013). However, its context is also radically different from that of PSA screening. While the PSA test might actively produce a sense of anxiety and vulnerability, these feelings are integral to the experience of life post-diagnosis, regardless of the form surveillance takes. As Comaroff and Maguire (1981) note, the meaning of the term 'remission' is profoundly ambiguous, both clinically and experientially. Is the retreat of symptoms partial or total? This condition thus raises problems of meaning, especially for women diagnosed with ovarian cancer, where rates of recurrence are high. Thus, the absence of *symptoms* of disease provides little reassurance regarding the absence of disease itself. According to Jain (2007: 80):

> Cancer is creepy. After it shows up one realizes that it must have been there for a while, growing, dispersing, scattering, sending out feelers and fragments. After the treatments, often one hasn't any idea if it is still there, slinking about in organs or through the lymph system – those parts of the body you can't really even visualize.

Absence here is semiotically loaded. In such a context, it's hardly surprising that CA125 levels come to take on such significance for many women – and that losing access to them would be experienced as acutely distressing.

If anything, these accounts demonstrate the agency of the technology, as opposed to the agency of the individual patient. Yet, the two are often conflated in the ways that these tests are written about. For example, the well-documented tendency of women treated for ovarian cancer to become 'preoccupied' with their CA125 levels (see Bell 2013) is treated as a problem of patient misunderstanding, not an effect of the technology itself, with observers consequently pointing to the ways that patients *misuse* the technology. To quote the director of a Massachusetts gynaecologic oncology programme, 'Some physicians will treat (a patient) solely on an elevated CA125 with chemotherapy when patients are upset' (Chitale 2009: 1234). The underlying discourse here is of the emotional and misinformed patient (and the complicit physician who panders to her whims) inappropriately drawing on health care services – a focus that becomes explicit in the emphasis on health care costs that has accompanied debates about these markers (see Chitale 2009). The displacement of agency from the technology onto the patient therefore serves to actively *pathologise* the patient, while simultaneously affirming the value of agency itself as a means of overcoming the pathology it instils. The end result is the assertion of an individual will whose potency and value seem to become ever more absolute as every grounding possibility for its coming into existence recedes further away (cf. Sedgwick 1993).

Conclusion

While informed consent has been enshrined as an overarching value in patient care, it clearly relies on a number of assumptions: about the nature of decision-making, the ideal relationship between the physician and the patient, and, indeed, the ideal patient. In this framework, the patient has the right to make informed choices, but this entails responsibilities – not just to *actively* make choices but to make the *right* ones. Indeed, although the rise of evidence-based medicine hasn't dislodged the emphasis on patient choice, it has inflected it in particular ways, such that an 'informed' choice is one that ideally echoes its own calculus and logic. This notion of choice also relies on a conception of agency that reifies that of the individual patient and displaces that of everything else in such a way that evidence of deviations from it only serve to further entrench it as an ideal. In Chapter 9 I will be considering a companion concept to informed choice: that of 'rights', and the ways it too inscribes a particular view of individual agency and personhood.

Notes

1 Of course, the question doesn't just take an ethical form but an economic one as well, given that 'worth' is also being measured in economic terms. This economic logic has been thoroughly naturalised in bioethics, where, as I noted in Chapter 7, the notion of medical scarcity forms a core orienting concept.
2 That this framework maps directly onto autonomous action is evident in their definition of such: 'X acts autonomously only if X acts: 1) intentionally, 2) with understanding, and 3) without controlling influences' (Faden and Beauchamp 1986: 238).
3 However, as I mentioned in Chapter 7, the Constitution of the World Health Organization, which was circulated a year earlier, also stressed the importance of 'informed opinion' as a broader value.
4 They are talking specifically about cancer patients, but the point applies more broadly.
5 Reubi is talking specifically about conceptions of informed consent in research; however, much of the literature he discusses focuses on the clinical encounter as opposed to research contexts per se and it's clear that Reubi's points apply equally to both contexts.
6 Of course, we know from other research that this isn't always the case, as oncologists do often give recommendations on what treatment they think the patient should have (see, for example, Sanders and Skevington 2004).
7 Given that both tests involve similar problems as population-level screening tools, one might legitimately ask why the PSA test is much more commonly used. First, prostate cancer is a far more common malignancy than ovarian cancer, so its potential utility as

a population-level screening tool is seen to be higher. Second, PSA is a protein that's specific to the prostate, whereas CA125 is found in a variety of cells, although it's present in higher concentrations in ovarian cancer cells than other types. In other words, PSA is a more specific test than CA125. However, I suspect that other factors are also responsible – especially the rise of prostate cancer advocacy groups, many of which strongly endorsed the test and campaigned to increase awareness of it among the public. Ovarian cancer, on the other hand, has a far lower profile than breast cancer, for reasons that likely connect with the politics of cancer advocacy as much as its lower prevalence (see Klawiter 2008). The utility of the PSA test in prostate cancer screening was also studied earlier than the utility of CA125 in ovarian cancer screening. Notably, especially given the thrust of this book, its use in primary care settings began in the 1980s – before the EBM movement officially emerged. Thus, evidence of its limitations came to light *after* its usage had already become widespread instead of preceding it, as occurred with the CA125 test.

8 Harold has unwittingly found himself a character in a novel written by Karen Eiffel (Emma Thompson), an author who is famous for killing off her protagonists under tragic circumstances. He discovers this when his life starts to be audibly narrated (although no one except him can hear the narrator's voice). After ruling out schizophrenia, he seeks the counsel of Jules Hilbert, a literature professor.

9 All names are pseudonyms.

10 I didn't think to raise this at the time, because I had only recently embarked on the study and was not yet aware of the controversy surrounding it. However, the PSA test is not covered under the provincial medical services plan unless the patient has a family history of the disease, so there is a brochure given to patients who request it. Other men I talked with had been given the brochure, so I assume this is fairly standard, although Richard clearly would have qualified for coverage.

11 This speaks to my earlier points about the ways that choice can be experienced as a kind of violence.

References

Ablin, R.J. (2010) The great prostate mistake. *New York Times*. Available at: www.nytimes.com/2010/03/10/opinion/10Ablin.html?_r=1 (accessed 13 May 2012).

Ablin, R.J. and Piana, R. (2014) *The Great Prostate Hoax: How Big Medicine Hijacked the PSA Test and Caused a Public Health Disaster*. New York: Palgrave Macmillan.

Beaulac, J.A., Fry, R.N. and Onysko, J. (2006) Lifetime and recent prostate-specific antigen (PSA) screening of men for prostate cancer in Canada. *Canadian Journal of Public Health* 97(3): 171–176.

Bell, K. (2009) 'If it almost kills you that means it's working': Cultural models of chemotherapy expressed in a cancer support group. *Social Science and Medicine* 68 (1): 169–176.

Bell, K. (2013) Biomarkers, the molecular gaze and the transformation of cancer survivorship. *BioSocieties*, 8: 124–143.

Berlant, L. (2011) *Cruel Optimism*. Durham, NC: Duke University Press.

CPAC (2009) *PSA Toolkit: PSA Screening and Testing for Prostate Cancer*. Available at: www.sasksurgery.ca/pdf/psa-toolkit-prostate-screening-cpac-2009.pdf (accessed 22 October 2015).

Chitale, R. (2009) Monitoring ovarian cancer: CA125 trial stirs controversy. *Journal of the National Cancer Institute*, 101(8): 1233–1235.

Comaroff, J. and Maguire, P. (1981) Ambiguity and the search for meaning: Childhood leukaemia in the modern clinical context. *Social Science and Medicine*, 15B: 115–123.

Dale, W., Bilir, P., Han, M. and Meltzer, D. (2005) The role of anxiety in prostate carcinoma: A structured review of the literature. *Cancer*, 104(3): 465–478.

Edwards, A.G.K., Naik, G., Ahmed, H., Elwyn, G.J., Pickles, T., Hood, K. and Playle, R. (2013) Personalised risk communication for informed decision about taking screening tests. *Cochrane Database of Systematic Reviews*, 2. Art no.: CD001865.

Faden, R.R. and Beauchamp, T.L. (1986) *A History and Theory of Informed Consent*. New York: Oxford University Press.

Fox, R.C. and Swazey, J.P. (2008) *Observing Bioethics*. New York: Oxford University Press.

Fung, M.F., Bryson, P., Johnston, M., Chambers, A., Cancer Care Ontario Practice Guidelines Initiative Genecology Cancer Disease Site Group (2004) Screening post-menopausal women for ovarian cancer: A systematic review. *Journal of Obstetric and Gynaecology Canada*, 26(8): 717–728.

Gillespie, C. (2012) The experience of risk as 'measured vulnerability': Health screening and lay uses of numerical risk. *Sociology of Health and Illness*, 34(2): 194–207.

Gillespie, C. (2015) The risk experience: The social effects of health screening and the emergence of a proto-illness. *Sociology of Health and Illness*, 37(7): 973–987.

HHS (1979) *The Belmont Report: Ethical Principles and Guidelines for the Protection of Human Subjects of Research*. U.S. Department of Health and Human Services. Available at: www. hhs.gov/ohrp/humansubjects/guidance/belmont.html (accessed 15 May 2010).

Ilic, D., Neuberger, M.M., Djulbegovic, M. and Dahm, P. (2013) Screening for prostate cancer. *Cochrane Database of Systematic Reviews*, 1. Art no.: CD004720.

Jain, S.L. (2007) Living in prognosis: Toward an elegiac politics. *Representations*, 98: 77–92.

Jain, S.L. (2013) *Malignant: How Cancer Becomes Us*. Berkeley: University of California Press.

Karam, A.K. and Karlan, B.Y. (2010) Ovarian cancer: The duplicity of CA125 measurement. *Nature Reviews Clinical Oncology*, 7(July): 335–339.

Klawiter, M. (2008) *The Biopolitics of Breast Cancer: Changing Cultures of Disease and Activism*. Minneapolis: University of Minnesota Press.

Lilja, H., Ulmert, D. and Vickers, A.J. (2008) Prostate-specific antigen and prostate cancer: Prediction, detection and monitoring. *Nature Reviews Cancer*, 8: 268–278.

McLeod, D.G. (2005) The effective management of biochemical recurrence in patients with prostate cancer. *Urology*, 7(Suppl. 5): S29–S36.

Marcus, C.S., Maxwell, G.L., Darcy, K.M., Hamilton, C.A. and McGuire, W.P. (2014) Current approaches and challenges in managing and monitoring treatment response in ovarian cancer. *Journal of Cancer*, 5(1): 25–30.

Mendrick, N., Young, B., Holcombe, C. and Salmon, P. (2010) The ethics of responsibility and ownership in decision-making about treatment for breast cancer: Triangulation of consultation with patient and surgeon perspectives. *Social Science and Medicine*, 70: 1904–1911.

Mol, A. (2008) *The Logic of Care: Health and the Problem of Patient Choice*. London: Routledge.

Moyer, V.A. and US Preventive Services Taskforce (2012) Screening for ovarian cancer: U.S. Preventive Services Task Force reaffirmation recommendation statement. *Annals of Internal Medicine*, 157(12): 900–904.

Murray, S.J. and Holmes, D. (2009) Introduction: Towards a critical bioethics. In S.J. Murray and D. Holmes (eds), *Critical Interventions in the Ethics of Healthcare: Challenging the Principle of Autonomy in Bioethics*. Farnham: Ashgate, pp. 1–14.

Pepin, K., del Carmen, M., Brown, A. and Dizon, D.S. (2014) CA 125 and epithelial ovarian cancer: Role in screening, diagnosis, and surveillance. *American Journal of Hematology/Oncology*, 10(6): 22–29.

Reubi, D. (2012) The human capacity to reflect and decide: Bioethics and the reconfiguration of the research subject in the British biomedical sciences. *Social Studies of Science*, 42(3): 348–368.

Rustin, G.J., van der Burg, M.E., Griffin, C.L., Lamont, A., *et al.* (2010) Early versus delayed treatment of relapsed ovarian cancer (MRC OV05/EORTC 55955): A randomised trial. *The Lancet*, 376(9747): 1155–1163.

Sanders, T. and Skevington, S. (2004) Participation as an expression of patient uncertainty: an exploration of bowel cancer consultations. *Psycho-Oncology*, 13: 675–688.

Sedgwick, E.K. (1993) *Tendencies*. London: Routledge.

Sinding, C., Hudak, P., Wiernikowski, J., Aronson, J., Miller, P., Gould, J. and Fitzpatrick, D. (2010) 'I like to be an informed person but . . .': Negotiating responsibility for treatment decisions in cancer care. *Social Science and Medicine*, 71: 1094–1101.

Sontag, S. (1990) *Illness as Metaphor and AIDS and its Metaphors*. New York: Picador.

US Military Tribunal (1949) *Trials of War Criminals before the Nuremberg Military Tribunals under Control Council Law*. 10(2): 181–182.

US Preventive Services Task Force (2004) Screening for ovarian cancer: Recommendation statement. *Annals of Family Medicine*, 2(3): 260–262.

White, D. (1995) Divide and multiply: Culture and politics in the new medical order. In P.A. Komesaroff (ed.), *Troubled Bodies: Critical Perspectives on Postmodernism, Medical Ethics and the Body*. Durham, NC: Duke University Press, pp. 20–37.

Wolpe, P.R. (1998) The triumph of autonomy in American bioethics: A sociological view. In R. De Vries and J. Subedi (eds), *Bioethics and Society: Constructing the Ethical Enterprise*. Upper Saddle River, NJ: Prentice Hall, pp. 38–59.

9

HEALTH, CHOICE AND HUMAN RIGHTS

Introduction

Electronic cigarettes, better known as 'e-cigarettes',[1] are battery-powered devices that deliver varying levels of nicotine via an inhaled vapour. Launched internationally in 2006[2] by a Chinese electronics company, their extraordinary rise in popularity over the past decade has been accompanied by intense debate about their harms and benefits. Compounding the debates is the legislative confusion these products have engendered: should they be treated as medical devices (like nicotine replacement therapy) or recreational tobacco products (like cigarettes and smokeless tobacco) or something else entirely?

For many working in the field of tobacco control, e-cigarettes are merely the latest incarnation of the tobacco 'menace': an untested product with the potential to enslave ever-greater numbers of people – especially adolescents – to a dangerous addiction. This position has been adopted by the World Health Organization (WHO 2014), which recommends that party countries to the Framework Convention Alliance on Tobacco Control prohibit manufacturers from making claims about the potential of e-cigarettes as smoking cessation aids until they have been approved by a 'suitable regulatory agency' (e.g., based on existing standards for medical devices). It also advises that advertising, promotion and sponsorship be restricted and that use of the products be banned in places with existing smoke-free policies.[3]

For e-cigarettes advocates, on the other hand, they are an indisputably safer product than cigarettes, which have the potential to dramatically reduce the toll currently exacted by smoking. In their view, the opposition to e-cigarettes is based on overstated concerns and is symptomatic of the long-standing unwillingness on the part of public health organisations to take the possibility of tobacco harm reduction seriously. In response to efforts to restrict the use of e-cigarettes, access to them is increasingly framed as an issue of human rights. 'Ex-smokers have rights; and their rights include being allowed to stay alive and stay healthy' proclaims the *E-cigarette Politics* website (Price 2013): one of a growing number run by e-cigarette users, or 'vapers'. Likewise, the Consumer Advocates for Smokefree Alternatives Association states that the organisation was 'formed in 2009 by members of an online forum as an advocacy group to raise awareness and protect our right to access reduced harm alternatives' (CASAA 2012). 'I vape. I vote' has become an international catch-phrase for the vaping movement, with vapers urged to rally against local restrictions on usage and legislative efforts to restrict the sale of e-cigarettes.

My interest in this chapter is in exploring the ways in which 'rights' have increasingly been invoked in relation to health. Following a general overview of the rise of the concept of human rights, I focus specifically on their invocation in the field of harm reduction, focusing first on illicit drugs more broadly before discussing tobacco harm reduction in particular. In some respects, tobacco harm reduction isn't a very obvious context through which to explore the ways that human rights have been invoked in relation to health; after all, nicotine is a legal product and smokers can hardly claim to have been subject to the sorts of discrimination, abuse and neglect that typically accompany assertions of human rights. But for this very reason it crystallises in a particularly acute fashion the assumptions underpinning the concept of human rights itself. Indeed, the debate about e-cigarettes has come to centre on precisely the issues that form the heart of this book: namely, questions of health, evidence and ethics. Increasingly framed through the lens of 'evidence-based rights', it illustrates the ways in which these three values often serve to bolster each other and to what effect.

'Human rights' and its discontents

As noted in Chapter 7, contemporary conceptions of human rights are a product of the post-Second World War era (Asad 2003; Rabinow 2003; Reubi and Mold 2013; Zigon 2014). The explicit language of human rights dates from the formation of the United Nations and the subsequent Declaration of Human Rights. However, Jarrett Zigon (2013a: 56) argues that

> the language of human rights as established in the 1948 UN Universal Declaration of Human Rights fits perfectly into a number of already well-established discursive traditions such as natural law, liberalism, socialism, independence and liberation movements, and Catholicism to name only a few.

Indeed, rights discourses, like the discourses on ethics they accompanied and bolstered, have been around for centuries. For example, some historians date the 'invention' of human rights to the 1789 'Declaration of the Rights of Man and of the Citizen' adopted by France's National Constituent Assembly, and a key document in the French Revolution (Reubi and Mold 2013). However, what was distinctively new about the post-Second World War period was the notion that rights must be defended and protected in an extra-discursive institutional context – prior to 1945 there was no international legal framework for protecting individual human rights (Rabinow 2003: 22).

As with the field of bioethics, a linear narrative of hope and progress is typically invoked in discussions of the concept of human rights, with such rights represented as the self-evident and natural outcome of advances in social and political thought (Rabinow 2003; Reubi and Mold 2013; Zigon 2013b). However, as Paul Rabinow (2003: 23) points out, although proponents often claim that human rights discourses dominate the moral landscape, secular rights cultures, cultures of consumption and a diverse range of religious moral discourses 'remain potent contenders for the privilege of defining who speaks morally, how to speak morally, and what moral speaking is about'. Nevertheless, although human rights isn't the only language in which 'social crises might be diagnosed, the weak defended and substantial reform called for' (Asad 2003: 145), no other secular discourse is accorded the same legitimacy and power (Rabinow 2003; Zigon 2013b).[4] The ubiquity of this idiom has led to a veritable 'cornucopia of universal human rights' (O'Neill 2005: 428) replete with claims about abstract rights to all manner of goods and services (tobacco harm reduction being a case in point). Indeed, the sheer diversity of contexts in which human rights are invoked speaks to the ways that the concept functions as a floating signifier, one whose meaning is open to contestation and re-articulation by diverse (and even contradictory) parties (Zigon 2013a).

Health is one area where an abstract human right has been claimed, although the indeterminate nature of the concept as it was defined in the Constitution of the World Health Organization made such claims essentially aspirational (see Chapter 7). The notion of a discrete right to health coalesced further in the 1966 International Covenant on Economic, Social and Cultural Rights (see O'Neill 2005) and the Alma-Ata declaration of 1978 (see Tarantola 2008; Meier 2013; Reubi and Mold 2013),[5] but it wasn't until the rise of the HIV/AIDS epidemic in the late 1980s that health came to be more concretely articulated in terms of human rights. In activist responses to HIV/AIDS we see the first clear attempt to operationalise human rights, with the concept deployed in order to protect people from stigma and discrimination (Fee and Parry 2008; Tarantola 2008; Reubi 2011; Meier 2013; Reubi and Mold 2013; Zigon 2013b). Jonathan Mann, mentioned in Chapter 7, was a key figure in promoting HIV/AIDS as a human rights issue. The inaugural head of the World Health Organization's Global Programme on AIDS, Mann became concerned with tackling the discriminatory and punitive measures taken by medical agencies against people who were HIV positive, which he argued merely served to drive those infected underground (Fee and Parry 2008). He went on to establish a human rights office within the Global Programme, emphasising non-discrimination and equitable access to health care.

Such discourses on a 'human right to health', as with human rights discourses more broadly, assert a polemical contrast between notions of power and freedom;[6] in this framing, health is conceptualised as something to be defended, even, if necessary, against the authorities designated to protect it (Greco 2004). However, various social critics have challenged the view of power and freedom upon which this assertion rests. First, commentators have pointed to the ways in which human rights discourses become yet another form of power and domination (Reubi and Mold 2013). For example, the philosopher Slavoj Žižek (2004, 2005) has argued that this framing effectively depoliticises human rights and transforms them into a pre-political opposition between good and evil. Thus, 'while human rights pretend to be universal, they secretly privilege a western set of values so that their global imposition promotes western cultural imperialism' (Žižek 2004). Clearly, this is an extension of the arguments about bioethical imperialism discussed in Chapter 7 and the field's inability to recognise its own cultural embeddedness. Indeed, human rights discourses arguably *rely* on the elision of social and cultural context. In the words of Annelise Riles (2006: 54),

> Human rights rhetoric is effective only to the extent that it negates such contextually derived distinctions – to the extent that it is possible to claim that a human rights violation anywhere is of the same epistemological order and of the same moral, political, or legal significance as a human rights violation elsewhere.

The assumption that human rights claims represent freedom from power has also been heavily critiqued in the growing body of literature on their relationship with neoliberal forms of governance (see Goodale 2009; Zigon 2011, 2013a; Mold and Reubi 2013). As Reubi and Mold (2013) observe, health rights assemblages have engendered new subjectivities and notions of citizenship that presuppose and advance the figure of the individual subject who is free and responsible in relation to her health, body and life. In many respects, discourses on human rights are the flip side of the discourses on citizenship that preceded them – although the latter emphasised responsibilities and the former emphasises rights, these are two sides of the same coin (Seymour 2013). Petersen and Lupton (1996) have connected this conception of the 'right to health' with the rise of the new public health (see Chapter 1), pointing to the ways it has been 'rephrased as taking on personal responsibility for one's health by accepting and adopting imperatives issuing forth from the state and other health-related agencies concerning the maintenance and protection of good health' (p. 63).

Intersections between health, human rights and harm reduction

As Zigon's (2011, 2013a, 2013b, 2014) work illustrates, one area where human rights have increasingly been invoked is in relation to drug use, where the concept has been promoted as a way of advancing harm reduction agendas.[7] Indeed, in recent years, the global harm reduction movement has explicitly moved towards a human-rights-based approach (Ezard 2001; Keane 2003; Hunt 2004; Chen 2011). However, the intersections between the two movements exist on a variety of levels, as there are clear parallels between the growing prominence of the assertion of a human right to health in the 1990s and the mainstreaming of the concept of 'harm reduction' in the same period.

Although the philosophical roots of harm reduction can be traced to at least the 1960s,[8] its development into a coherent set of practices and ideas is connected with the rise of HIV/AIDS in the late 1980s, and the threat that injecting drug users were perceived to pose to the general population (Ezard 2001; Hunt 2004; Roe 2005; Smith 2012). Here, we effectively see the institutionalisation of harm reduction as public health policy (Smith 2012), although this occurred to differing degrees across national settings. For example, 'harm reduction' and 'harm minimisation' became catchphrases in national drug strategies in Australia in the mid-1980s (see Miller 2001) and in Canada in the late 1980s and early 1990s (see Roe 2005; Smith 2012). However, the concept of harm reduction has remained largely absent from US policy discourse – where invoked, it has often been utilised to support prohibitionist agendas (Hathaway 2001).

Various scholars have argued that the institutionalisation of harm reduction in public health policy has domesticated its central principles (see especially Roe 2005; Smith 2012), although there have always been tensions within the movement between those perceiving harm reduction as a medical means of promoting health and those seeing it as a platform for broader social and structural change (Roe 2005; see also Hathaway 2001; Miller 2001; Hunt 2004; Smith 2012). From a strategic perspective, the harm reduction movement has tried to navigate a middle ground between 'right-wing prohibitionists and anarchic libertarians, staking out the common ground between them' (Hathaway 2001: 126). In consequence, there are numerous versions of harm reduction; indeed, much like the concept of human rights, harm reduction seems to operate to some degree as a floating signifier, with a meaning open to contestation and re-articulation by diverse parties (cf. Zigon 2013a).

Such tensions are apparent in the ways that the concept of human rights has been incorporated into the harm reduction movement. Neil Hunt (2004) identifies two conceptually distinct versions of human rights in the field: a 'weak rights' version that prioritises health and a 'strong rights' version that more fully recognises people's rights to use drugs – even if they cause harm. The latter version of rights has its roots in the liberal philosophy of John Stuart Mill (1863), who argued that it was only acceptable to exercise power over an individual against his will when it involved potential harms to others. However, although the strong rights framing is often treated as prioritising individual rights over public health, this version of harm reduction *also* tends to be framed in terms of health. While the emphasis may have shifted from the 'endangerment' of the public to the 'entitlement' to use drugs (Hathaway 2001), many proponents of legalisation base their position on the net health and social benefits that will accrue for both the individual and the population (e.g., Wodak and Owens 1996).

Žižek (2004, 2005, 2012, 2014) argues that contemporary appeals to human rights within liberal-capitalist societies rest on the assumption that the two most fundamental rights are freedom of choice and the right to dedicate one's life to the pursuit of pleasure – as opposed to sacrificing it for a higher ideological cause. However, in this framework pleasure is conceptualised in very particular ways. Using the analogy of the 'chocolate laxative': 'a product that contains the agent of its own containment', Žižek argues that today's hedonism combines pleasure *with* constraint.

> Enjoyment is tolerated, solicited even, but on condition that it is healthy . . . chocolate, yes, but fat-free; Coke, yes, but diet; coffee, yes, but without caffeine; beer, yes, but without alcohol; mayonnaise, yes, but without cholesterol; sex, yes, but safe sex.
>
> *Žižek 2014*

Thus, contemporary pleasures are strictly regulated ones, deprived of their 'passionate excess' (Žižek 2012). In other words, this version of human rights has the pursuit of health *at its very core*.

Many observers have pointed to the shift that harm reduction paradigms evidence from coercive forms of power to 'more productive or even seductive techniques to elicit compliance through self-regulation' (Roe 2005: 245). Indeed, just as the human rights paradigm has been linked to neoliberal forms of governance (especially neoliberalism-as-governmentality), the same is also true of discourses on harm reduction (e.g., Miller 2001; Fischer *et al.* 2004; O'Malley and Valverde 2004; Roe 2005; Moore and Fraser 2006; Chen 2011; Smith 2012; Elliott 2014). In both instances, we see a particular conceptualisation of the sovereign individual centred on ideals of autonomy and rationality (Keane 2003). Thus, while the language of human rights could conceivably be used to legitimise actions that *counter* health as a kind of overarching master value (as in a right to use drugs, regardless of their personal costs), such rights are articulated in a manner that invariably bolsters a certain vision of the self and citizenship. This becomes particularly evident in the debate about e-cigarettes and the specific ways that tobacco harm reduction advocates have invoked the concept of 'rights'.

The 'right' to tobacco harm reduction

Today, cigarettes hold the dubious distinction of being the most lethal of all drugs, with morbidity and mortality rates exponentially higher than for alcohol and illicit drugs combined (Single *et al.* 1999; Rehm, Taylor and Broom 2006). As Nick, the tobacco lobbyist in Christopher Buckley's satirical novel *Thank You For Smoking*, observes in an argument with Polly, an alcohol lobbyist,

> I'll put my numbers against your numbers any day. My product puts away 475,000 deaths a year. That's 1,300 a day . . . So how many alcohol related deaths a year? A hundred thousand, tops. Two hundred and seventy something a day. Well wow-ee.
>
> *Buckley 1995: 128*

Although nicotine is the addictive ingredient in tobacco, the harms associated with smoking stem primarily from the carcinogens in cigarette smoke rather than nicotine itself. While the long-term effects of nicotine haven't been well studied, and both its potential therapeutic benefits and carcinogenic properties remain contested, available evidence suggests that nicotine is not in itself particularly harmful (e.g., Waldum *et al.* 1996; Le Houezec 1998). Nor does it impair consciousness in the manner of other licit and illicit drugs; indeed, it often enhances it. Thus, in contrast to recreational drugs such as alcohol, heroin or cocaine, tobacco's main advantage is its compatibility with the requirements of everyday life (Keane 2002). For these reasons, it's perhaps the clearest instance of a drug where the mode of delivery rather than the drug itself causes harm; indeed, it has become a truism in tobacco harm reduction that 'people smoke for nicotine but they die from the tar' (Russell 1976: 1431).[9]

Despite the distinctive attributes of cigarettes and nicotine, as Britton and Edwards (2008: 442) observe: 'Effective harm reduction strategies, and particularly the option of providing nicotine without smoke as an acceptable long-term or even lifelong substitute for smoking, have not been widely applied to tobacco smoking'. This careful statement disguises the passions that the topic of tobacco harm reduction currently arouses. Today there are two distinct and mutually hostile camps working in the fields of public health and tobacco control: the majority who oppose tobacco harm reduction as a myth and a minority who support it as a way of reducing smoking and its associated health effects. Thus, the current debates about e-cigarettes have merely exacerbated fault lines that have long existed regarding the best ways to respond to the smoking 'problem' and the viability of alternative forms of nicotine in reducing its impact.

Since the turn of the twenty-first century, tobacco harm reduction advocates have increasingly invoked the concept of human rights as a way of challenging the continuing marginalisation of harm reduction approaches within tobacco control. In essence, the language of human rights has been explicitly deployed to present tobacco harm reduction as a more *ethical* approach to tobacco use. To quote Lynn Kozlowski:

> The principle of protecting the health of the public has been offered, then, as one guiding principle in the development of harm reduction products; but these major works offer no consideration of another established principle: the human right of individuals to receive information relevant to their health and their health choices . . . If people are deprived of information relevant to their health, they will necessarily be deprived of choices that might protect their health.
>
> *Kozlowski 2002: S55–S56*

Elsewhere, Kozlowski and Edwards (2005: ii3) expand on this point, arguing that depriving people of their right to reduced-harm tobacco products undermines the principles of autonomy and self-determination. They continue: 'The principles of autonomy and self determination are also the basis of the doctrine of informed consent. Individuals cannot make autonomous, informed choices about their lives without pertinent and accurate information' (Kozlowski and Edwards 2005: ii3). Here, the terminologies of human rights, bioethics and public health (and, indeed, evidence-based medicine[10]) are utilised as mutually reinforcing principles. The central thrust of Kozlowski and Edwards' argument is that the prevailing tobacco control message that 'there is no safe tobacco product' is misleading because it obfuscates the fact that while smokeless tobacco products might not be 'safe' in an absolute sense, they are unquestionably much safer than cigarettes. Therefore, disguising this information violates the human right of individuals to receive honest and accurate health information. Once again, we see the ways in which (evidence-based) information is seen to facilitate autonomy (see Chapter 8), and, by implication, better *choices*. Here, the human right to tobacco harm reduction is invoked using the logic of choice outlined in Chapter 7.

This is precisely the position taken by e-cigarette advocates. For example, in response to the World Health Organization's conservative stance on e-cigarettes, 53 researchers (including many leading harm reduction advocates) from 18 countries sent an appeal to the Director General, Dr Margaret Chan, in May of 2014. The open letter lists 10 principles that the authors suggest should underpin public health approaches to e-cigarettes and includes statements such as:

> Tobacco harm reduction is strongly consistent with good public health policy and practice and it would be *unethical and harmful to inhibit the option to switch to tobacco harm reduction products*. As the WHO's Ottawa Charter states: 'Health promotion is the process of enabling people to increase control over, and to improve, their health'. Tobacco harm reduction allows people to control the risk associated with taking nicotine and to reduce it down to very low or negligible levels.
>
> *Abrams* et al. *2014, emphasis added*

Notably, evidence-based arguments are given equal weight to ethics- and rights-based arguments in the letter; indeed, they are treated as inextricably linked. For example, a second principle states that: 'Tobacco harm reduction policies should be evidence-based and proportionate to risk, and give due weight to the significant reductions in risk that are achieved when a smoker switches to a low risk nicotine product' (Abrams *et al.* 2014). In the first instance, recourse is made to the language of ethics and in the second to the language of evidence, but both are invoked as a means of expressing the same idea: that e-cigarettes enable people to *control* and *minimise* risks to their health.

E-cigarettes and evidence-based rights

As discussed in Chapter 4, advocacy movements are increasingly articulating their goals and agendas in terms of 'evidence' rather than explicit ideological or moral claims. Thus, it should come as little surprise that where human rights claims are made, they are expected to be backed up by evidence – especially of the kind prioritised in the hierarchies established by evidence-based medicine (Storeng and Béhague 2013; Storeng and Béhague 2014). Drawing on their work with an advocacy group aiming to galvanise international action on the high levels of maternal mortality in the global South, Storeng and Béhague (2013) highlight the rise of what they term 'evidence-based rights': 'a new type of "rights-based approach" that brings together legal and scientific rationales to substantiate their claim that maternal mortality is a human rights issue' (p. 163).

It's this same notion of 'evidence-based rights' that we see articulated in e-cigarette advocacy, with an ideological battle essentially couched in technocratic language (cf. Storeng and Béhague 2013). Indeed, the authors of the letter present their principles as an 'evidence-based' intervention into prevailing orthodoxy, with Principle 9 asserting: 'WHO and national governments should take a *dispassionate* view of scientific arguments and not accept or promote flawed media or activist misinterpretations of data' (Abrams *et al.* 2014, emphasis added). The problem, of course, is that critics of tobacco harm reduction *also* claim to be dispassionate assessors of the evidence. For example, in a response to the letter, Stanton Glantz, a long-standing tobacco control advocate, submitted a second letter – this one signed by 129 'experts' from 31 countries. The letter begins:

> Recently, media attention was focused on a statement by a group of 'specialists in nicotine science and public health policy'. Unfortunately, the statement makes several assertions about ENDS' [electronic nicotine delivery systems] marketing, emissions, harms, and use that are either contradicted by available evidence or for which no evidence is currently available. (Indeed, the statement does not cite a single scientific study.)
>
> *Aktan* et al. *2014*

The authors cite 43 studies to support their assertion that the WHO's hard-line stance on e-cigarettes is warranted, in a tactic clearly designed to demonstrate that *they* are the 'evidence-based' side and their interlocutors are the biased ones. The response will hardly surprise the reader: the original letter writers responded with a *third* letter challenging the claims made by their critics and systematically interrogating their analysis of the evidence.

This pattern of claims and counter-claims (and counter-counter-claims) has been replicated, virtually unchanged, in a variety of publications on e-cigarettes and the commentaries they have generated.[11] In attempting to explain these disparate interpretations of the evidence, Fairchild and Bayer (2015: 375) argue that: 'it is not evidence alone that accounts for this pitched battle. The opposing letters reflect very different understandings of what the protection of public health requires.' They assert that these contrasting interpretations are largely an effect of two clashing ethical principles: harm reduction versus the precautionary principle, with the former supporting a pragmatic stance in relation to risk and the latter encouraging a conservative one, based on the view that endorsing a product with lesser harms is tantamount to giving the tobacco industry a carte blanche.[12] However, this analysis assumes that 'facts' are separable from 'values', a view I have taken some pains to challenge throughout this book. Indeed, if the debates about e-cigarettes have shown us anything, it is that these products are so 'beautifully complex and entangled' (cf. Latour 2004: 234) they resist attempts to separate the two.

Embracing evidence-based rights is clearly a pragmatic response to altered political realities in public and global health that have accompanied the rise of evidence-based medicine, but it fosters a heavy reliance on purportedly objective claims rather than explicitly challenging the ideological basis upon which decision-making takes place (Storeng and Béhague 2013). In other words, ethics and rights become discursively transformed into second-order issues tied to questions of evidence. As I discussed in Chapter 4, advocacy becomes redefined as the translation of research into action, with proponents required to set themselves up in the role of 'neutral purveyors of evidence'.

It also has the effect of naturalising a number of assumptions about why people smoke (and vape). As I outlined in Chapter 2, prevailing approaches to smoking as a 'health behaviour' are underpinned by a causal, linear narrative: that people use tobacco because they are addicted and can't stop; that they lack an awareness of the health consequences of tobacco use; and they lack the self-control or self-efficacy to resist peer pressure and/or manipulation by the tobacco industry (Mair and Kierans 2007). These assumptions, in turn, manifest in two seemingly contradictory views of the smoker: the 'rational agent' view and the 'Pavlovian automaton' view (see Macnaughton, Carro-Ripalda and Russell 2012).

Tobacco harm reduction narratives and the invocation of a right to 'reduced-harm' products similarly invoke the rational agent and the Pavlovian automaton fuelled by addiction. In this framework, 'Most people continue to smoke because they are addicted to nicotine' (Britton and Edwards 2008: 441). However, this 'fact' is perceived not only as the heart of the problem, but also the key to solving it. The goal therefore is to wean people off cigarettes by 'allow[ing] smokers to buy satisfying nicotine substitutes' (Laugesen *et al.* 2010: 3). Smokers are thus presented as rational consumers, who, if presented with the option for less harmful (albeit equally addictive) alternatives to smoking, will invariably take them. Here, the figure of the 'health conscious citizen capable of rational decision making, self-determination, self-regulation and risk management in order to minimise drug-related harm' (Moore and Fraser 2006: 3037) once again appears.

Rethinking the harm-reducing, nicotine-addicted subject

But what if people smoke for reasons beyond addiction? What if the pleasures of smoking are inextricably bound up with its risks? What if not everyone is attracted to vaping merely out of a desire to choose a healthier 'nicotine delivery device'? (Indeed, what if such medicalised framings themselves put some smokers off e-cigarettes?[13]) These questions are almost impossible to reconcile with the smoker/vaper articulated in the dominant tobacco harm reduction discourses on e-cigarettes. On one level, this is hardly surprising, given the alarmist claims about e-cigarettes as a 'gateway' to smoking that characterise much of the mainstream opposition to these products (see Bell and Keane 2014) and the alacrity with which any talk of pleasure is immediately used to condemn them.[14] However, it's also a product of the discursive transformation of smoking into 'nicotine addiction' (see Bell and Keane 2012; Hughes 2014; Elam 2015). As Jason Hughes (2014) notes, 'we have come to think of smoking as *essentially a means of nicotine self-administration*' (p. 177, emphasis in original).

David Moore (2008) has observed that in the field of harm reduction the pleasures of drug use are subjugated knowledges elided by the dominant discourses of medicine, psychology and epidemiology (see also O'Malley and Valverde 2004; Race 2008 for similar points). Echoing mainstream harm reduction discourse, the pleasures of smoking tend to be articulated exclusively in terms of the nicotine hit cigarettes provide. The language here is that of 'satisfying cravings' and pleasure is reframed as a neurological disorder produced by the release of dopamine; for the most part, a positive element of actively seeking pleasure or enjoyment doesn't enter into the picture (Keane 1999; O'Malley and Valverde 2004). For example, Laugesen *et al.* (2010: 7) argue that: 'At low doses, nicotine loses its ability to provide smoking pleasure. Smoking a reduced nicotine content cigarette . . . though sufficient to relieve cravings . . . does not release dopamine, the pleasure drug, and so the cigarette does not satisfy'. Thus, advocates focus exclusively on finding a product that delivers the benefits of nicotine with the fewest harms; in other words, they search for tobacco's equivalent of the 'chocolate laxative' (Žižek 2004). While I have no doubt that many smokers have indeed turned to e-cigarettes as a healthier alternative to smoking, framing e-cigarettes exclusively in terms of a human right to reduced-harm products entails the assumption that there are 'right' (and wrong) reasons for using them and that smokers will make the decision to 'choose' health. This has the effect of delegitimising engagements with the products outside of these terms.

Although I haven't specifically sought out vapers to interview, in the course of other research projects I have occasionally stumbled across smokers who have tried and are actively using e-cigarettes. One such encounter occurred in the summer of 2014 when I met Grace as she was enjoying a cigarette outside a Vancouver pub before heading inside to meet her husband. A well-preserved white woman of 66, Grace was originally from Scotland – her family had migrated to Canada when she was nine years old. Grace started smoking when she was about 15 and had been doing it 'off and on' ever since. When I asked how much Grace was smoking at the moment, she indicated that she had recently cut back on her cigarette consumption. In her words, 'Ah, I smoke about a pack every two days, because I use the – also the – what do you call 'em? Those menthol – those electronic [ones].'

Excited, I informed her that she was the first smoker I'd interviewed who was actively using them and then asked, 'How are you finding them?', acknowledging that this question was 'a bit off topic' (the interview was ostensibly about her views on cigarette packaging). Grace responded, 'Oh, they're wonderful! Because my husband's a non-smoker, so when we go home, have a glass of wine on the weekends or something I can sit and have a puff inside.' Rather than follow up on that line of thought, I interrupted, saying somewhat dismissively: 'Right, right. So have you noticed for you if it's helped you cut back?' Having effectively cut her off, it's little surprise that Grace responded with a monosyllabic 'Yes.' I prompted again: 'Okay, because there's so much debate happening about e-cigarettes at the moment.' Another 'yep' from Grace followed. Wanting her to say more, but unsure of how to encourage her, I continued: 'There's all this scare-mongering.' 'It's so silly.' Grace agreed. I nodded and observed: 'It's a bit of a pity because it seems like if it's working for people why – ?' At this point, Grace interrupted with: 'It's steamed – and it's nice. Smoking as a habit is just putting something in our mouth and going out and smoking.'

In hindsight, what I find noteworthy about this exchange is that I was the one who kept trying to draw e-cigarettes into a health frame, not Grace. Although she politely agreed with my rather leading statements about cutting back, scare-mongering and the like, her own responses (when I let her make them!) focused on aspects of vaping *entirely removed from questions of health*. For Grace, e-cigarettes were 'wonderful' because they allowed her to have a glass of wine with her husband, who was a non-smoker, rather than being banished outdoors if she wanted to have a drink and 'a puff' at the same time (much as she was having to do at the pub where we met). She also thought they were 'nice' to use: she liked the steamed aspect of e-cigarettes and the way they replicated the hand-to-mouth action of smoking. During our conversation it became clear that she didn't see e-cigarettes as a permanent 'replacement' for smoking; nor was her exclusive goal in using them to improve her health – although she clearly saw this as a side benefit.

Interestingly, when she invoked the language of 'rights' and 'choice' in the interview, it wasn't to justify her *vaping* but her *smoking*. For example, when I asked Grace about her views on cigarette warning labels, she emphatically asserted that they had no effect on her smoking, continuing: 'It's my decision. No one else's! And it *is* legal.' This led to a discussion about attitudes towards smoking in Vancouver, with Grace observing the irony that an ostensibly legal activity seemed to be more frowned upon than marijuana use.[15] In her words, 'What I find, too, is that some of the people that *really* go against people who are smoking, they go and they toke a bit. I mean, hello?!?' She concluded, 'we should just let people have their choice!' Thus, Grace essentially invokes her right to choose *against* health. However, although smokers frequently invoke the notion of rights in this fashion, such claims are not treated as credible. Instead, they are dismissed as mimicking tobacco industry rhetoric (which has long marketed smoking as an 'adult choice'),[16] based on the underlying assumption that the autonomy of smokers has been compromised by their addiction. What rational person would *choose* to go against health? The very assertion of such a right thus becomes proof positive of their imperfect autonomy. This speaks to the ways in which the legitimacy of rights-based claims have become tied to a certain kind of 'rational' subject.

However, one of the effects of the discourse on the 'right' to a 'reduced-harm' product is that it entirely prefigures the terms of engagement with these products (something I clearly played into myself in my conversation with Grace). For example, the International Tobacco Control Survey is an ongoing longitudinal survey that evaluates key policies of the WHO's Framework Convention on Tobacco Control; it is therefore extremely influential in terms of setting international tobacco control agendas. In light of their growing popularity, questions on e-cigarettes are now incorporated into the survey, but in very particular ways. Smokers who indicate that they have used e-cigarettes are asked why they started using them and are given six 'yes' or 'no' responses to choose from: 1) they may not be as bad for your health; 2) they taste better; 3) they are cheaper than regular cigarettes; 4) you can smoke in places where smoking regular cigarettes is banned; 5) to make it easier to cut down on the number of cigarettes you smoke; and 6) as a way to help you quit (Hummel *et al.* 2015). As should be evident, the reasons why people might choose to vape e-cigarettes are predefined in ways that emphasise health and downplay other reasons for using them beyond price. The only question that moves outside this frame (#2) does so indirectly; questions of pleasure and enjoyment are almost entirely elided. Through such renderings, e-cigarettes become discursively transformed into a 'smoking cessation intervention' and are evaluated exclusively on this basis.

But the reality is that some smokers may not want tobacco harm reduction's version of the chocolate laxative, where nicotine is permitted, so long as it is deprived of the substance that makes it dangerous. As Richard Klein (1993: 1) has observed, understanding the health effects of smoking is not usually sufficient reason to cause anyone to quit or resist starting in the first place. Moreover, the rapid rise of a vaping subculture, where e-cigarette enthusiasts come together at regional festivals and share nicotine solution recipes and product reviews suggests there are serious pitfalls with treating them merely as a healthier alternative to smoking. While some distributors of e-cigarette products tout their health benefits, others speak only of pleasure – such as Pink Spot Vapors in Las Vegas, whose slogan is 'Happy vaping! This juice will hit the spot'. Thus, while the assertion of a 'human right' to 'safer' forms of nicotine is potentially a politically useful tool for legitimising e-cigarettes (although time will tell on that front), it provides an extremely narrow base on which to advocate them, one that links them to the evidence hierarchies established by evidence-based medicine and conceptualises their effects solely in terms of health. It also configures rights in such a way that they advance an all-too-familiar subject – one who makes a 'rational' decision to 'choose' health. As Klein (1993: 185) asks: 'What is the value assigned to health that makes it, in this case, the criterion of what is good and beautiful?'

Conclusion

While the invocation of human rights may be a powerful way of calling for reform, it comes at a price. The concept of human rights is clearly premised on certain assumptions about the relationship between power and freedom, and the individual and the state. But instead of 'liberty' and 'health' being treated as oppositions, as they tend to be conceptualised in public health ethics (see Chapter 7), here they collapse into each other. Thus, we see another kind of invocation of the subject at the heart of the concept of informed consent: one who is rational and autonomous, but whose rationality and autonomy are simultaneously linked with their capacity to make certain kinds of 'choices' (and seen to be in jeopardy if they don't). It seems that we simply can't get away from the figure of the health conscious citizen who rationally chooses health.

Notes

1 The term 'e-cigarettes' covers a variety of quite different products – from devices that look like traditional cigarettes ('cig-a-likes'), to larger devices that bear little physical resemblance to cigarettes and look more like large pens or even small torches.

2 Different dates are given for the launch of e-cigarettes – both 2003 and 2006 are commonly cited.

3 In response, many local jurisdictions have extended existing smoke-free legislation to cover e-cigarettes. For example, the City of Vancouver has banned them in all public spaces where smoking is prohibited (e.g., indoor environs, parks, beaches, semi-enclosed bus stops, etc.) and they are subject to the same advertising and sales restrictions as tobacco products.

4 Unless, that is, one includes scientific discourses on 'evidence'.

5 This declaration was adopted at the International Conference on Primary Health Care, held in Almaty, Kazakhstan (then, Alma-Ata, Kazakh Soviet Socialist Republic) and became the basis of the WHO's optimistic goal of 'Health for All by 2000'.

6 This same view of the relationship between power and freedom pervades the field of bioethics, and is particularly evident in its conception of 'autonomy'. Thus, 'informed consent' and 'human rights' are paradigmatically connected.

7 As I go on to discuss, providing a straightforward definition of harm reduction is complicated; however, it's typically glossed as efforts aiming to ameliorate the negative impacts of drug use, as opposed to ending it entirely.

8 According to Hunt (2004), the philosophical origins of the movement can be traced back to the Rolleston Report of 1926, which helped to establish British policy towards opiates.

9 I will have more to say about these assertions later in the chapter.

10 This is evident in the reference to 'accurate information'.

11 For a recent illustration, see the report commissioned by Public Health England titled *E-cigarettes: An Evidence Update* (McNeill et al. 2015), the commentary on it published in the *British Medical Journal* (McKee and Capewell 2015), and the many responses it generated.

12 In these accounts, the tobacco industry and e-cigarette industries tend to be collapsed. Although a growing number of e-cigarette companies have been purchased by the tobacco industry, and many companies are experimenting with their own e-cigarette products, the e-cigarette industry emerged independently from the tobcaco industry.

13 As Jason Hughes (2014: 179) observes, it's precisely because e-cigarettes are 'not sanitised, not associated with illness and recovery, and are perhaps even glamorous, that for some users, they are a far more appealing alternative to combustible tobacco than NRTs [nicotine replacement therapies]'.

14 For example, one of the few pieces on e-cigarettes and tobacco harm reduction to explicitly tackle the topic of pleasure (Farsalinos and Stimson 2014) was criticised on precisely these grounds in a follow-up commentary, with the author noting, in tones

of deep suspicion, 'it is both remarkable and unusual to ever see researchers in the field of smoking and health mention "the positive experience of nicotine" and the "joy and pleasure" of cigarettes' (Shatenstein 2014: 1148). He goes on to accuse the authors of being in the pocket of the e-cigarette and, by implication, tobacco industry.

15 This is a frequent observation among smokers I've interviewed in Vancouver (see Bell 2013), where medical use of cannabis has been legalised and open recreational consumption is widespread.

16 Smokers' rights groups (e.g., Forest) are typically dismissed as industy mouthpieces based on the fact that they receive industry funding.

References

Abrams, D., Axéll, T., Bartsch, P., Bauld, L. *et al.* (2014) Statement from specialists in nicotine science and public health policy. Available at: http://nicotinepolicy.net/documents/letters/MargaretChan.pdf (accessed 10 December 2015).

Aktan, O., Alexanderson, K., Allebek, P., de Araugo, A.J. *et al.* (2014) 129 public health and medical authorities from 31 countries write WHO DG Chan urging evidence-based approach to ecigs. Available at: https://tobacco.ucsf.edu/129-public-health-and-medical-authorities-31-countries-write-who-dg-chan-urging-evidence-based-appro (accessed 10 December 2015).

Asad, T. (2003) *Formations of the Secular: Christianity, Islam, Modernity.* Stanford, CA: Stanford University Press.

Bell, K. (2013) Where there's smoke there's fire: Outdoor smoking bans and claims to public space. *Contemporary Drug Problems*, 40(1): 99–128.

Bell, K. and Keane, H. (2012) Nicotine control: E-cigarettes, smoking and addiction. *International Journal of Drug Policy*, 23(3): 242–247.

Bell, K. and Keane, H. (2014) All gates lead to smoking: The 'gateway theory', e-cigarettes and the remaking of nicotine. *Social Science and Medicine*, 119: 45–52.

Britton, J. and Edwards, R. (2008) Tobacco smoking, harm reduction, and nicotine product regulation. *Lancet*, 361: 441–445.

Buckley, C. (1995) *Thank You For Smoking.* New York: Harper Perennial.

CASAA (2012) About CASAA. *Consumer Advocates for Smokefree Alternatives Association.* Available at: http://casaa.org/About_CASAA.html (accessed 5 December 2015).

Chen, J-S. (2011) Beyond human rights and public health: Citizenship issues in harm reduction. *International Journal of Drug Policy*, 22: 184–188.

Elam, M.J. (2015) Nicorette reborn? E-cigarettes in light of the history of nicotine replacement technology. *International Journal of Drug Policy*, 26(6): 536–542.

Elliott, D. (2014) Debating safe injecting sites in Vancouver's inner city: Advocacy, conservatism and neoliberalism. *Contemporary Drug Problems*, 41: 5–40.

Ezard, N. (2001) Public health, human rights and the harm reduction paradigm: From risk reduction to vulnerability reduction. *International Journal of Drug Policy*, 12: 207–219.

Fairchild, A.L. and Bayer, R. (2015) Smoke and fire over e-cigarettes. *Science*, 347(6220): 375–376.

Farsalinos, K.E. and Stimson, G. (2014) Is there any legal and scientific basis for classifying electronic cigarettes as medications? *International Journal of Drug Policy*, 25: 340–345.

Fee, E. and Parry, M. (2008) Jonathan Mann, HIV/AIDS, and human rights. *Journal of Public Health Policy*, 29: 54–71.

Fischer, B., Turnbull, S., Poland, B. and Haydon, E. (2004) Drug use, risk and urban order: Examining supervised injection sitres (SISs) as 'governmentality'. *International Journal of Drug Policy*, 15: 357–365.

Goodale, M. (2009) *Surrendering to Utopia: An Anthropology of Human Rights*. Stanford, CA: Stanford University Press.

Greco, M. (2004) The politics of indeterminacy and the right to health. *Theory, Culture and Society*, 21(6): 1–22.

Hathaway, A.D. (2001) Shortcomings of harm reduction: Toward a morally invested drug reform strategy. *International Journal of Drug Policy*, 12: 125–137.

Hughes, J. (2014) E-cigarettes and the 'civilising' of smoking. *Cambio*, IV(7): 169–181.

Hummel, K., Hoving, C., Nagelhout, G.E., De Vries, H., van den Putte, B., Candel, M.J.J.M., Borland, R. and Willemsen, M.C. (2015) Prevalence and reasons for use of electronic cigarettes among smokers: Findings from the International Tobacco Control (ITC) Netherlands survey. *International Journal of Drug Policy*, 26(6): 601–608.

Hunt, N. (2004) Public health or human rights: What comes first? *International Journal of Drug Policy*, 15: 231–237.

Keane, H. (1999) Adventures of the addicted brain. *Australian Feminist Studies*, 14(29): 63–77.

Keane, H. (2002) Smoking, addiction, and the making of time. In J.F. Brodie and M. Redfield (eds), *High Anxieties: Cultural Studies in Addiction*. Berkeley, CA: University of California, pp. 119–133.

Keane, H. (2003) Critiques of harm reduction, morality and the promise of human rights. *International Journal of Drug Policy*, 14: 227–232.

Klein, R. (1993) *Cigarettes are Sublime*. Durham, NC: Duke University Press.

Kozlowski, L.T. (2002) Harm reduction, public health, and human rights: Smokers have a right to be informed of significant harm reduction options. *Nicotine and Tobacco Research*, 4 (Suppl. 2): S55–S60.

Kozlowski, L.T. and Edwards, B.Q. (2005) 'Not safe' is not enough: Smokers have a right to know more than there is no safe tobacco product. *Tobacco Control*, 14 (Suppl II): ii3–ii7.

Latour, B. (2004) Why has critique run out of steam? From matters of fact to matters of concern. *Critical Inquiry*, 30(2): 225–248.

Laugesen, M., Glover, M., Fraser, T., McCormick, R. and Scott, J. (2010) Four policies to end the sale of cigarettes and smoking tobacco in New Zealand by 2020. *The New Zealand Medical Journal*, 123(1314): 1–13.

Le Houezec, J. (1998) Nicotine: Abused substance and therapeutic agent. *Journal of Psychiatry and Neuroscience*, 23(2): 95–108.

McKee, M. and Capewell, S. (2015) Evidence about electronic cigarettes: A foundation built on rock or sand? *British Medical Journal*, 351: h4863.

Macnaughton, J., Carro-Ripalda, S. and Russell, A. (2012) 'Risking enchantment': How are we to view the smoking person? *Critical Public Health*, 22(4): 455–469.

McNeill, A., Brose, L.S., Hitchmans, S.C., Hajek, P. and McRobbie, H. (2015) *E-cigarettes: An Evidence Update*. London: Public Health England. Available at: www.eciginfo.us/uploads/2/5/1/1/25116158/ecigarettes_an_evidence_update_a_report_commissioned_by_public_health_england_final.pdf (accessed 10 December 2015).

Mair, M. and Kierans, C. (2007) Critical reflections on the field of tobacco research: The role of tobacco control in defining the tobacco research agenda. *Critical Public Health*, 17(2): 103–112.

Meier, B.M. (2013) The political evolution of health as a human right: Conceptualizing public health under international law, 1940s–1990s. In A. Mold and D. Reubi (eds), *Assembling Health Rights in Global Context: Geneaologies and Anthropologies*. London: Routledge, pp. 73–93.

Mill, J.S. (1863) *On Liberty*. Boston, MA: Ticknor & Fields.

Miller, P.G. (2001) A critical review of the harm minimization ideology in Australia. *Critical Public Health*, 11(2): 167–178.

Mol, A. (2008) *The Logic of Care: Health and the Problem of Patient Choice*. London: Routledge.

Mold, A. and Reubi, D. (eds) (2013) *Assembling Health Rights in Global Context: Geneaologies and Anthropologies*. London: Routledge.

Moore, D. (2008) Erasing pleasure from public discourse on illicit drugs: On the creation and reproduction of an absence. *International Journal of Drug Policy*, 19: 353–358.

Moore, D. and Fraser, S. (2006) Putting at risk what we know: Reflecting on the drug-using subject in harm reduction and its political implications. *Social Science and Medicine*, 62: 3035–3047.

O'Malley, P. and Valverde, M. (2004) Pleasure, freedom and drugs: The uses of 'pleasure' in liberal governance of drug and alcohol consumption. *Sociology*, 38(1): 25–42.

O'Neill, O. (2005) The dark side of human rights. *International Affairs*, 81: 427–439.

Petersen, A. and Lupton, D. (1996) *The New Public Health: Health and Self in the Age of Risk*. London: Sage.

Price, C. (2013) About us. *E-cigarette Politics*. Available at: www.ecigarette-politics.com/about-us.html (accessed 5 December 2015).

Rabinow, P. (2003) *Anthropos Today: Reflections on Modern Equipment*. Princeton, NJ: Princeton University Press.

Race, K. (2008) The use of pleasure in harm reduction: Perspectives from the history of sexuality. *International Journal of Drug Policy*, 19(5): 417–423.

Rehm, J., Taylor, B. and Room, R. (2006) Global burden of disease from alcohol, illicit drugs and tobacco. *Drug and Alcohol Review*, 25(6): 603–613.

Reubi, D. (2011) The promise of human rights for global health: A programmed deception? *Social Science and Medicine*, 73: 625–628.

Reubi, D. and Mold, A. (2013) Introduction: Global assemblages of virtue and vitality: Genealogies and anthropologies of rights and health. In A. Mold and D. Reubi (eds), *Assembling Health Rights in Global Context: Geneaologies and Anthropologies*. London: Routledge, pp. 1–19.

Riles A. (2006) Anthropology, human rights, and legal knowledge: Culture in the iron cage. *American Anthropologist*, 108(1): 52–65.

Roe, G. (2005) Harm reduction as paradigm: Is better than bad good enough? The origins of harm reduction. *Critical Public Health*, 15(3): 243–250.

Russell, M.A.H. (1976) Low-tar medium-nicotine cigarettes: A new approach to safer smoking. *British Medical Journal*, 1: 1430–1433.

Seymour, J.K. (2013) Not rights but reciprocal responsibility: The rhetoric of state health provision in early twentieth-century Britain. In A. Mold and D. Reubi (eds) *Assembling Health Rights in Global Context: Geneaologies and Anthropologies*. London: Routledge, pp. 23–41.

Shatenstein, S. (2014) Asking the wrong questions about e-cigarettes: The case for cautious classification. *International Journal of Drug Policy*, 25: 1147–1148.

Single, E., Robsin, L., Rehm, J. and Xi, X. (1999) Morbidity and mortality attributable to alcohol, tobacco, and illicit drug use in Canada. *American Journal of Public Health*, 89(3): 385–390.

Smith, C.B.R. (2012) Harm reduction as anarchist practice: A user's guide to capitalism and addiction in North America. *Critical Public Health*, 22(2): 209–221.

Storeng, K. and Béhague, D.P. (2013) Evidence-based advocacy and the reconfiguration of rights language in safe motherhood discourse. In A. Mold and D. Reubi (eds), *Assembling Health Rights in Global Context: Geneaologies and Anthropologies*. London: Routledge, pp. 149–168.

Storeng, K.T. and Béhague, D.P. (2014) 'Playing the numbers game': Evidence-based advocacy and the technocratic narrowing of the Safe Motherhood Initiative. *Medical Anthropology Quarterly*, 28(2): 260–279.

Tarantola, D. (2008) A perspective on the history of health and human rights: From the Cold War to the gold war. *Journal of Public Health Policy*, 29: 42–53.

Waldum, H.L., Nilsen, O.G., Nilsen, T., Rørvik, H. *et al.* (1996) Long-term effects of inhaled nicotine. *Life Sciences*, 58(16): 1339–1346.

WHO (2014) *Electronic Nicotine Delivery Systemas: Report by WHO*. Geneva: World Health Organization. Available at: http://apps.who.int/gb/fctc/PDF/cop6/FCTC_COP6_10Rev1-en.pdf?ua=1 (accessed 12 February 2016).

Wodak, A. and Owens, R. (1996) *Drug Prohibition: A Call for Change*. Sydney: University of New South Wales Press.

Zigon, J. (2011) *HIV is God's Blessing: Rehabilitating Morality in Neoliberal Russia*. Berkeley: University of California Press.

Zigon, J. (2013a) Rights, responsibility and health services: Human rights as an idiomatic language of power. In A. Mold and D. Reubi (eds), *Assembling Health Rights in Global Context: Geneaologies and Anthropologies*. London: Routledge, pp. 55–70.

Zigon, J. (2013b) Human rights as moral progress? A critique. *Cultural Anthropology*, 28(4): 716–736.

Zigon, J. (2014) Maintaining the 'truth': Performativity, human rights, and the limitations on politics. *Theory and Event*, 17(3).

Žižek, S. (2004) Iraq war, chips and chocolate laxatives. *Times Higher Education Supplement*. Available at: www.timeshighereducation.co.uk/story.asp?storyC (accessed 22 January 2013).

Žižek, S. (2005) Against human rights. *New Left Review*, 34: 115–131.

Žižek, S. (2012) The hedonist ideal. *Big Think*. Available at: http://bigthink.com/ideas/47376 (accessed 22 January 2013).

Žižek, S. (2014) Fat-free chocolate and absolutely no smoking: Why our guilt about consumpton is all consuming. *The Guardian*, 21 May. Available at: www.theguardian.com/artanddesign/2014/may/21/prix-pictet-photography-prize-consumption-slavoj-zizek (accessed 15 December 2015).

CONCLUSION

In this book my goal has been to understand how health is currently conceptualised, researched and intervened into. Grasping this topic requires an examination of a number of distinct areas, namely: epidemiology, evidence-based medicine and ethics (the three Es, if you will). But this isn't just a matter of epidemiology and evidence-based medicine shaping our 'facts' and ethics shaping our 'values'. As Steven Shapin (2010: 47) observes, 'Verity and virtue march in lock-step through history, as do error and evil.'

Throughout *Health and Other Unassailable Values* I have consistently tried to illustrate the ways in which these phenomena intersect. For example, there's no point in singling out evidence-based medicine for enshrining the randomised controlled trial as the gold standard evidence of efficacy. Without the rise of the 'new' epidemiology and the notions of probabilistic causality it introduced, the RCT could not have emerged, and without the ethical imprimatur bioethics accorded it, it could not have flourished. Likewise, without the concept of a 'health behaviour' in place, evidence-based medicine couldn't have taken a behavioural turn: complex social practices needed to be conceptualised as analogous to human physiology (i.e., isolable, intervenable) for 'behavioural' interventions to emerge and for the RCT to become a meaningful way of demonstrating their efficacy. The point is that the *unassailability* of health, evidence and ethics depends on the ways in which 'facts' and 'values' co-constitute each other. Indeed, I would suggest that one of the reasons why certain ideas and assumptions have been so intractable, despite the energetic critiques levelled against them, is because they are bolstered by a variety of different (albeit interconnected) edifices – it's just that some are more visible than others.

In some respects, the story I have told has been about standards and what happens as they solidify and become naturalised. What is evidence-based medicine if not an attempt to create *standards* for evidence and medical care?[1] And what are the fields of bioethics and human rights if not an attempt to create *standards* for human relationships – both in medical contexts and beyond them? As the growing body of research into the sociology of standards reveals, standards order the world in particular ways, with far-reaching social and political consequences (see Bowker and Star 1999; Lampland and Star 2009; Busch 2011).

This literature provides important insights into many of the topics I have explored in this book. As Star and Lampland (2009) observe, standards are nested and integrated: pull any strand and its effects are recursive throughout the system. Star and Lampland also point out that standards embody ethics and values – values that quickly become invisible. They also contain, and taxonomically constrain, messy reality: ordering it, simplifying it. Indeed, without standards, the contemporary world couldn't exist. But, once in place, standards are difficult to dislodge. According to Star and Lampland, in many cases they become functionally irreversible. (Imagine the effort required to change the meaning of a red light to 'go' and a green light to 'stop'!) Thus, it has become almost impossible to imagine how we could discuss evidence of efficacy *without* the RCT, despite its clear limitations. Abandoning the concept of informed consent becomes equally unfathomable. However, although it hasn't been a central preoccupation in this book, people don't just passively comply with standards. As Star and Lampland point out, they develop workarounds and engage in formal rather than substantive compliance. For example, as a number of empirical studies have demonstrated, the relationship between the *formal* rationality of EBM and *actual* clinical reasoning is complex rather than straightforward (e.g., Tanenbaum 1994, 1996; Armstrong 2002; Mykhalovskiy 2003; Timmermans and Berg 2003). Moreover, despite the rise of 'evidence-based policy', policies and practices in medicine and public health continue to veer from what research findings suggest to be desirable (Lin and Gibson 2002; Smith 2013) – to the extent that a whole field, 'knowledge translation', has emerged to attend to the problem.

A certain kind of human being is posited in all of this, one that crops up again and again throughout this book: the rational, autonomous subject. This ideal has its origins in the European Enlightenment and its conception of reason as exercised by an isolated, monadic subject (Komesaroff 1995; Mol 2008; Murray and Holmes 2009). According to Murray and Holmes (2009: 5),

> if we glance beyond medicine, we can begin to see that nearly every facet of life in the West presumes – and relies on – the fiction of this modern, rational, autonomous subject: our legal and judicial systems, so-called 'free market' capitalism, democracy, and education, to name just a few.

Although the self of the liberal tradition has only ever existed in narrowly conceived theoretical spaces (Code 2001: 263), it's reified as an objective entity in epidemiology, evidence-based medicine and ethics. While it reaches its apotheosis in concepts such as 'informed choice' and 'human rights', it equally animates the concepts of 'lifestyle', 'health behaviour' and the 'teachable moment', and the attendant notion of the subject who 'chooses' health. Evidence-based medicine is also premised upon it, both in terms of its goal to produce a more rational medicine and in the methodologies it prioritises, with their assumption of the possibility of 'controlling' for complexity and context to get at the 'pure' effect of an intervention.

But behind the figure of the rational human always lurks its opposite: the *irrational* one. As Shapin notes, equally part of the Enlightenment vision is the assumption that:

> human beings are intellectually imperfect and limited; they are subject to tidal currents of passion and interest. These currents flow against their rational faculties and hinder or distort the operation of rationality. Instead of reckoning rightly or seeing what is authentically there to be seen, passion- and interest-influenced human beings tend to think and see not what is but what they wish to be the case.
>
> *Shapin 2010: 47–48*

The spectre of irrationality is repeatedly invoked in the discourses of epidemiology, evidence-based medicine and ethics: the individual who refuses to modify his 'health behaviours', despite being aware of their epidemiological risks; the physician who bases her practice on intuition and tradition; the patient who makes a health care decision at odds with what the evidence suggests is the best course of action. Sometimes this irrationality is seen as something to be made use of – such as the individual whose 'optimistic bias' can be rectified via an anxiety-inducing health event and the purposeful intervention of a physician, or when choice architecture is transformed to 'nudge' people towards healthier behaviours. However, the paradigm itself is rarely challenged.

Consider, for example, the concept of 'therapeutic misconception' – itself a product of the convergences between health, evidence and ethics. Introduced by Appelbaum and colleagues (Appelbaum, Roth and Lidz 1982; Appelbaum *et al.* 1987), it was initially articulated in the context of randomised controlled trials, and the ways in which the 'care' of individual subjects is to some extent sacrificed for the experimental design. Appelbaum *et al.* observed that unless subjects were explicitly informed otherwise, they generally assumed that decisions about their care were being made exclusively with their individual benefit in mind[2] – a view incompatible with the principle of randomising subjects to control and care conditions (and, indeed, the nature of experimental research itself). This assumption, they argued, compromised patients' ability to assess the benefits of the research, thus jeopardising the truly informed nature of consent.

One interpretation of the 'therapeutic misconception' is that the principle of informed consent itself is fundamentally flawed. Indeed, Dixon-Woods and colleagues (2007) have shown that such 'misunderstandings' are an incorrigible feature of research participation because (among other things) lay and scientific understandings of research are largely incommensurate. Nevertheless, instead of challenging the notion of informed consent and the underlying premises upon which it is based, Appelbaum *et al.* (1987: 22) attribute the therapeutic misconception to 'distortions' in subjects' reasoning. Thus, they advocate resolving it via recourse to the principle of informed consent itself. In their words, 'with careful planning, the therapeutic misconception can be dispelled, leaving the subjects with a much clearer picture of the relative risks and benefits of participation in research' (Appelbaum *et al.* 1987: 24). This type of reasoning – where challenges merely serve to reinforce the prevailing paradigm – is one we have seen consistently repeated, whether the context is epidemiology, evidence-based medicine or ethics itself.

The problem is that the ideal being strived for in all three fields is an *illusion*. Some concepts, like 'informed consent', are mirages: they beckon tantalisingly but continually recede further into the distance, the closer we try to get. Others, like 'health behaviours', are phantasms: they have the appearance of solidity but no substance underneath. Thus, invoking the 'rational human' paradigm and its attendant separation of 'facts' and 'values' invariably leads to befuddlement and disappointment. For example, instead of asking 'why is public health policy not evidence-based?' the far more pertinent question is why on earth would we ever assume that it *could* be? (Smith 2013: 4).

Now don't get me wrong. I certainly think it's possible to speak of better and worse evidence and more and less ethical practice. Nor am I attempting to deny or downplay the vast inequalities in health and access to health care both within and across countries – these are very real issues and they have been tackled extensively elsewhere. But these are inherently 'wicked' problems in the sense that Rittel and Webber (1973) define.[3] Although the term has been widely taken up as an identifier for certain types of complex social issues that have no obvious solution, in many respects the 'wicked problem' wasn't so much the assertion of a new idea or paradigm but a *rejoinder* to prevailing orthodoxy. It is in this sense that I invoke the concept here. What Rittel and Webber were primarily reacting to was an ongoing allegiance to an idealised image of how the systems they were concerned with functioned. In their view, this image was one that everybody in the field knew was unattainable; indeed, some even questioned whether it was desirable. However, despite this awareness everyone continually sought to approximate the ideal. It was this *disjuncture*, as much as the nature of the problems themselves, which they sought to highlight. In their words,

> We use the term 'wicked' in a meaning akin to that of 'malignant' (in contrast to 'benign') or 'vicious' (like a circle) or 'tricky' (like a leprechaun) or 'aggressive' (like a lion, in contrast to the docility of a lamb). We do not mean to personify these properties of social systems by implying malicious intent. But then, you may agree that it becomes morally objectionable for the planner to treat a wicked problem as though it were a tame one, or to tame a wicked problem prematurely, or to refuse to recognize the inherent wickedness of social problems.
>
> *Rittel and Webber 1973: 160–161*

In my view, the topics I have dealt with in this book are not just 'wicked' because they are complex and irresolvable (although they are both of these things) but because the terms of engagement with these phenomena have been so *prefigured*. While epidemiology, evidence-based medicine and ethics may appear to have 'tamed' certain problems, they have done so in very particular ways that have produced very particular answers.

In closing, I'll end where I began, with another scene from *The Princess Bride*. In this scene, Westley has just caught up with Vizzini, a Sicilian criminal mastermind Prince Humperdinck has employed to kidnap and kill his fiancé, Buttercup (and Westley's true love). Vizzini has Buttercup bound and is threatening to kill her if Westley takes a step closer to his picnic table, so Westley challenges him to battle of wits for Buttercup's life. Vizzini, confident in his intellectual superiority, accepts the challenge and Westley instructs him to pour two goblets of wine, producing a small vial of iocane powder: 'It's odourless, tasteless, dissolves instantly in liquid and is among the more deadly poisons known to man.' Away from Vizzini's view, Westley deposits the poison and returns the goblets to the table, announcing: 'Alright, where is the poison? The battle of wits has begun. It ends when you decide and we both drink and find out who is right and who is dead.' A dazzling display of intellect follows, with Vizzini pontificating on whether Westley is the sort of man 'who would put the poison into his own goblet or his enemy's'. After he surreptitiously switches the goblets, they both take a sip, with Vizzini convinced that he has won. Gleeful, he is in the process of explaining that he has tricked Westley when he unceremoniously keels over, quite dead. Why? Because contrary to all *rational expectation*, Westley has put the poison into both vials. 'They were both poisoned. I spent the last few years building up an immunity to iocane,' he explains to a confused Buttercup. While Vizzini's starting premise may have been rational and his conclusions sound, they were flawed in a literally fatal sense.

Notes

1 This, of course, is precisely the point Timmermans and Berg (2003) make.
2 This is often conceptualised as a manifestation of 'optimism bias', discussed in Chapter 3 (e.g., Barnett and Katz 2015).
3 The concept of the 'wicked problem' was first written about (as far as I'm aware) by Churchman (1967), although he attributes it to Rittel.

References

Appelbaum, P.S., Roth, L.H. and Lidz, C. (1982) The therapeutic misconception: Informed consent in psychiatric research. *International Journal of Law and Psychiatry*, 5: 319–329.

Appelbaum, P.S., Roth, L.H., Lidz, C.W., Benson, P. and Winslade, W. (1987) False hopes and best data: Consent to research and the therapeutic misconception. *The Hastings Center Report*, 17(2): 20–24.

Armstrong, D. (2002) Clinical autonomy, individual and collective: The problem of changing doctors' behaviour. *Social Science and Medicine*, 55: 1771–1777.

Barnett, S.J. and Katz, A. (2015) Patients and partners in innovation. *Seminars in Pediatric Surgery*, 24(3): 141–144.

Bowker, G.C. and Star, S.L. (1999) *Sorting Things Out: Classification and its Consequences*. Cambridge, MA: MIT Press.

Busch, L. (2011) *Standards: Recipes for Reality*. Cambridge, MA: MIT Press.

Code, L. (2001) Rational imaginings, responsible knowings: How far can you see from here? In N. Tuana and S. Morgen (eds), *Engendering Rationalities*. Albany: State University of New York Press, pp. 261–283.

Churchman, C.W. (1967) Wicked problems. *Management Science*, 14(4): B141–B142.

Dixon-Woods, M., Ashcroft, R.E., Jackson, C.J., Tobin, M.D., Kivits, J., Burton, P.R. and Samani, N.J. (2007) Beyond 'misunderstanding': Written information and decisions about taking part in a genetic epidemiology study. *Social Science and Medicine*, 65(11): 2212–2222.

Komesaroff, P.A. (1995) From bioethics to microethics: Ethical debate and clinical medicine. In P. Komesaroff (ed.), *Troubled Bodies: Critical Perspectives of Postmodernism, Medical Ethics, and the Body*. Melbourne: Melbourne University Press, pp. 62–86.

Lampland, M. and Star, S.L. (2009) *Standards and their Stories*. Ithaca, NY: Cornell University Press.

Lin, V. and Gibson, B. (eds) (2002) *Evidence-Based Health Policy: Problems and Possibilities*. Melbourne: Oxford University Press.

Mol, A. (2008) *The Logic of Care: Health and the Problem of Patient Choice*. London: Routledge.

Murray, S.J. and Holmes, D. (2009) Introduction: Towards a critical bioethics. In S.J. Murray and D. Holmes (eds), *Critical Interventions in the Ethics of Healthcare: Challenging the Principle of Autonomy in Bioethics*. Farnham: Ashgate, pp. 1–14.

Mykhalovskiy, E. (2003) Evidence-based medicine: Ambivalent reading and the clinical recontextualization of science. *Health: an Interdisciplinary Journal*, 7(3): 331–352.

Rittel, H.W. and Webber, M.M. (1973) Dilemmas in a general theory of planning. *Policy Sciences*, 4: 155–169.

Shapin, S. (2010) *Never Pure: Historical Studies of Science as if It Was Produced by People with Bodies, Situated in Time, Space, Culture, and Society and Struggling for Credibility and Authority*. Baltimore, MD: Johns Hopkins University Press.

Smith, K. (2013) *Beyond Evidence-Based Policy in Public Health: The Interplay of Ideas*. Basingstoke: Palgrave Macmillan.

Star, S.L. and Lampland, M. (2009) Reckoning with standards. In M. Lampland and S.L. Star (eds), *Standards and their Stories*. Ithaca, NY: Cornell University Press, pp. 3–24.

Tanenbaum, S. (1994) Knowing and acting in medical practice: The epistemological politics of outcomes research. *Journal of Health Politics, Policy and Law*, 19(1): 647–662.

Tanenbaum, S. (1996) 'Medical effectiveness' in Canadian and US health policy: The comparative politics of inferential ambiguity. *Health Services Research*, 31(5): 517–532.

Timmermans, S. and Berg, M. (2003) *The Gold Standard: The Challenge of Evidence-Based Medicine and Standardization in Health Care*. Philadelphia, PA: Temple University Press.

INDEX